ROUTLEDGE LIBRAR`
LITERARY TH

Volume 5

POST-STRUCTURALIST CLASSICS

POST-STRUCTURALIST CLASSICS

Edited by
ANDREW BENJAMIN

Routledge
Taylor & Francis Group

LONDON AND NEW YORK

First published in 1988 by Routledge

This edition first published in 2017
by Routledge
2 Park Square, Milton Park, Abingdon, Oxon OX14 4RN

and by Routledge
711 Third Avenue, New York, NY 10017

Routledge is an imprint of the Taylor & Francis Group, an informa business

© 1988 Andrew Benjamin
'Beyond Aporia' is a translation of *Comment S'en Sortir* by Sarah Kofman
© Editions Galilee 1983

British Library Cataloguing in Publication Data
A catalogue record for this book is available from the British Library

ISBN: 978-1-138-69377-7 (Set)
ISBN: 978-1-315-52921-9 (Set) (ebk)
ISBN: 978-1-138-68951-0 (Volume 5) (hbk)
ISBN: 978-1-138-68952-7 (Volume 5) (pbk)
ISBN: 978-1-315-53759-7 (Volume 5) (ebk)

Publisher's Note
The publisher has gone to great lengths to ensure the quality of this reprint but points out that some imperfections in the original copies may be apparent.

Disclaimer
The publisher has made every effort to trace copyright holders and would welcome correspondence from those they have been unable to trace.

Post-structuralist classics

edited by

Andrew Benjamin

Routledge
London and New York

First published in 1988 by
Routledge
11 New Fetter Lane, London EC4P 4EE
29 West 35th Street, New York NY 10001

'Beyond Aporia' is a translation of Comment S'en Sortir by
Sara Kofman, © Editions Galilee 1983

Printed in Great Britain by
T J Press (Padstow) Ltd, Padstow, Cornwall

Library of Congress Cataloging in Publication Data

Post-structuralist classics/edited by Andrew Benjamin.
p. cm.—(Warwick studies in philosophy and literature)
Includes index.
Contents. Beyond Aporia?/Sarah Kofman—Hesiod's mimetic Muses
and the strategies of deconstruction/Giovanni Ferrari—Desire
and the figure of fun/Simon Goldhill—Time and interpretation in
Heraclitus/Andrew Benjamin—Banter and banquets for heroic death
/Pietro Pucci—Knowledge is remembrance/David Farrell Kent—
On the saying that philosophy begins in the thaumazein/John
Llewelyn—Entertaining arguments/John Henderson—Sunt aliquid
manes/Rowland Cotterill—Concealing revealing/David
Halliburton.
1. Classical literature—History and criticism. 2. Philosophy,
Ancient. 3. Structuralism (Literary analysis) I. Benjamin, Andrew
E. II. Series.
PA3003.P64 1988
180—dc19 88—4384

ISBN 0–415–00922–7

Contents

· 1 ·

Introduction

ANDREW BENJAMIN

In recent years a number of new approaches to the reading of literary and philosophical texts has emerged. This emergence, while it has its origin in French and German thought, has come if not to dominate then at least to exert a profound influence on Anglo-American philosophical and literary studies. If the use of the 'post' to indicate such a departure has any function at all then what it marks is a textual practice which takes place in the wake of a critique of (amongst other things) humanism, intentionality and historical reductionism. A number of proper names have come to play a major role in these recent adventures. In the case of German thought these names are Heidegger and Gadamer. The impact of French thought offers us no one proper name as such. There is rather a persuasive influence that comes, for example, from Lacan, and hence the inclusion of psychoanalysis within textual studies; there is also the influence of Derrida and of a number of other and perhaps less well known philosophers and literary critics. The importance of French thought is that it has provided a domain of experimentation. In the wake of the critique of the certainties that have dominated the reading of texts which were for the most part based in the concept of the subject, there is now a freedom in which the rules of evaluation and assessment are in the process of being negotiated.

The case of Heidegger is of course more complex. On the one hand Heidegger has given rise to a new orthodoxy, and on the other the use of his work has occasioned developments – especially in philosophy – which have in part overcome the hinderances and restrictions that analytic philosophy imposed on the development of philosophy itself. Even the emergence of a new orthodoxy presents an exciting stimulus to philosophical thought. It is situated in the 'post' because it inherently contains those critical moments which mark the beginning of the post-structuralist adventure. The clearest example of this is Heidegger's *Letter on Humanism*[1] which is an attempt to free philosophical thought from its dependence on Cartesian subjectivity and hence the certitude of the *cogito*. Even if one does not wish to accept the consequences of Heidegger's critique of Descartes, the nature of the critique locates Heidegger's philosophical enterprise within the ambit of post-structuralist thought, a location which is strengthened by the importance that is presently given to Derrida's reading of Heidegger. Derrida has read Heidegger in a way that frees much of his writings from any easy reincorporation into German hermeneutic theory. Indeed, today it is perhaps possible to say that Heidegger's survival – the capacity of Heidegger to live on – is in no small part due to the meticulous reading of his texts undertaken by Derrida.

Classical studies have always been concerned with meticulous readings. Even though the Anglo-American tradition has failed to understand the inherently theoretical dimension of reading and interpretation, the German and French philosophers concerned with classical studies have been deeply concerned with the prob-lems of interpretation. This is especially the case with the originator of contemporary hermeneutics, F. Schleiermacher. His introduction to his own translation of Plato's works[2] is an attempt to draw important connections between the scholarly activity of translating Greek and the philosophical activity of interpretation. Both Heidegger and Gadamer have demonstrated their recognition of the important philosophical issues at stake in translation and even in discussions concerned to establish a correct edition of a particular philosophical or literary text. Once again, even if one wanted either to resist or disagree with Heidegger or Gadamer's reading of Greek philosophical texts, what can never be denied is the active interplay between the establishing, translating and interpreting of texts and philosophy itself.

One of the major characteristics of post-structuralist thought is the growing interdependence and hence inseparability of philos-ophy and literary theory. While the distinction is maintained by the structure of university departments, it is no longer the case that philosophers have nothing to say about literary texts or that literary critics are silent about philosophical texts. While in the Anglo-American academic world this development is new and – for some – potentially disturbing, for the European tradition it is a commonplace. Even leaving Heidegger and Gadamer to one side in the German tradition, philosophers and critics such as Walter Benjamin, Theodor Adorno and Peter Szondi were always concerned with the interplay between the philosophical and the literary. Recently in the USA the work of Paul de Man also exemplifies this refusal to be limited by the institutionally inspired and maintained distinction between philosophy and literature. This refusal cannot be restricted to de Man; indeed, there is a whole new generation of both critics and philosophers whose work refuses any straightforward distinction between the philosophical and the literary. One major consequence of which is that the concern with textuality which is lacking in analytic philosophy is overcome in current philosophical and literary studies that derives its orientation from the European tradition. Reciprocally, of course, the severing of the link between the analysis of texts and interpretation that marks the work of many writers in the domain of literary theory (and especially in classical studies) is joined in the work which takes place under the general rubric of post-structuralism. The papers included in this volume all exemplify these contemporary concerns. This is not to suggest that they all offer the same approach and all agree in matters of interpretation; rather that they all exhibit a concern with topics and the modes of approach afforded by a critique of conventional methods of analysis and philosophical activity.

While it is obviously problematic to try to delimit the specificity of individual papers by allocating them to a general group, the papers in this volume reveal three different, though at times related, points of departure. The papers by David Krell, John Llewelyn and Andrew Benjamin all situate themselves around the work of Heidegger. Although they disagree as to the importance or indeed the viability of Heidegger's philosophical project, his philosophy and especially his reading of Greek philosophical texts forms a general locus of investigation. This Heidegger, it must be stressed, is a post-Derridian Heidegger. The importance of Derrida cannot be overestimated. Not only have his writings provided a new approach to Heidegger, but also they stand in their own right as perhaps the most powerful contemporary philosophical influence.

Derrida has to some degree influenced all the papers in this volume, but this influence is most evident in the papers by Giovanni Ferrari and Pietro Pucci. Once again it is not a question of a tacit and uncritical acceptance of Derrida; indeed Ferrari's paper is concerned in part with a critique of Pucci's use of Derrida in his now famous reading of Hesiod, *Hesiod and the Language of Poetry*[3] The important point in this instance is the recognition by both not simply of the contribution made by Derrida to the now interrelated domain of philosophical and literary studies, but the inevitability of coming to terms with his philosophical point of departure. The other paper which shows the influence of Derrida is Sarah Kofman's discussion of Plato. It must be said, of course, that the paper is not a simple essay in applying Derrida's work to Platonic texts. Kofman is an important thinker in her own right, and her various books, which include studies of Freud and Nietzsche amongst others,[4] have established her as one of France's most important contemporary philosophers. None the less, her point of departure can be described as an acceptance of Derrida's approach to the reading and analysis of texts. Kofman's paper will emerge as one of the most important and influential readings of Plato in recent years and as such it is both a delight and a privilege to be able to include it in this volume.

The papers by John Henderson, Roland Cotterill, Simon Goldhill and David Halliburton can all be described as incorporating and exemplifying the experimental possibilities occasioned by post-structuralism. The acceptance of post-structuralist approaches is neither unified nor complacent. John Henderson and Simon Goldhill offer readings of specific texts. They both draw on philosophical and psychoanalytic sources to offer their detailed and perhaps controversial readings of Terence's *Adelphoe* and Theocritus 11. David Halliburton and Roland Cotterill are concerned with larger topics. Halliburton's reading of Sophoclean tragedy makes persuasive use of the work of Rene Girard in order to offer both an important reading of texts as well as a significant and original discussion of tragedy itself. Cotterill's critical stand in relation to some of the problems which emerge in post-structuralist conceptions of history informs his reading of Augustan poetry. He offers a counterargument to the all-too-easy evacuation of any concern with the historical. Not only, therefore, does his paper provide an important interpretation of poetical texts, but also it serves to reintroduce the problem of the historical.

In sum, all the papers offer an exciting and important challenge to the conventional practice of classical studies and ancient philosophy and yet they do so with the same care and concern for scholarship which has always characterized these domains of intellectual research. Consequently these papers incorporate a futural dimension. Instead of scholarship being condemned to the repetition of repetition, where the division between philosophy and literature is not only reinforced by its place within the university structure but also repeated in academic work, there has emerged a domain of intellectual endeavour which refuses any essential characterization and allows, if not demands, experimentation. The importance and viability of post-structuralism, therefore, lies in its twofold challenge: a challenge on the one hand to the tradition and hence to intellectual complacency, and on the other the redefinition of intellectual activity as itself a challenge.

A note needs to be made concerning the transliteration of Greek. A standard transliteration procedure has been followed in most instances. However accents have been included only where their retention is vital in order to distinguish between different words or where an interpretative point depends upon the retention of the accent, or more simply where an author has deemed it necessary. For readers without a working knowledge of Greek this method of presentation will I hope prove helpful. While readers of Greek may find it slightly frustrating it is consistent with the overall intention of making these papers available to an academic though not necessarily classically trained audience.[5]

Notes

1 The English translation of Heidegger's text is in David Farrell Krell (ed.) *Martin Heidegger: Basic Writings*, London, Routledge & Kegan Paul, 1978, pp. 189–243. It was translated by Frank A. Capuzzi.
2 In F. Schleiermacher (trans.), *Platons Werke Ersten Theiles Erster Band*, Berlin, Georg Reimer, 1855, pp. 5–56.
3 Pietro Pucci, *Hesiod and the Language of Poetry*, Johns Hopkins University Press, Baltimore, Md, and London, 1977.
4 Sarah Kofman has published approximately seventeen books of which

some of the most important are: *Nietzsche et la metaphore*, Paris, Galilée, 1983; *Nietzsche et la scène philosophique*, Paris, Galilée, 1986; and *L'Énigme de la femme*, Paris, Galilée, 1980. The paper translated here as 'Beyond Aporia' was first published in France as a book entitled *Comment s'en sortir*, Paris, Galilée, 1983.

5 The majority of these papers were first given in a series of lectures organized by the Centre for Research on Philosophy and Literature at the University of Warwick, on the general theme of the relationship between classical studies and post-structuralism. In looking for other papers to complement the original lecture series I have tried to include papers covering a wide range of topics. Clearly this volume is only a beginning but it will serve to indicate the presence of a new direction now being taken in classical studies. It must also be said that the volume could not have been completed without the goodwill of all the contributors, the help of Tamra Wright, the editorial assistant at the Centre, and the continual encouragement of David Wood, the general editor of the series.

· 2 ·

Beyond Aporia?

SARAH KOFMAN

Translated by David Macey from
Comment s'en sortir?, Paris, Galilée, 1983

Translator's note

The Republic, The Symposium, Phaedrus, Charmides and *Euthyde-meus* are cited in Benjamin Jowett's translation; in the case of *The Symposium*, W. Hamilton's translation has also been consulted (Harmondsworth, Penguin, 1951). *Parmenides, Theaitetos* and *The Sophist* are cited in John Warrington's translation, London, Every-man's Library, 1961. *Meno* and *Protagoras* are cited in W. K. C. Guthrie's translation, Harmondsworth, Penguin, 1956; *Philebus* in Robin A. H. Waterfield's translation, Harmondsworth, Penguin, 1982; *Phaedo* in Hugh Tredennick's translation (in *The Last Days of Socrates*, Harmondsworth, Penguin, 1954). *Menexeneus* and *The Laws* are cited in R. G. Bury's translation, London, Heine-mann, Loeb Classical Library, 1929 and 1926.

Existing translations have occasionally been modified to take into account discrepancies between the French and English versions.

Nightmare at the Margins of Medieval Studies first appeared in *SubStance* 49, 1986, translated by Frances Bartkowski.

Men, a strange species, would like to escape death. And some cry, 'Oh, to die, to die!' because they would like to escape death. 'What a life. I will kill myself; I give up.' This is pitiful, strange, and a mistake. (Blanchot, La Folie du jour)

Poros, son of Metis

Marcel Detienne and Jean-Pierre Vernant conclude their remark-able study of the Greek *metis* by emphasizing the supposed exclusion from within philosophy of the wily iintelligence which progresses by twists and turns.[1] It is claimed that, in the name of truth, Plato in particular relegated to the outer darkness and condemned this entire sector of intelligence, its ways of under-standing and its practical modalities; more specifically, he is said to have denounced its devious, approximate and uncertain methods by contrasting them with the one exact and rigorous science, with the philosophical *episteme*, which is by its very nature contempla-tive. Science, which stands at the summit of the hierarchy of knowl-edge, is deemed to have distinguished between true and untrue, between oblique and straight, to have divided human productions into those which depend upon uncertain knowledge and those which result from accuracy, to have dismissed with a lordly gesture most *technes*, along with rhetoric and sophistics. Quite explicitly. The condemnation of everything derived from *stochastic* (conjec-tural) understanding, from *metis*, is, we are told, 'quite unequivocal'. This conclusion, seems irrefutable and classical.

And yet, if philosophy itself could not do without *metis*, if its 'contemplative' understanding did not make a radical break with 'technical' understanding, perhaps Plato's gesture would not be so simple or so unequivocal — even if it cannot be denied that he does make a hierarchical distinction between philosophy and other sciences, between philosophy and *techne*, between philosophy and sophistry.

I will begin with the celebrated myth of the birth of Love in *The Symposium* (203b, f). In a parody of earlier encomia which, rather than investigating the essence of love, give it a divine origin, Socrates (Diotima) in his turn indulges in a genealogical fantasy. He gives Love a father and a mother: Poros and Penia. We are given no information as to the ancestry of Love's mother; it is as though, in her distress, Penia could have no ancestors, as though she had to be always already an orphan. His father Poros, on the other hand, is, we are told, the son of Metis. This genealogical asymmetry is not, it seems to me, without its significance: to stress the tie of kinship that exists between Love, Poros and Metis is to state that the wily resourceful intelligence that lies at the origin of

8

all *technes* is also one of the ancestors of philosophy, of the love of *sophia*. For Love is a philosopher, 'a philosopher at all times.' He is at one with philosophy, for 'wisdom is a most beautiful thing', 'and therefore Love is also a philosopher or lover of wisdom, and being a lover of wisdom is a mean between the wise and the ignorant' (204b).

Its kinship with Metis gives philosophy the same soteriological finality as a *techne*: to discover *poroi* which can free men from aporia, from all sorts of difficult situations from which there is no way out. It is in effect Metis who allows us to blaze a trail, a *poros*, a way, to find a path through obstacles, to discover an expedient (*poros*), to find a way out (*poros*) of a situation from which there is no way out, which is aporetic. Wherever indeterminacy (*apeiras*) reigns, wherever there are no limits and no directions, whenever we are trapped, encircled or caught in inextricable bonds it is, according to Detienne and Vernant, Metis who intervenes, who discovers stratagems, expedients, tricks, ruses, machinations, *mechane* and *techne* which allow us to move from the absence of limits to determinacy, from darkness to light. The kinship between Poros and Metis provides an indissoluble link between journey, transition, crossing, resourcefulness, expediency, *techne*, light and limits (*peiras*).

(This is sufficient to indicate the difficulty of 'translating' *poros* and the related term *aporia*, and to stress the *aporia* into which the terms plunge translators, who usually escape their perplexity by translating *poros* as 'expediency' and *aporia* as 'difficulty'; yet these translations leave the reader in the dark as to all the semantic richness of *poros* and *aporia*, and give no hint as to their links with other words belonging to the same 'family', with, for example, *euporia*, the term Plato introduces into his dialectical approach so as to facilitate his interlocutor's understanding of inaccessible ideas. Above all, they obscure the link with the radical *perao*, 'to traverse', and the close connection between *mechane* and journey, crossing, light and limit. To translate, to open up a path through a language by using its resources, to decide upon *one* meaning, is to escape the agonizing, aporetic impasses of any translation, to make the philosophical gesture *par excellence*: the gesture of betrayal. To recognize the untranslatability of *poros* and *aporia* is to indicate that there is something about the terms, which Plato borrows from a whole tradition, which breaks with a philosophical conception of translation, and with the logic of identity that it implies.)

Poros is not to be confused with *odos*, a general term designating a path or a road of any kind. *Poros* refers only to a sea-route or a route down a river, to a passage opened up across a chaotic expanse which it transforms into an ordered, qualified space by introducing differentiated routes, making visible the various directions of space, by giving direction to an expanse which was initially devoid of all contours, of all landmarks.

To say that a *poros* is a way to be found across an expanse of liquid is to stress that a *poros* is never traced in advance, that it can always be obliterated, that it must always be traced anew, in unprecedented fashion. One speaks of a *poros* when it is a matter of blazing a trail where no trail exists, of crossing an impassable expanse of territory, an unknown, hostile and boundless world, an *apeiron* which it is impossible to cross from end to end; the watery depths, the *pontos*, is the ultimate *apeiron* (*paron* because *apeiron*); the sea is the endless realm of pure movement, the most mobile, changeable and polymorphous of all spaces, a space where any way that has been traced is immediately obliterated, which transforms any journey into a voyage of exploration which is always unprecedented, dangerous and uncertain.[2] The sea is, to use Detienne and Vernant's magnificent expression, 'widowed of routes' (*veuve de routes*), and it is analogous with Hesiod's Tartarus, with the image of chaos itself; Tartarus is a realm of wild swirling squalls where there are no directions, no left and no right, no up and no down, where there are no fixed directions, where one can find no landmarks, no bearings to travel by. In this infernal, chaotic confusion, the *poros* is the way out, the last resort of sailors and navigators, the stratagem which allows them to escape the impasse and the attendant anxiety. Sea-lanes, those roads to safety, are to be related to the *peirata*, the landmarks, the points of light that mark the sailor's course. *Peirata* are also links; for the Greeks, a certain kind of path, of *poros*, can take the form of a link that binds, just as the action of linking can sometimes take on the appearance of making a traverse, of making one's way. Tartarus, the aporetic place *par excellence* (Plato says that no *mechane* can overcome the irresistible violence of the winds that rage there; *Phaedo* 112c), is also the place where one comes into contact with inextricable bonds that are impossible to break, with a realm of shadows without exit. It links forever. It is impossible to flee; Tartarus extends to form a gigantic mesh which has no end and no bounds, a *peiras apeiron*, the aporia of an undefined circular space; the most adequate image for it is that of the hunting nets and fishing nets which the *metis* of men invents to defeat the *metis* of animals and to trap them.

The ocean of discourse

Now there is no discontinuity between the various 'technical' traps which men weave to protect themselves and the traps sophists set in their discourses to overcome and master their adversaries. There is no break between fishermen, hunters, weavers and the sophists who 'specialize' in discourse (even though the sophist, a specialist in *mimesis*, does not rely upon any one *techne* that is bound up with any determinate need or function, can take refuge in any *techne*, and escapes by perpetually sliding from one to the next). Yet the philosopher, who tracks down the sophistic beast and drives him from his every lair in a pitiless pursuit, is closely related to his prey, and has to display a *metis* which is at least as cunning as that of the sophist if he is to escape the aporia inherent in the discourses his adversary exploits to his own advantage. For discourses are forces which are no less disturbing and no less dangerous than the sea and its depths: like the sea and like Tartarus, the aporia of discourse are endless; they are *apeirania*, not because there is no limit to their number, but because they cannot be crossed; not one of them can be pursued to the end because one can see no end to them; such, for example, are the aporia into which the doctrines of Being plunge the interlocutors in *The Sophist* (245e). In general, Plato describes aporia as a veritable 'storm of difficulties' which has to be faced at one or another moment in a dialogue (*chei mazometha gar ontos up' aporias*; *Philebus* 29b). When, in Book V of *The Republic*, Socrates takes up the fearful and formidable question of the education of women, he invites his interlocutor to 'swim', to attempt against the odds to emerge safe and sound from the perilous discussion (*sozesthai ek tou logou*), for

the fact is that when a man is out of his depth, whether he has fallen into a little swimming bath or into mid-ocean (*eis to megiston pelagos meson*), he has to swim all the same . . . . And must we not swim and try to reach the shore: we will hope that Arion's dolphin or some other miraculous help may save us (*aporon soterian*), let us see if any way of escape can be found. (453e)

The way out of discourse, the exit, is a way to safety, a *poros* which appears unexpectedly, which no one can be sure of finding, and which is itself always aporetic: a true miracle, an encounter with a dolphin in mid-ocean! But if we refuse to swim, if we stay where we are, we must abandon all hope of ever meeting a dolphin that might save us. In order to persuade Theaitetos to continue his investigations when he comes up against·an idea that blocks his progress (science as true belief), Socrates uses a similar image, but this time it refers to a river and not to the sea:

Well, Theaitetos, 'We can but try', as the man said when asked if the river could be forded. So in this case, if we go ahead with our enquiry we may come across something that will reveal the object of our search: we shall discover nothing by just standing still. (200e–201a)

At the beginning of the dialogue, old Parmenides quivers with fear because, at his age, he dreads having to swim through 'such a formidable sea of words' (*pelagos logou*; *Parmenides* 137a).

The same image is used in *The Laws* (892a) to describe the panic of the old men who feel 'faint and dizzy' when they are faced with a 'torrent of questions they are unused to answering'. Faced with this situation, the Athenian resolves to go on alone, to leave the old men in a safe place and to take the risk of crossing the fast-flowing river alone; if he proves that it is fordable, he will then help them across.

Although, like the sea, rivers are liquid spaces which are difficult to cross and which are full of dangerous currents and whirlpools, the sea is still the aporetic place *par excellence*, and it is still the best metaphor for the aporia of discourse. Certain texts therefore contrast the sea and its salinity with the fresh waters of rivers, just as they contrast philosophical discourses with sophistical discourses, discourses 'taken from some haunt of sailors': 'I desire to wash the brine (*almuran*) out of my ears with water from the river' (*Potimo logo*; *Phaedrus*, 243c-d). For the sea is also the best image to describe the corrosion and sterility of the sensible world.

The *Phaedo* (109) compares men with fishes which from time to time put up their heads out of the sea in order to see our world, while the earth is described as a region in which everything is marred and corroded, 'just as in the sea everything is corroded by the brine (*osper ta en thallate upo tes alles*)'; 'there is no vegetation worth mentioning (*axion lougou en te thalatte*)', 'and scarcely any degree of perfect formation (*teleion*), but only caverns and sand and measureless mud, and tracts of slime wherever there is earth as well; and nothing is in the least worthy to be judged beautiful by our standards.'

The sensible world is a sea that is alive with dangerous creatures like the sophist, that 'monster of a sea-crab' (*Euthydemeus* 297c) which bites the philosopher; more generally, the life of a sea-creature imprisoned in a shell is, according to Plato, 'not fit for the life of a human being', and is unworthy of man (*Philebus* 21c).

Confronting discourses is therefore doubly dangerous: language itself is an ocean alive with aporia and, because the sophistic beast has made it his lair, it has become a maritime kingdom which is corroded and sterile. Thanks to a veritable conjuring trick, the prestigious power of the sophist has transmuted the fresh life-giving water of a river that can be forded into bitter, sterile brine.

Wonders

The metamorphosis is all the more fearful in that the sophist exhibits the aporia of discourse as though they were real wonders. For example, the aporetic principle which states that the one is many and infinitely so, and that the many are one, appears to him to be a source of wonder. The principle is indeed stupefying, paralysing and 'highly obstructive to discussion' (*Philebus* 14 e); it makes swimming difficult, but it also makes it easy to set traps which force one to make 'monstrous assertions' and to create all sorts of aporias (*apases aporias*). When they relate to the sensible world, these aporia are false wonders, childish difficulties which are easily resolved. But when the contradictions of the one and the many are applied at the level of ideas themselves, the aporia are true wonders. They are wonderfully stupefying, seem to be inextricable, and give rise to endless discussion.

In the first place, the question arises whether such units should be supposed truly to exist. Second, how these units, each of which is always the same and admits neither generation nor destruction, should be supposed reliably the unit that each is, despite also being present in the infinite number of things which *are* generated – the same unit, you see, is simultaneously in the one and in the many. Should one suppose that this occurs through its being divided up and having become many, or through the whole of its being separated from itself – which seems absolutely impossible? (*Philebus* 15 b)

Being inherent in language, these aporia can be introduced at every opportunity, and crop up in every single utterance. This will never stop being the case, nor has it begun; the phenomenon is an immortal and ageless feature of human speech itself. How does one escape these eternal aporia? Assuming, of course, that men do want to escape them. For all men, and especially young men, delight in playing with them and in using them to catch out others, as though they were true wonders.

As soon as a young man gets wind of this feature of speech, he is delighted: he feels he has discovered a treasure-trove of ingenuity. He is in his seventh heaven, and he loves to worry every sentence, now shaking it to and fro and lumping it together, now rolling it out again and tearing it apart. Above all, he confuses himself, but he also confuses anyone he ever comes across, be he younger, older or of the same age as himself. He spares neither his father nor his mother, nor anything which can hear – not even animals escape, let alone men: he wouldn't have mercy on a foreigner, if only he could get hold of an interpreter. (15 d–e)

In the face of this youthful enthusiasm which spares no one there is no option but to discover some trick (*tropos*) or subterfuge (*mechane*) to put an end to a game which disturbs and depresses – or so it would seem – only the philosopher, to find some 'better route' to escape this dizzying wordplay, whose counterpart is a stupefying paralysis.

Plato does not examine the underlying reasons behind the profound jubilation that arises from eternally introducing trouble, disorder and chaos into the ordered world of adult reason at every opportunity, from leading mothers and fathers into an infernal dance, from reducing to a second childhood those who brought you up from infancy by forbidding you to play with language and to enjoy it. Jubilating in the aporia of language always means enjoying setting traps for one's parents, succeeding in trapping them in bonds similar to the chains Haephestus forged to trap Ares and to surprise him in the arms of Aphrodite. It is well known that that spectacle made all the gods who had come down from Olympus to watch the primal scene burst out laughing.

Traps

The sophist exploits this 'parricidal' delight to his own advantage by erecting the use of aporia into a system. His method is a *technique of disorientation*: by 'wriggling in and out of every hole' (*Republic* 405 e) he reduces the *logos* to a state of chaos, to the chaos of the sea or of Tartarus, where all directions merge. Like Hermes, that wily god who, in order to cover his tracks, draws a tracery of conflicting marks on the ground,[3] the sophist uses every possible device to give his discourse at least two conflicting meanings. His discourse, unlike the sound discourse of the Phaedrus, has neither head nor tail to it; true and false, being and non-being are hopelessly mingled and confused. By weaving together contradictory theses, the sophist can make the same things appear to his hearers like and unalike (*Phaedrus* 261d); he turns opinions into their opposites, transforms the weakest argument into the strongest, turns his adversary's arguments against him. His slippery discourse, which is as mobile as the sensible world, is the discourse of *doxa* itself, a discourse which, by definition, can hold contradictory and enigmatic positions (*Republic* 497c, 498c).

The Greek for enigma is *ainigma* or *griphos*, a word which also applies to a certain kind of fishing net. An enigma is woven, like a basket or a hoop-net; the sophist who intertwines and twists discourses and artifices is a past master at the arts of bending and interweaving things. One of the subdivisions of *The Sophist* (226b f) classifies sophistics amongst the 'diacritical' arts, and relates it to the arts of weaving and plaiting, 'to the most ancient techniques and tricks which use the suppleness of vegetable matter and its capacity for torsion to make knots, ligatures and knots which allow men to snare, trap and catch animals'.[4] The wily discourses of the sophist are traps (*Theaitetos* 194b), and he himself is a living snare, a 'net which catches everything and is never caught by anything';

he simultaneously floors his adversary without difficulty, paralyses him with his aporia, and eludes his grasp by taking on the shape of other living forms, like a veritable Proteus. In *The Sophist* he finds a resting place within his own paradigm, that of the angler, but he is also the elusive animal that is the fisherman's prey: a crab, a cuttlefish or an octopus, a creature whose head cannot be distinguished from its tail, whose very being defies directionality. Mottled, polymorphous and hydra-headed, it cannot be placed in any category, is irreducible to any definite species, and possesses the wiles of both hunter and hunted; its form is ambiguous; it operates through inversions and reversals, and is always the opposite of what it appears to be, elusiveness made flesh, as bizarre and as dangerous as the 'mad becoming' (*le devinir fou*).

Suppleness, polymorphy, duplicity, equivocity, tortuous and oblique ambiguity – these characteristics of the sophist are also those of *metis*, of the resourceful technical intelligence which progresses by twists and turns; being a veritable living aporia, the sophist is always capable of tracing his own *poros*, of finding a way out, no matter what the situation may be.

Although Plato denounces the devices of the sophist because of their kinship with the sensible world, their duplicity and their obliquity (in *The Laws*, at 823d and 824a, he denounces in the name of truth and morality fishing with hooks and all hunting which involves the use of nets and traps because they encourage deception), they can still be *incorporated* by the philosopher; just as Zeus swallows Metis and integrates her into his own sovereignty to prevent her giving birth to wily children who might dispossess him of his power,[5] so the philosopher is forced to swallow the *metis* of the sophists in order to use it against them and so as not to be dispossessed of his mastery (it will not be forgotten that, in the *Phaedrus* myth, he tries to imitate Zeus and to take him as a model by following his chariot through the heavenly procession of souls as best he can; 246e f).

The only way to invert the balance of power, to track the mottled beast to his lair and to bring him bound hand and foot to the *basilikos logos* (*Sophist* 235c) is to outdo him by adopting his wiles. *The Sophist* in particular can be read as a fantastic tale in which two brothers fight to the death: two doubles, one good and the other bad (they resemble each other 'like dog and wolf'), have to assimilate one another's properties; each has to become his other, and must drink his blood in order to exterminate him more thoroughly.[6] The various dichotomous divisions are so many traps which the good double, the 'noble sophist', sets for the bad double, for the 'vile sophist', and the final trap is the mimetic genre, which is especially aporetic (*aporon genos*). This is the sophist's last refuge, his last bolthole; it is a place for which there is no place, which is aporetic because it is a-topic, which belongs to neither the genre of being nor to that of non-being, which forces Plato to commit a symbolic parricide, the symbolic murder of Father Parmenides, which forces him, in other words, to break with the logic of identity. For it is in the name of that logic, which he borrows from Parmenides in order to turn it against the philosophers and to paralyse them, that the sophist can deny the existence of the mimetic genre, of the simulacrum, of falsity and error; that he can block all discussion, all research, and can reduce everything to chaos. The murder of Parmenides allows the prestigious power of the sophist to be reduced to that of a charlatan who can do no more than throw dust in the eyes of the young, or of those who view truth from afar: it has as its correlate the putting to death of the sophist.

As in all stories about doubles, the death of the one signs the other's death warrant. Trapping the sophist means trapping oneself. For renouncing the logic of identity means losing the certainty of one's identity, of one's authenticity. It is in a sense to commit suicide.[7] It means renouncing philosophical purity and recognizing that the philosophical is always-already sullied and tainted by the mimetic. No one resembles the sophist more closely than the philosopher. Indeed, this is why, in order to safeguard reason from madness, and in order to master a mimesis that cannot, ultimately, be mastered, Plato makes a salutary distinction between good and bad mimesis,[8] between noble and base sophistry, between dog and wolf; this is why he attempts to distinguish between philosophical aporia and sophistical aporia, which are as alike as rival brothers.

The double aporia

It is in fact because Socrates too makes systematic use of aporia that he is often seen as a sophist and that he is forced to make it clear that he is not one.

At the end of the *Protagoras*, which is of course an 'aporetic' dialogue, for example, both interlocutors find themselves in an impasse; it is as though each of them had been forced to contradict himself, and the dialogue ends with a complete reversal of their initial positions: Socrates, who has demonstrated that virtue relates to the science of measurement, is now forced to admit that virtue can be taught, while Protagoras is forced to go against his own premises and to admit that it cannot be taught. Neither of them knows where he stands. Their dialogue has turned everything upside down (*ano kato taratomena*), has led to an extraordinary confusion of ideas, and has plunged both of them into bewilderment, into a confusion worthy of Tartarus. A reversal of positions, a tragic loss of direction . . . or perhaps it is merely comical:

It seems to me that the present outcome of our talk (*exodus ton logon*) is pointing at us, like a human adversary, the finger of accusation and scorn. If it had a voice it would say 'What an absurd pair you are, Socrates and Protagoras'. (361b; literally 'you are *atopoi*')

In the *Meno* it is stressed that, before he met Socrates, Meno regarded him as a real sophist because he had been told that 'You are a perplexed man and reduce others to perplexity' (*autoste aporeis kai tous allous poieis aporein*; 80a). And Meno, who has spoken about virtue hundreds of times and who has always been able to come up with an answer to everyone, finds himself powerless to argue with Socrates. Socrates must be an enchanter who uses drugs (*pharmaka*) and incantations if he can trap a man of his abilities in an aporia (*Meston aporian*) and leave him powerless; only magic and witchcraft can leave a man like Meno speechless and directionless (*sans voix/voie*), and if this were anywhere but Athens Socrates would most likely be arrested for sorcery. The complaint levelled against Socrates is the very same complaint that he lodges against the sophists, the orators and the poets, against all the mimetic powers which use their formal charms of their discourse to trap men in magical bonds and to pin them down:

And they [funeral orators] praise in such splendid fashion, that . . . with the variety and splendour of their diction, they bewitch our souls . . .. every time I listen fascinated . . . so persistently does the speech and voice of the orator ring in my ears that it is scarcely on the fourth or fifth day that I recover myself and remember that I really am here on earth, whereas till then I almost imagined myself to be living in the Islands of the Blessed. (*Menexeneus* 235a – c)

Mimetic discourses which are designed to intimidate an adversary have the same aporetic, paralysing and petrifying effect as the Gorgon's head; Agathon's encomium, which parodies Gorgias's rhetorical speeches, has, for example, precisely that effect:

Must not I or anyone be in a strait who has to speak after he has heard such a rich and varied discourse? It culminated in the beautiful diction and style of the concluding words – who could listen to them without amazement? . . . I was reminded of Gorgias, and at the end of his speech I fancied in my terror that Agathon was shaking at me the Gorginian or Gorgonian head of the great master of rhetoric, which was simply to turn me and my speech to stone. (*Symposium* 198b)

Now in the *Meno* it is Socrates who plays the part of Medusa or, rather, of the sting-ray. It is said that his drugs have the same narcotic, numbing effects:

Whenever anyone comes into contact with a sting-ray it numbs him, and that is the sort of thing that you seem to be doing to me now. My mind and my lips are literally numb, and I have nothing to reply to you. (80a)

And yet, before he approached Socrates, before he came into contact with his paralysing magic, Meno thought he knew what virtue was.

The sting-ray: a fish with *metis*, a veritable living trap; it has all the appearance of a flaccid body with no vigour, but Oppian tells us that 'Its flanks conceal a trick, a *dolos*, which is the strength of its weakness. Beneath its harmless appearance it has a *dolos*; a sudden electrical discharge which surprises its enemy, puts it at its mercy, paralyses and stuns it.'[9]

Like the sophists, Socrates draws his interlocutors into a situation from which there is no escape, makes them *fall* into a directionless space where they become disoriented and dizzy. The aporetic state always arises as one moves from a familiar environment or space to a space to which one is unaccustomed, during a *transition* from below to above or from above to below, from darkness to light or from light to darkness. In both cases, falling into an aporia is like falling into a well of perplexity and becoming a laughing stock for bystanders. Thus, the *Theaitetos* describes a double aporia, a double laugh.

It describes the aporia of the philosopher who makes himself look ridiculous when he has to defend himself before a court. He is like Thales, who could not see what was at his feet; his inexperience leads him into every kind of pitfall (*pasan aporian*). 'The philosopher is derided by the common herd, partly because he appears arrogant, and partly because he is hopelessly at sea (*aporon*) in day-to-day affairs' (175).

A *well*: a sort of dark pit from which there is no escape. A Thracian maidservant bursts out laughing when she sees the philosopher fall in. Fitting revenge for a woman, for a sister to Pandora, the first woman, whom Hesiod compares with a steep-sided pit from which there is no exit. Woman, the veritable living aporia whom the wily Zeus wove during his struggle against Prometheus, is a piece of bait which allows Epithemeus and all men to be caught: the same word applies to her genitals and to the cuttlefish, a particularly slippery, devious, polymorphous and ambiguous creature.

But the laughter of a woman, and of a maidservant at that, is of no consequence to the philosopher. All that matters to him is the laughter of men, of the educated. And they do not laugh at the philosopher's embarrassment; they do, however, laugh when a man 'with a small mind' stumbles into an aporia, when he is subjected to dialectical questioning and has to render his account. Here again, the passage from below to above is a very bad passage. In his turn, he is disoriented, overcome with dizziness, and he tumbles into a well of perplexity which is at least as deep — if not deeper — as Thales' well, or even the seductive well of a woman's belly. He is 'dizzy from hanging at such an unwonted height and gazing down from midair. Dumbfounded (*aporon*), stammering, he becomes a laughing-stock' (175 b).

The myth of the cavern also represents a double aporia and provokes a double laugh. It must first be noted that the captives' initial situation is not, for them, aporetic: the chains that bind them are invisible to them; they do not know that they are in chains because they do not know that they know nothing, because they see their ignorance as certainty. Like Poros who, in *The Symposium*, gets drunk on nectar and falls into the arms of sleep, the prisoners think that they are resourceful, and would have spent their entire lives in this oneiric, hallucinatory state, had not a spoilsport gone into the cavern: the philosopher. It is the philosopher who, by forcefully awakening them from their blissful slumbers, plunges them into a revolting aporia: 'If any one tried to loose another and lead him up into the light, let them only catch the offender, and they would put him to death' (517a). Their aporia begins with the dialogue that loosens their tongues, as well as their necks and heads. Before the arrival of the philosopher, the captives' very posture prevented them from conversing: 'If they were able to converse with one another', says the text, using an unreal optative (*ei oun dialegesthai oioi t'eien pros allelous*, 515b). But as their legs and necks are in chains, they cannot change places and can see only what is in front of them; their heads are immobilized, and they cannot even turn to one another; they cannot catch one another out in a productive contradiction which would make them aware that they know nothing. Paradoxically the one thing that can save them is an aporia; only an aporia can make visible the chains of pleasure and of the sensible world, which bind their souls to their bodies and prevent them from thinking; only an aporia can make them aware of the aporetic state into which they were initially plunged without realizing it. It is only when he returns to cavern that the former captive compares his old abode to Hades and his chains to the chains of death. Like Achilles, he will then say, ' "Better to be the poor servant of a poor master" and to endure anything, rather than think as they did and live in this miserable manner' (516e).

There can be no aporia, in the true sense of the word, without a transition from a familiar state which affords one every security to a new, and therefore harrowing, state. When, for example, one moves from darkness to light, the transition causes suffering, perplexity and aporia:

When any one of them is liberated and compelled suddenly to stand up and turn his neck round and walk and look towards the light, he will suffer sharp pains; the glare will distress him, and he will be unable to see the realities of which in his former state he had seen the shadows; and then conceive someone saying to him, that what he saw before was an illusion, but that now, when he is approaching nearer to being and his eye is turned towards more real existence, he has a clearer vision – what will be his reply? And you may further imagine that his instructor is pointing to the objects as they pass and requiring him to name them — will he not be perplexed? (*aporein*) Will he not fancy that the shadows which he formerly saw are truer than the objects which are now shown to him?

The transition from light to darkness, in its turn, produces the same suffering, perplexity and dizziness. A captive who returned to the cavern would be unable to see in the dark and would be a laughing-stock; it would be as though he had ruined his eyesight by going into the upper world:

And is there anything surprising in one who passes from divine contemplations to the evil state of man, misbehaving himself in a ridiculous manner; if while his eyes are blinking and before he has become accustomed to the surrounding darkness, he is compelled to fight in courts of law, or in other places, about the images or shadows of images of justice? (517)

The bewilderment (*epitaratto*) that affects the eyes or the soul can, then, take one of two forms; there are two symmetrical but inverse ways of falling into an aporia. And yet, for Plato, they are not equivalent: one aporia is better than the other; there are good and bad aporia. The fearful aporia comes about because the soul is troubled and bewildered by the darkness. If, on the other hand, it is dazzled by the light, one should, he says, rejoice at one's perplexity, at one's aporia. One should not be afraid of making Thracian maidservants laugh.

The hierarchy established between the two types of aporia is consistent with all the Platonic hierarchies, which privilege the visible at the expense of the sensible, above at the expense of below, and which make light dominant over darkness, male over female. It introduces a decisive division between sophistical aporia and philosophical aporia, and only ignorant, uneducated people can confuse the two. For his part, Socrates always stresses the differences that mark the superiority of the philosophical aporia rather than the similarities which confuse his interlocutors. Of course the *Protagoras* ends in an impasse. But that is precisely because the dialectical method has gone astray, has strayed from the strait and narrow: Socrates and Protagoras began to discuss whether or not virtue could be taught without first asking themselves about the nature of science. They rushed into things, tried to go too fast, and forgot the essential point: the question of essences. They behaved like Epithemeus in Protagoras' myth, whereas they should have taken Prometheus as their guide and model. Had they done so, they could have guarded against

the possibility that your Epithemeus might trip us up und cheat us in our enquiry, just as according to the story he overlooked us in the distribution. I liked Prometheus in the myth better than Epithemeus, so I follow his lead and spend my time on all these matters as a means of taking fore-thought for my whole life. (361d)

The final aporia is not, moreover, the desired end: the interlocu-tors do not part without having formulated the project of meeting again to continue their discussion. The end of the dialogue is purely contingent: Protagoras is temporarily called by another appoint-ment. Similarly, at the end of the *Theaitetos* the participants agree to meet again the next day to pursue their discussion. The aporia is no more than a shadowy passage which is brief but necessary, as the perplexity it causes stimulates the desire to find a way out of the impasse. 'When I see the subject in such utter confusion (*deinos*) I feel the liveliest desire to clear it up' (*Protagoras* 361c). Aporetic perplexity alone awakens the desire for deliverance. Because it is untenable, the aporetic state, far from paralysing, encourages one to find, stimulates one to invent some *mechane*, some *poros* in attempt to find a way out; it forces one to jump into the water, to swim in the hope of encountering a miraculous dolphin. For no one possesses the *poros*, neither Socrates nor his interlocutors. It has to be 'found' anew each time, in each case. It has to be traced, woven, in some new way, and that involves an element of risk. This is why the comparison between Socrates and the sting-ray rests upon a confusion between the numbing aporia (that of the sophist) and the stimulating aporia (that of the philos-opher – and in the *Apology* Socrates compares himself not with a sting-ray, but with a gadfly or a goad which excite and arouse); and that in turn presupposes, wrongly, that Socrates possesses knowledge, that he is a resourceful man, which is to confuse him with Poros:

As for myself, if the sting-ray paralyses others only through being paralysed itself, then the comparison is just, but not otherwise. It isn't that, knowing the answers myself, I perplex other people (*tous allous poio aporein*). The truth is rather that I infect them also with the perplexity (*aporein*) I feel myself. So with virtue now. I don't know what it is. You may have known before you came into contact with me, but now you look as if you don't. (*Meno* 80d)

In the *Theaitetos* Socrates counters the arguments of ignorant men who describe him as having the sophist's ability to paralyse and as trapping men in aporia (*poio tous anthropous aporein*) by describing his true art: the fertile art of bringing forth souls. The art of midwifery consists of bringing on and stilling labour pains; the pains which fill men are more agonizing than those felt by women in labour.

There is another way in which my associates can be likened to women with child; night and day they are in travail and distress, far more so indeed than are women; and my art (*e eme techne*) can bring on or still these labour pains. (151a)

Like a midwife, Socrates uses drugs and magical incantations to lead men from their bad past to clear a passage, a *poros*, for the child, to bring it into the world and to expose it to the light. The art of the midwife in fact implies no abstract knowledge (*savoir*) and Socrates, like her, is sterile, and knows only that he does not know; that is his only superiority over those who think they know and whom he delivers, like an obstetrician, of their pseudo-knowledge. The midwife has no knowledge, but she does have a certain practical understanding which implies the ability to achieve the goal she has set herself because she has an expert eye; she can tell at a glance precisely when a woman is going into labour and can tell whether the new-born child is fit to live or whether it must die.

Aristotle states that the wisdom of the midwife is no different from that of the politician,[10] that she possesses an approximate, conjectural knowledge, the kind of knowledge that one assimilates during a long journey across a desert where no path is marked, where one must guess one's way and navigate by taking bearings from a far-off point on the horizon, where one must take devious roundabout paths to reach the desired goal. Now an expert eye and cleverness or quickness of soul are, according to Plato, the very qualities of the true natural philosopher (*Charmides* 160a; *Republic* IV) who brings forth souls, and whose *techne* he

compares, point for point, with the art of the midwife: their functions, their means and their ends are all comparable. Like a
midwife, Socrates can tell at a glance when someone is going into
labour, when someone whose soul is about to give birth begins to
experience aporetic pains. The moment in which the soul is full/
pregnant (*pleine*) and needs the help of the philosopher–midwife
if it is to be saved, if it is to be delivered of an aporia, is precisely
the moment when it is emptiest. It is the dizzying emptiness that
awakens the tormenting desire to know, that brings on labour
pains.

'I cannot convince myself that I have reached a solution, or that I have
ever heard anyone else put forward the kind of answer you require. On
the other hand I cannot put the subject from my mind.' ... 'My dear
Theaitetos, that is because you are in pain ... not from emptiness but
fullness (plénitude)'. (148d)

Aporia, Penia, Poros and Eros

Those who are in labour are always in the same position as Penia.
It is because she is in a wretched condition (*dia ten autes aporian*;
Symposium 203b) that she feels the need to have a child; she was
not invited to the splendid feast the gods held on the day when
Aphrodite was born, and had to go begging around the doors like
a shade or a ghost. (The Greek *skia* refers to a shade, but also an
uninvited guest at a feast; in *The Symposium*, the same could be
said of Socrates' shade Aristodemus, who passes on the 'story',
and of Alcibiades, who is also in love with Socrates; it is true, that
is, of both his good and his bad double.) In order to escape her
wretched condition, her feeling of poverty and emptiness, and also
because she has been abandoned by the gods, Penia plots to have
a child by Poros who, drunk on nectar, is imprisoned by the links
of sleep. The child of poverty (Penia), the child born of her ruse,
is Eros, and he inherits the contrasting characteristics of his parents.
Because he takes after his mother Penia, he is not, as Agathon,
Phaedrus and all those who thought that they could best praise
him by giving him all sort of qualities claimed, 'tender and fair':
'He is rough and squalid, and has no shoes, nor a house to dwell
in; on the bare earth exposed he lies under the open heaven, or in

the streets ... and like his mother he is always in distress'. And because he takes after his father Poros,

He is always plotting against the fair and good. He is virile, enterprising, strong, a mighty hunter, always weaving some intrigue (*mechane*) or other, keen in the pursuit of wisdom, fertile in resources (*porimos*), a philosopher at all times, terrible as an enchanter, sorcerer, sophist. He is by nature neither mortal nor immortal, but alive and flourishing at one moment when he is in plenty (*euporiste*), and dead at another moment in the same day, and again alive by reason of his father's nature. . . . But that which is always flowing in is always flowing out (*to porizmenon*), and so he is never in want and never in wealth. (203d ff)

Neither mortal nor immortal, Love is a daemon, an intermediary being. Neither wise nor ignorant, he is a philosopher, forced to invent all kinds of ruses; he is fertile in resources, like an enchanter, a sorcerer or a sophist. Because the philosopher does not possess knowledge, and because Eros is not to be confused with Poros, he neither has nor possesses any wealth. He retains nothing; wherever he finds himself, he always has to find a new path, to find new expedients. For that which is always flowing in is always flowing out. But, because he is not ignorant, Eros the philosopher can invent and seek, and he is not trapped or paralysed by any aporia. He does not have the same wealth of knowledge as the gods, the immortals or Poros who, enchained by the links of sleep and the toils of drunkenness, do not need to seek, and nor does he live in penury, in an extreme aporia, like one who does not know that he is in an aporia, not knowing that he does not know, trusting in the certainties of opinion, who does not seek that which he thinks he already possesses. Love, the philosopher and the daemon are intermediaries between, I would say, between Poros and Aporia rather than between Poros and Penia as the mythical story suggests in simplistic fashion by claiming that the child Eros takes after both his parents and that they have different characters because they are of different sexes. Indeed, everything in the story places this opposition 'under erasure' and tends to disassociate Penia from Aporia – who is seen simply as Poros's opposite. If Penia were in fact the paralysing Aporia, she would never even have tried to escape her distressing situation. If there had not been some *poros* in Penia's *aporia*, she would never have been able to plot, to think up the stratagem of lying down at the side of Poros, who is too full, too rich, who is asleep and passive, and who plays the so-called 'female' role in this primal scene. The 'virility' which love inherits from his father Poros is indeed embodied in Penia; it is she who is active, who takes the initiative, who is aggressive, who hatches plots, who is fertile in resources. It is her and not Poros who sleeps peacefully. All the characteristics which the myth attributes to Poros in fact belong in practice to Penia, and vice versa. In other words, Penia is no more the opposite of Poros than is the aporia; the true, philosophical aporia, or Penia, is always fertile; in her all opposites are placed under erasure; she is neither masculine nor feminine, neither rich nor poor, neither a transition nor the absence of a transition, neither resourceful nor without resources. (This is why *Aporia*, which breaks with the logic of identity, and which pertains to the logic of the intermediary, is an untranslatable term.) This indicates that Penia must always-already be pregnant with Love if she is to be able to give birth to him; she is not – to use an Aristotelean formula which is itself simplified – a passive receptacle, a raw material which receives form and all its determinations, all its riches, from an active, virile father. It is she who weaves the intrigue, who hatches the whole plot. The myth distributes these characteristics amongst three characters – Poros, Penia and Eros – but it also undoes that distribution and attributes them to one character: Eros. His parents are simply 'inventions' designed to try to convey the a-topic and daemonic nature of the intermediary (something that had already been discovered by the dialectical method), and of the human soul itself, that other *skia* whose condition is neither that of the gods nor that of animality, which is neither truly immortal nor mortal, which neither knows nor does not know, but which desires knowledge, which is, by its very nature, a philosopher. For man, who is neither Poros nor Penia/Aporia, the only *poros* is Eros.

Love gives neither wealth nor wisdom. He neither keeps nor owns anything. He offers only the possibility of incessant and imperishable generation. Acting as a midwife to souls does not mean delivering them of a wisdom, a *poros* which they possess without knowing it. It means creating within them an aporetic vacuum, a vacuum of plenitude which gives them an infinite desire to give birth to that with which they are always-already pregnant: Love.

The *Meno* counters the lazy arguments of sophists who use the sterile logic of opposition to frustrate all inquiries by asking:

But how will you look for something when you don't in the least know what it is? How on earth are you going to set up something you don't know as the object of your search? To put it another way, even if you come right up against it, how will you know that what you have found is the thing you didn't know. (80d)

The *Meno*'s answer is the myth of recollection, and *The Symposium*'s is that of Love, the daemon, the intermediary between gods and men, between ignorance and knowledge. Its answer is the infinite inventiveness of this child of Poros and Penia, who dies and who rises again from his ashes. For the logic of Love, of the intermediary, is a deliverance from all paralysing aporia. The two answers are in fact one and the same, if we accept that the *Meno*'s recollection is none other than *The Symposium*'s 'new memory': thought always dies when it is forgotten, but it rises again from its ashes; it is always able to find new internal resources, to think again, to give birth to itself; it is always the same and always new; it leaves behind it a new and different thought which resembles it like a brother. 'For what is implied in the word "recollection", but the departure of knowledge, which is ever being forgotten, and is renewed and preserved by recollection, and appears to be the same although in reality new' (208a).

In order to escape a sophistical aporia, it is therefore enough to love, that is to have the desire for a child; it is enough to remember oneself as a thought, to release one's soul from oblivion; it has been disfigured by the banquets of the sensible world, has become unrecognizable, corporeal, but it can be restored to its true nature if it is released from the body in which it is imprisoned.[11] A soul which forgets itself, say the myths, is reincarnated in the body of an animal when it is born again; this is the destiny of the tyrant whose soul is incurable; it is his misfortune to be too resourceful for, being unable to experience the aporia of indigence or distress, he never desired to have a child and loved only himself. His radical solitude makes him the most wretched of men, for only a meeting with a kindred soul can kindle the desire to beget a child in harmonious congress, 'in beauty'. It is the misfortune of the tyrannical soul to have no travelling companion who will agree to follow it to Hades and it is this which damns it to an eternal aporia, despite all its resourcefulness: it is hurled into Tartarus, which will never cast it up, for even a soul burdened with crimes can escape that infernal place, provided that it calls another soul to its aid and obtains its pardon. If a soul has not been cleansed of its crimes it is

shunned and avoided by all; it has no travelling companion (*euneporos*) and none will guide it; and it wanders alone in utter desolation (*en aporia*). But every soul that has lived throughout its life in purity and soberness enjoys divine company and guidance, and each inhabits the place which is proper to it. (*Phaedo* 108)

The souls of those who are judged incurable because they have committed many gross acts of sacrilege or many wicked and lawless murders are hurled into Tartarus, and never emerge. Those whose souls are judged curable are also cast into Tartarus

but when this has been done and they have remained there for a year, the surge casts them out. . . . And when, as they are swept along, they come past the Acherusian lake, they cry aloud and call upon those whom they have killed or misused, and calling, they beg and entreat for leave to pass from the stream. . . . If they prevail, they come out . . . but if not, they are swept once more into Tartarus. (114)

Winning or losing the immortality of your soul is a matter of finding – or not finding – a companion who awakens love in you. Philosophy is nothing less than the conquest of immortality. And this, in effect, is Love's ruse: to have discovered a stratagem, an expedient, an artifice, a *mechane* which procures men an Ersatz immortality, Ersatz because only the gods, by their very nature, enjoy true immortality. The ingenious *poros* which Love weaves to release men from the radical *aporia* of their mortality is child-birth, which is a divine act because all fecundity makes men immortal, as gods. Corporeal or spiritual generation is the *mechane* invented by Love to preserve the human race

according to the law by which all mortal things are preserved, not absol-utely the same, but by substitution, the old worn-out mortality leaving another new and similar existence behind – unlike the divine, which is wholly and eternally the same. And in this way, the mortal body, or mortal anything, partakes of immortality; but the immortal in another way. (*Symposium* 208a–b)

The union of man and woman is a procreation; it is a divine thing, for conception and generation are an immortal principle in the mortal creature. . . . And this is the reason why, when the hour of procreation comes, and the teeming nature is full, there is such a flutter and ecstasy about beauty whose approach is the alleviation of the bitter pain of travail. (206c, d)

For love is 'the love of generation and of birth in beauty. . . . Because to the mortal creature, generation is a sort of eternity and immortality' (206e).

Prometheus: the first philosopher

And yet the fecundity of the soul is declared to be 'more glorious' than that of the body: people worship the memory of poets who give birth to works, of those who invent just laws, and of craftsmen only if they are truly 'Fecund', only, that is, if they are inventors. For his part, Plato privileges philosophical fecundity above all others (it is the only form to which the term 'fecundity' fully applies, for it alone also implies coupling). Only this fecundity is truly 'divine', for it constantly gives birth to the divine part of the soul: thought. Its children are fairer and more immortal, for their seed was implanted in the soul by discourses and they will in their turn beget other discourses by other souls by planting a seed which will 'render immortal' its possessors and make them 'happy to the utmost extent of human happiness' (*Phaedrus* 277a).

At the touch and in the society of the beautiful which is ever present to his memory, even when absent, he [who finds a fair and noble and well-nurtured soul] brings forth that which he had conceived long before, and in company with him tends that which he brings forth; and they are married by a far nearer tie and have a closer friendship than those who beget mortal children, for the children who are their common offspring are fairer and more immortal. (*Symposium* 209c)

The hierarchy established between different types of fecundity can only really be justified by the always-already established hierarchy which posits the superiority of the soul over the body. It tends therefore to efface the very thing that it has established, namely the similarity between all kinds of fecundity: the search for immortality. The philosophical division which proclaims the superiority of philosophical fecundity above all others can be read as a gesture which breaks with anything that might contaminate its purity; the wish to make a break masks the strict continuity between the finality of philosophy and that of any other *techne*, of all inventiveness: to find expedients, *poroi*, to release man from the most fearful aporia of all: death. It disguises the Promethean nature of the philosophical undertaking.

Prometheus, of course, is the hero who narrowly saved the human race by stealing fire from Zeus, who liberated mankind and who paid for his deed by being bound.[12] Going against the will of Zeus, he saves men from death, undoes their fearful bonds and, like the philosopher in the myth of the cavern, leads them into the light of the day. In certain versions of the myth Prometheus is Haephestus' double; like him, he is the master of a liberating magic, and creates the human race by bringing inert matter to life. He moulds clay moistened with water, fashions arms and legs, and breathes life and movement into it. More generally, he is a figure who binds and unbinds. According to Aeschylus, it was he who taught men how to subdue the wild beasts of the fields and make them 'slave in pack and harness'.[13] He owes his mastery of bonds to his wily intelligence, to his shrewdness, to his multi-faceted *metis*, to his foresight. The art of this most resourceful (*pantoporos*) of heroes is the art of traps and tricks, of fraudulent plots. He can find a new *poros*, whatever the situation: 'His wit can circumvent the closest strait'.[14] His extreme shrewdness gives him a hold over all things, even over time itself. Because of his *metis*, Prometheus is a direct rival to Zeus; but he also helps Zeus when he gives birth to Athena, the daughter of Metis, whom he had devoured.[15] His role as an obstetrician indicates his kinship with Socrates, who is related to him in many other respects: at the end of the *Protagoras*, it will be recalled, he proposes Prometheus as a model because of his foresight. Socrates (who also frees men, invents *poroi*[16] to help them escape their *aporia*, leads them from darkness into light, and invites them to be as gods) 'imitates' Prometheus in many other ways. If we refer back to the *Protagoras* myth we find that Prometheus is described primarily as the hero who saves the human race from inextricable aporias, the myth is in fact the story of the birth of mortal creatures. It describes how the gods made different types (*tupousin*) of mortal beings in artisanal fashion by mixing earth and fire, and how mortal beings were truly born when they were brought out of the earth into the light. Before they were brought out, Epithemeus and Prometheus equipped each type of being with suitable powers at the behest of the gods. Epithemeus, who had no foresight, carried out the task alone, leaving the vigilant and far-sighted Prometheus to review it when he had done. The division of labour is, to say the least, ominous, and foreshadows the many difficulties that were to come. And indeed, the aporia are not slow to appear. The principle whereby the qualities are distributed amongst the various species is governed by the necessity to safeguard them from death, their 'natural qualities' are machinations, machines or artifices (*emechanato*) designed to ensure that no species will be destroyed (*dunamin eis soterian*) by guarding against the threat of mutual destruction and against external dangers. Epithemeus's ruse consists of providing each of them with appropriate food, and of ensuring that those species which devour others are less prolific, and that their victims, on the other hand, are fertile. The path to salvation (*soterian to genei porizon*) is the same as that invented by Love in *The Symposium*: generation as a *poros* granting immortality.

But Epithemeus is not perfectly wise, and is not as far-sighted as his brother; he distributes qualities without showing any sense of measure. He begins with the aloga, the animals, providing them with all the powers of survival and is impoverished and restricted when he comes to the human race. Epithemeus's aporia prefigures the aporia in which his lack of foresight would have plunged the human race, had it not been for the intervention of Prometheus to whom he appeals at the last moment as a saviour. Despite all his ingenuity, Prometheus himself is at a loss (*aporia oun echomenos*), for it is time to lead the human race out into the light of day. In order to save mankind, Prometheus hits upon the plan to steal the gift of skill in the arts, together with fire, from Athena and Haephestus, for it is impossible for anyone to use or possess skill without fire; skill is vain and impracticable (*amechnon*) without fire. He bestows the gift of fire upon man who, thanks to this fraudulent trick, acquires all the wisdom (*sophian*) required for life; only political wisdom remains in the possession of Zeus for, in his haste, Prometheus did not have time to enter his citadel, and crept only into the dwelling shared by Haephestus and Athena, both of whom possess *metis*, and stole fire without being seen by them as they lovingly practised their arts.

Thanks to this stratagem Prometheus puts human beings in a state of *euporia* and blesses them with every resource.

In Aristophanes' myth in *The Symposium*, men were originally gifted with prodigious strength and vigour and, in their Promethean arrogance, they scaled Olympus to attack the gods; Zeus punished them for their indiscipline by castrating them – by cutting them in two. Their punishment had the effect of diminishing their strength and of increasing the number of sacrifices made to the gods (190b ff). The only result of Prometheus' theft is the binding of man's liberator, who is left powerless and quite destitute, even though he has provided the human race with every expedient it might need. The theft of something divine completely reverses the situation in man's favour: the weakest of all mortal beings is now the strongest, the animal which was least provided for is now the best provided for; *aporia* is transformed into *euporia*; the human animal becomes a divine creature, the only one to possess the art of language, of uttering sounds and articulate speech, the only one capable of honouring the gods. And yet, because they have no political wisdom, men live in scattered groups; they are inferior to the animals which devour them, and when they come together and found cities, they injure one another. Having resolved to save the human race (in Aristophanes' myth, Zeus also takes pity on men and sends them a remedy to heal their scars: Love), Zeus delegates Hermes, another god possessed of *metis*, carrier of justice and respect which enchain men in harmonious links. These 'political' virtues, which are intended to safeguard the cities of men, are, unlike the 'technical virtues' distributed to all. All must have their share of respect for others and of justice under pain of being excluded from humanity and of being liable to death. The fact that the gift of politics was distributed to all explains why the Athenians, like other peoples, listen to every man's opinion when political wisdom is involved, whereas institutions address themselves to specialists in all other matters.

Protagoras – and this, for him, is one of the finalities of this whole story – then tries to demonstrate that it is neither an accident nor natural than all should possess this virtue, and that it has been taught them. The subsequent dialogue with Socrates leads to an impasse, to a complete reversal of the interlocutors' respective positions; both have acted like Epithemeus, and have lost their sense of measure, have distributed things badly; they have become lost because they let themselves be enchained and were seduced by the poetic spell of the myth. Prometheus, a model of foresight, is to be preferred to Epithemeus, who allows the soul to forget itself. This final convergence between dialectical aporia and the 'technical' aporia facing Epithemeus in the myth suggests that there is no solution of continuity between them, and that Prometheus, the benefactor who by stealing fire and technical skill has provided mankind with all the resources of life, is also a philosophical model; a twofold figure of salvation. Another of Plato's myths takes the same suggestion even further. This time it is not a sophist but Socrates himself who tells the myth, and he figures Prometheus as the founder of dialectics. This is the *Philebus* myth (16c f), a perfect companion piece to the Protagoras myth. The companion piece to the story of the theft of fire is that of the theft of dialectics, the most precious of gifts and the only one which really saves the human race by immortalizing it.

In both the *Philebus* and the *Protagoras* the figure of Prometheus appears at the moment when a way out of the aporia has been found; to be more specific, the aporia concerns the unity and plurality inherent in language. Socrates states then that there is no better path (voie) to salvation than the route (route) of dialectics; a path (voie) of which he has always been enamoured even if it has often eluded him, leaving him in the aporia (aporon) without a guide or a way out (issue). The best path (voie) is never man's possession. He can only eternally desire it as though it were a woman. He can only be enamoured of a poros which always flees from him; of a path (voie) which he has always to trace anew whenever he takes it, for it is always being obliterated and always leaves him disordered. The path of dialectics is in effect divine in origin, and to follow it is to become as the immortal gods. Dialectical aporia are, as it were, the inevitable punishment for man's hubris, a permanent reminder of Prometheus's sin. Though the dialectical gift came down to men from the gods, it was not given as a present; it was 'hurled from the heavens alone with the brightest of fire, thanks to some Prometheus' (18c). It was stolen in an act of fraudulent theft.

Legend has it that originally men and gods lived together and sat down together at the same feasts, until the day came when Prometheus was given the task of giving them appropriate nourishment. He tried to fool the gods and to favour men. Zeus then took over the task: each category of beings was to have the food which suited it and which it deserved. Mortal men were given the cooked flesh of dead animals; the immortals, nectar and ambrosia. Men, like Penia, could not be invited to the feasts of the gods. Prometheus's sin was to have tried, by deception, to let them partake of the feasts and to grant them immortality. We can therefore understand why, in the *Protagoras* myth, Epithemeus has sole responsibility for distributing the qualities. Prometheus would have shaped a type of human being identical to the divine type; the mimetic rivalry between Zeus and men would, sooner or later, have resulted in the destruction of the human race. Zeus would have swallowed up the human race completely, just as he swallowed Metis, or he would have bound it for ever, just as he bound Prometheus. Unable to let men partake directly of the divine feast, Prometheus steals fire, pays for it by being tortured, and makes men a gift of dialectics. He commits a double theft, and makes men a double gift of an Ersatz immortality for both body and soul, a substitute for the true immortality he could not give them as their portion.

This is why dialectics provide a good road, but this is also why that road is full of pitfalls; it is a *poros* which leads men out of their aporia, but it is also strewn with aporia and always leaves them in an aporia. It is too good a way, too divine a way for human thought, which must not seek to go beyond its limitations, which must strive only to remember itself, and which can repeat itself only by reinventing itself, by being always new and always the same.

Although too good, the dialectical *poros* is still the best one for men. It is the best way 'to investigate, learn and teach one another' (16d). The gift of dialectics spares men from having to behave like Epithemeus, from having to distribute things wrongly for lack of foresight; for if Prometheus sinned by acting beyond measure, he did so in order to give men a sense of measure. It prevents them from positing 'unity' too early or too late, from placing the one immediately after the multiple, makes them respect the intermediates that come between the one and the multiple, and allows them to count accurately. For it is 'the intermediates that make all the difference between dialectical discourse and eristic discourse'. The art of dialectics, defined as the art of numerical division and as the science of intermediates, is stated to be at the origin of all the sciences – 'anything which is a suitable object of science and has ever been discovered has been brought to light by this process' (16c) – and two *techne* are said to provide it with its paradigm. Both the art of music and that of grammatics are *techne* which are capable of counting and of specifying diversity within unity, of distinguishing intermediates and of arranging them into a hierarchy of classes and sub-classes. The former art distinguishes high-pitched notes from low-pitched notes within the confused variety of sound, knows the precise number of intervals that separate them, understands the limits of those intervals, and the combinations and harmonies that they can form. It finds similar features in bodily movements and can measure them numerically (17d). It is only its understanding of numbers that makes the art of music a true science; and it is that alone which makes who understands the art a real expert (*sophos*). Similarly, what constitutes grammatics as a true science is its ability to identify precise numbers of vowels and non-vowels within the indeterminacy of sound and to understand the multiple combinations to which they give rise. In order to be able to read, to be a *sophos* in the domain of letters, it is not enough to experience sound either as indeterminate or as one; 'literacy comes from knowing the number and nature of its parts' (17b). At 18b it is pointed out that it was Theuth, the god of writing, who was the first to perceive that vocal sound is indeterminate, that there are several vowels and not just one, and that there are other letters which do not have a sound, but which do make noise and do have number,

and he distinguished a third class of letters, which we nowadays call 'mutes'. Next he divided these noiseless, mute letters until he reached each unit; and he divided the vowels and the intermediate letters in the same way until, once he had seen their number, he gave the name 'letter' to each and every unit. . . . He further concluded that this interdependence is a factor which unifies all the letters in some way.

This implies that, in so far as it is a science of numerical division, dialectics cannot be contrasted with that which provides it with its paradigm; that it can no more be contrasted with writing, as in the *Phaedrus*, than writing can be contrasted with vocal sound, which is defined in the *Philebus* as a system of differences.[17] The paradigm of grammatics allows us to establish a kinship between the figure of Theuth and that of Prometheus (and therefore with that of Socrates), between the father of all *techne* and of the art of dialectics, and the father of writing and arithmetic, who also discovered astronomy, another science of measurement; between the fire which is necessary if technical skills are to be of any use, and the fire of writing and dialectics, which lies at the origin of all that has been brought to light in the domain of art and which is itself an art.[18]

At the end of the *Philebus*, the dichotomous method is used to arrange the *techne* in a hierarchy, and measurement is used as a criterion. *Techne* which use only conjecture, experience and habit, or a certain form of practical intelligence are placed at the bottom of the hierarchy, while dialectics is placed at the top, with those sciences and *techne* which use arithmetic, measurement and weighing occupying an intermediate position.

Suppose arithmetic, measurement and weighing were subtracted from all the sciences; the remainder of each science would be pretty trivial. . . . In fact only guesswork (*eikazein*) would be left, and the training of the senses by experience and habit. We would have to use guesswork (*stochastikos*), which is commonly called technas all of whose efficacity only came from laborious training. (55d).

This is followed by the example of flute-playing and, more generally, by that of music,[19] an art which is very approximate because it uses empirical conjectures and not measurement to establish its harmonies. The same is true of medicine, agriculture, helmsmanship and military command. On the other hand, ship-building, house-building and many other types of carpentry are much more precise, accurate and 'technical' (*technichoteron*) than most sciences (*epistemon*) because they use measurement and instruments. Plato thus makes a distinction between those arts – *techne* – which, like music, are lacking in precision, and those related to building, which are more precise. Arithmetic and the arts or sciences of measurement and weighing are placed at the top of the 'technical' hierarchy. The arts of arithmetic and measurement are in their turn subdivided in accordance with the criterion of their use: the vulgar forms are used in trade and building, and are distinct from the forms used for philosophical and scientific purposes. The latter are infinitely superior in terms of accuracy, precision and purity.

Although they have a single name, a distinction must therefore be made between two sciences of arithmetic and two sciences of measurement. Finally, the dialectical faculty (*dialegestai dunamin*) is elevated above even the most exact sciences. It is noteworthy that this hierarchical and dichotomous division does not introduce any solution of continuity between *techne* and *episteme*; the latter are merely stated to be included amongst the arts, to be more accurate and more precise forms of *techne*. The division established by Plato is not one between *techne* and *episteme* (and throughout this passage he uses the terms interchangeably) but one between that which relates to measurement and numeration and that which does not. And he uses the same criterion to award pride of place to dialectics. Yet it is only by virtue of a certain slippage that dialectics can be declared the supreme science, the most exact science of all. On the one hand, Plato abandons the 'Promethean' definition of dialectics as the art of numerical division (a definition which did allow a perfect continuity to be established between dialectics, the sciences and the arts) in favour of an older definition, which is used in *The Republic*, of dialectics as science of Being, as the science of a true reality which is perpetually self-identical; on the other hand, the superiority of dialectics, defined in this way, does not derive from the superiority of greater accuracy of its instruments, but from the superiority of its object, which is accurate, precise, true, constant and pure. 'Now, speaking with all truth and precision, could we attribute certainty to any of these things, when none of them has ever been, nor will be, nor is at the moment constant?' (59b).

It is as though Plato once more needed, despite the continuity he has established between *techne*, the sciences and dialectics, to exhibit a real break, as in *The Symposium*, where he declares philosophical fecundity to be superior to all other forms of fecundity. It is as though he needed to break with the 'impure' character of the *techne*, with their kinship with the sensible world and with profit: 'I hadn't got around to asking which science (*techne*) or which branch of knowledge (*episteme*) is outstandingly powerful or noble or profitable. I was simply asking which one surveys that which is certain, precise and most true' (*Philebus* 58c). If dialectics is the science of Being as always identical to itself, can it still take the art of music and grammatics as its paradigm? Can it still claim Prometheus, the Greek double of the Egyptian Theuth, as its founding father?

Is not the return to the familiar old definition of dialectics at the end of the dialogue ('Clearly, everyone would recognize the science in question to be the truest one', 58a) somehow akin to the return of a 'repressed'? Is it not because he is afraid that he will be accused of having repudiated the earlier dialogues ('dialectic would spurn us . . . were we to give precedence to any other science' 58a) that Plato suddenly reintroduces the old dialectics of the science of Being, which seemed to have been abandoned in favour of the new concept of dialectics as the art of numerical division, which implies a very different concept of Being, namely Being as a system of differences? A return of the repressed which acts, so to speak, as a screen, which counter-cathects the new Promethean definition of dialectics.

Having stated that dialectical science is superior, more exact and purer, having, so to speak, cleansed himself of any hint of impurity, of any suspicion of disavowing something, with one final gesture, Plato 'recuperates' what he seemed to have condemned, repressed or at least devalued. He 'throws the doors open' and allows even the most base, empirical and utilitarian techniques to 'pour in': any human life worthy of the name is a mixed life, and it implies the mingling of the purest science with the most impure techniques.

This is at least the case if one wants to be able to find one's way and to get home without tumbling into a well.

'Do you mean that, for all its unreliability and impurity, we should toss into our mixing bowl the science which uses imperfect rulers and circles as well?' 'We have to, if any of us is even to find his way (*odon*) home when he wants to.' 'Music-making too, when we said a short while ago that it is full of guesswork (*stochaseos*) and bluff and consequently lacks purity?' 'I think we have to, at least if our life is ever to be any kind of life at all.' 'It follows that you want me, like a doorman buffeted and pressed by a crowd, to give way – to throw the doors open and let *all* the branches of knowledge pour in together, the pure mingling with the less pure?' 'I don't see what harm all the other sciences (*epistemas*) can do . . . given possession of the first ones.' (*Philebus* 62b – 62d)

He therefore has to abandon his original intention of admitting only the pure sciences. The best life is a mixed life, which is not to be confused with a hotchpotch that is doomed to rot. A good mixture implies measure (*metron*) and proportion (*summetron*), both of which dethrone pleasure and which put paid to its claim to take first place amongst the virtues.

The final decision to throw open the doors to the impure sciences which are needed in life finally reconciles the two aspects of the Prometheus figure, who is a saviour in two senses: he stole both fire and technical skills, and the art of dialectics.

For man is an intermediate being whose love is dedicated not to Aphrodite Urania and nor to the earthly Aphrodite (the only two known to Pausanias), but to the third subterranean Aphrodite who is one with death — a figure concealed by all the protagonists of *The Symposium* except (indirectly) Socrates. And the only fitting life for him is a mixed life regulated by measure and proportion.

Method and way

Does not our reading of Plato contradict that made by Heidegger, who traces the beginnings of modern thought, of the technological era in thought whose main concern is with method and treatises on method, back to Descartes and to the affirmation of the subject as will? He makes a distinction between the method of thought and the way of thought, which cannot be reduced to a body of procedures and processes which treat things as objects, which pursue them and track them down so as to allow the concept to seize them: 'The way knows no procedures, no mediation'.

Yet the same text asserts that 'the rule of any kind of dialectic bars the way towards the essence of the way'.[20] It recognizes that the Platonic dialectic, which predates Cartesian method, is also essentially technological; that the Platonic *poros*, which is closely bound up with 'technical' understanding and with a Promethean will to mastery, is a way that has nothing to do with the essence of the way.

When Heidegger writes elsewhere that for the Greeks, it was not a matter of likening *praxis* to theory but, on the contrary, of understanding theory itself as the highest effectuation of authentic *praxis*, he is attacking the received view that *theoria* is a pure form of contemplation which is its own end. He adds that

according to an old story which circulated amongst the Greeks, Prometheus was the first philosopher and reports Aeschylus as having him pronounce a phrase which expresses the true essence of knowledge: '*Techne d'anagkes asthenestera makro*' ('But knowledge has much less strength than necessity'; 514).[21]

Is he thinking of the *Philebus* when he recounts this old story? Plato, in any case, is certainly thinking of the same story when he describes the 'gift' of dialectics as a fraudulent gift, and the 'best way' as a gift from Prometheus, that most resourceful, devious and shrewd of thinkers.

Which leaves us with the question of why Heidegger claims so strenuously that the modern, technological era of thought begins with Descartes . . .

Blanchot's *La Folie du jour* seems to me to demonstrate that, on the contrary, it dates back to at least Plato.[22] This text, which begins (and ends) with the very terms used to describe Eros in *The Symposium* ('I am neither wise nor ignorant') is perhaps one of those texts which does most to break with all 'technological thought', with all method, with all dialectical interrogation, all police interrogations, with all calling into question, and with all putting to the question, and therefore with all pretentions to immortality, with all 'Platonism'. Here, aporetic situations are no longer bad passages (mauvais passage) during a passage (poros). They are radically 'other', and have more to do with the thought of the 'way' than with that of method. There is no Promethean figure in this narrative, which breaks with all narrative,[23] and in which the *reprise* of the Platonic text is simply a means to displace it more radically.

Men, a strange species, would like to escape death. And some cry 'Oh, to die, to die!' because they would like to escape life. 'What a life. I will kill myself; I give up.' This is pitiful, strange, and a mistake. And yet I have met beings who have never told life to be quiet or told death to go away. Almost all of them are women, beautiful creatures.

Men are besieged by terror; night sees through them; they see their projects reduced to nought, their works reduced to dust. And they, who were so important that they wanted to build a world, are stupefied: everything collapses.

May I describe my trials? I could neither walk, breathe nor feed myself. . . . One day, they buried me in the ground, and the doctors covered me with mud. . . . I emerged from the muddy ditch with the vigour of maturity.

The worst thing was the harsh, frightful cruelty of the light; I could neither look nor turn my eyes away; to see was horrible; not to see tore me apart, cut me from forehead to throat. . . . Eventually, I became convinced that I had come face to face with the madness of light; the truth was that the light was going mad, that the brightness had lost its reason; it assaulted me irrationally, bound by no rules, with no purpose.

I walked down the street like a crab, clinging fast to the walls. As soon as I moved away from them, dizziness lay at my feet.

It is tempting to quote the whole tale. . . . 'A tale? No, no more tales. Nevermore.'

Notes

1 Marcel Detienne and Jean-Pierre Vernant, *Les Ruses de l'intelligence*, Paris, Flammarion, 1974, pp. 301 f. The following analyses owe an incalculable debt to this book, and I would like here to express – once and for all – my deepest thanks to its authors.
2 *Pontos.* cf. Emile Benveniste, *Problèmes de linguistique générale*, Paris, Gallimard, 1966, p. 297: 'In Greek, this is a poetic figure which likens the sea to a way'. If we refer back to the Vedic, and if we compare *pontos* with other words for way, we find that

The characteristic feature of *panthah* is that it is not simply a way in the sense that it is a space that has to be traversed from one point to another. It implies difficulty, uncertainty and danger; there are unexpected diversions; and it is not confined to land; it can .vary depending on who travels it; birds have their *panthah*, as do rivers. A *panthah* is therefore neither traced in advance nor used regularly. It is, rather, an attempt to cross an unknown and often hostile region, a way opened up by the gods for rushing water, the crossing of a natural barrier, the route that the birds find through space; in short, a way across a region that is closed to normal travel, a means of crossing dangerous or rough terrain. The closest equivalent appears to be 'crossing' rather than 'way'. . . . In Greek, it is an arm of the sea that is crossed, or, by extension, the expanse of water that allows one to pass from one continent to another.

3 cf. Detienne and Vernant, pp. 49, 50.
4 ibid.
5 ibid., p. 291.
6 cf. Sarah Kofman, 'Vautour rouge' in *Mimesis des articulations*, Paris, Flammarion, 1975.
7 cf. Jean-Luc Nancy, 'Le Ventrilogue', ibid.
8 cf. the writings of Jacques Derrida, in particular 'The double session' in Derrida, *Dissemination*, trans. Barbara Johnson, London, University of Chicago Press, 1981.
9 Cited, Detienne and Vernant.
10 Aristotle, *Historia Animalium*, VII, 9587a ff. Cited, ibid., p. 294.
11 cf. *Phaedo* 82d; *Republic* X.
12 Aeschylus, *Prometheus Bound*, trans. George Thomson, Cambridge, Cambridge University Press, 1932, 84; the 'iron girdle' which pins Prometheus to the rock is 'fixed inextricably'.
13 ibid., 462.
14 ibid., 60.
15 All these details about the Prometheus figure are taken from Detienne and Vernant.
16 Detienne and Vernant point out that the Greeks called the Pleiades 'the seven *Poroi*', the seven ways. By crossing the channels that lead from the depths of the sea to the sky, they open up paths of communication between the space of men and the space of the gods.
17 For all these problems, see Jacques Derrida, 'Plato's Pharmacy' in *Dissemination*, especially pp. 161 f.
18 The kinship between Theuth and Prometheus did not escape Rousseau. At the beginning of the second part of his *Discours sur les arts et les sciences*, he writes: 'According to an ancient tradition that was handed down from Egypt to Greece it was a god who did not want men to rest who discovered the sciences.' And he adds in a note:

The allegory of the fable of Prometheus is easy to understand, and it appears that the Greeks who chained him to the Caucasus did not think any more highly of him than the Egyptians did of their god Theuth. According to an ancient fable, when the satyr saw fire for the first time, he wanted to wrestle with it and to embrace it, but Prometheus called out to him: 'Satyr, you will mourn the beard on your chin, for it burns when you touch it.'

19 The art of music was previously described as the paradigm for dialectics, defined as the science of numerical division.
20 This final discussion of Heidegger's position was prompted by Jacques Derrida's seminar on method, during which this text (translated by R. Munier and P. Lacoue-Labarthe as *Le Défaut des noms sacrés*), and

its investigations into the relationship between method and way, was studied.

21 Heidegger, 'Discours du Rectorat', as cited by P. Lacoue-Labarthe in 'La Transcendence finit dans la politique', in *Rejouer le politique* (Cahier du Centre des recherches philosophiques sur le politique), Paris, Galilée, 1981.
22 Maurice Blanchot, *La Folie du jour*, *Montpellier*, Fata Morgana, 1973.
23 cf. Jacques Derrida's reading of the text in his 'La Loi du genre', *Le Colloque sur le genre*, Strasbourg, 1979.

· 3 ·

Hesiod's mimetic Muses and the strategies of deconstruction

GIOVANNI FERRARI

This essay has a narrow focus but a large penumbra. My focus is a current interpretation of the couplet spoken by the Muses in the prologue to Hesiod's *Theogony*, an interpretation avowedly influenced by the work of Jacques Derrida. I think it not just mistaken, but mistaken in an exemplary fashion. That is, in considering how it goes wrong I hope to reveal something more general about the impact of Derrida's work, actual and potential, bad and good, on classical studies. (This will eventually involve me in a quite detailed analysis of an exemplary piece by Derrida himself.)[1] In addition, I will offer the beginnings of an account of a significant and general pattern of archaic Greek thought evinced by Hesiod's couplet (one which has particular importance for the later development of Greek philosophy); a pattern which, I argue, is obscured by a certain pervasive anachronism that classicists engaged by Derrida have imported from his work.

i

When the Muses come to the shepherds on Helicon and confer upon the intrepid Hesiod the letters patent for his poetic mission, they formally declare their authority by means of an opposition. They inform their audience (at *Th.* 27–8) that they know how to say 'many false things that are like the genuine' (*pseudea polla etymoisin homoia*), but also, when they wish, how to 'speak true'

45

(*alêthea gêrysasthai*).[2] Which said, they give Hesiod a sceptre of laurel and invest in him the power to celebrate the gods in song (29–34). Pietro Pucci finds in the Muses' declaration a general thesis about the medium of their power, language (or, as he puts it, 'the *logos*'): namely, that 'the *logos* signifies things by *imitating* them with some obliquity, distortion, and addition', because 'the "original" signified is always absent'; a thesis he explicitly labels as Derridean, comparing 'Derrida's insight that the . . . "signified" is always caught in the web of the differential, deferring, negative relationships that allow the emergence of meaning and can never appear as present *hic et nunc*'.[3] Pucci's Derridean interpretation has been followed as such and developed by Marilyn Arthur. Summarizing Pucci's position, she asserts that in Hesiod's formulation 'both the true discourse and the false one are "imitations", but the true *logos* . . . imitates "things as they are", while "the concept of false discourse derives from the idea of imitation as *difference* from things, *simulation* of identity with things" '; and declares on her own account that 'in order to understand what Hesiod says' we must bring to bear 'the recognition that language itself – the *logos* – is a form of fiction, that representation itself is always, in some sense, a "lie" '.[4]

Both interpretations of the Muses' words have the merit of appreciating that in so generally phrased a statement, and one put on the lips of poetry's presiding spirits at the moment when the poet is confirmed in his craft, we would do well to look for an insight into how Hesiod conceived of the very workings of language – the mastery of which he here accepts as the Muses' gift. Alternative interpretations of these much-contested lines, by contrast, have long sought to make the allusion more specific and locate the truth and falsehood to which the Muses refer in particular poems or bodies of poetry, Hesiodic and Homeric. Of course, the two lines of interpretation are not mutually exclusive; Hesiod could perfectly well be putting out a general statement about poetic language with particular targets in mind, or he could be conducting a special polemic which nevertheless through its phrasing reveals how he conceives of poetic languages as such. And any attempt to settle for one or the other of these latter alternatives would swiftly be reduced to mere speculation. The important point is that the possibility of these lines having a particular target should not be allowed to block exploration of what they reveal, directly or indirectly, about Hesiod's more general conception of language.[5]

That the line of interpretation inspired by Derrida has vaulted this block is a significant achievement. However, the actual thesis that it distils from this passage of Hesiod seems to me to miss what is special – and especially interesting – about Hesiod's view of language. What I find striking in these two lines of the *Theogony* is that only of falsehoods, and precisely *not* of language in general, do the Muses say that they are '*like* the genuine'. In expressing their capacity for truth-saying, the Muses make no reference to a relation of likeness or a talent for imitation, but simply state that they know how to 'speak true' (or 'truths'). Pucci and Arthur, invoking Derrida, generalize the 'obliquity' of likeness or imitation to describe the metaphysical relation between words and world; but for Hesiod's Muses such indirectness seems to characterize only the false things we say about the world, not the true things.

In effect, Pucci and Arthur read the couplet as if the line in which the Muses mention their ability to imitate the genuine (or 'real' or 'true') were in fact a general statement of their mastery of language, of which the following line describes a special case: to wit, when the result of their imitation is itself something true. They treat the second line as subordinate to the first, rather than co-ordinate with it. This is no straightforward misreading on their part. I have reproduced in this section only their conclusions, and have not yet considered the steps by which they come to their opinion. Before I do so, however, I will fill out what I take to be the widespread and philosophically intriguing pattern of archaic Greek thought which shows through this text on my reading of it, and which I feel their reliance on Derrida has led them to miss. I can then appeal to the distinctive character of this material in order to resist their attempted assimilation of it to the Derridean model.

ii

I will take my examples primarily from Hesiod himself and from Theognis.[6] I am attempting to understand the asymmetry in the Muses' couplet: the fact that they do not dwell on the relation between language and world in general, but only in the case of a false or lying story do they emphasize the mechanism (of likeness to the genuine) by which a story of *that* sort accomplishes its effect, and say nothing one way or the other (*pace* the Derrideans) about how a true story comes to signify. I believe there is insight to be gained from seeing the linguistic asymmetry between truth and lies as one instance of a broader asymmetry between two types of exchange or substitution which structure the ethical position taken in these texts. Let us tag along with the culture and call them 'good' and 'bad' exchange; for this is what Hesiod does when he begins the *Works and Days* by distinguishing a praiseworthy from a blameworthy type of 'strife' or 'contention' (*eris*; see *Op.* 11–26).[7] The praiseworthy kind of contention is an emulative desire to match one's neighbour. Looking over at the next man's wealth, says the poet, we bestir ourselves to plough and plant and set our house in order (*Op.* 21–3). Moreover, since a cardinal fact of our existence is that the gods have 'hidden' our livelihood (42) – which is to say that our material resources are finite and require distribution and laborious production – what begins as a matching of one's neighbour is liable to end with our taking his place. Thus Hesiod envisions as the reward of a god-fearing life, and with no indication that it might be less than edifying as an ideal, the prospect that you should buy your neighbour's land, rather than he yours (341), and similarly that you should not need to look towards others, but that they should have to come to you to bail them out (477–8). The message would be that the mortal ledger is a zero-sum; that to do well, and to live as the gods intended, we cannot help but take from our fellows – take their place. Our gain is another's loss. And this is an example of what I am calling 'good' exchange or substitution.

The corresponding model of 'bad' exchange can be seen in the blameworthy contentiousness attributed by Hesiod to his brother Perses (27–41). Hesiod does not berate him for desiring 'another's property' (34) – for we have just seen that this is a desire shared by the god-fearing man[8] – but because he has come by that property (his own brother's share) dishonestly: not by worthy toil, nor by 'straight judgments' from the authorities (36), but by bribing the 'gift-eating' kings (39) into crooked litigation. Here, rather than match and take over from his fellow in a good exchange, Perses has imposed himself where he does not belong, in a position to which he has no just title; rather than making another's genuine loss his own genuine gain (where 'genuine' here refers to the results of labour, planning, luck, and of their absence), he has replaced the genuine with the spurious. This replacement of the genuine with the spurious is what I am calling 'bad' exchange. It is evident even in the means by which Perses has usurped his brother's place; for rather than labour to turn his land into food and fill his granary (30–2; cf. 299–301) – a good exchange, and a 'gift of the gods' (320) – he turns his wealth instead into 'gifts' for the kings to 'eat'; spurious food, that nourishes spurious justice. Nevertheless it is not an essential trait of bad exchange that it be effected through devious and deceptive means that can be viewed as bad exchange in its own right, as here. Violent force is an alternative means to devious speech; hence the blameworthy sort of contention is the spirit behind warfare (14) as well as Perses' double-dealing (and cf. 321–2). Bad exchange is a broader notion than deception.

Another sphere of good exchange – one more acceptable to a liberal mind than the unabashed jostling of landholders, because more inevitable – is that between parents and children, and between old and young in general. For a sign of the just society according to Hesiod is that its women bear 'children who resemble their parents' (*eoikota tekna goneusin*, *Op.* 235). Here again what begins as a matching between two parties will end with one party actually becoming what the other is: the child will become a parent in turn. Compare Theognis' conviction that the way to become good (or bad) is to keep the company of the good (or bad) (*Thgn.* 35–6; 563–6; 1,165–6); also his promise to Cyrnus that he is transmitting with good intent what he himself learnt as a child from the good (27–8), and his idea that 'no rose or hyacinth is born from squill, nor free child from a slave' (537–8) – that like generates like. The corresponding bad exchange here is the situation that Hesiod imagines overtaking the whole of society as our 'iron' race reaches the final stages of degeneration (*Op.* 180–201): 'father will not be like [or 'at one with', *oude* . . . *homoiios*][9] his children, nor the children like their father' (182). The younger generation will freely insult their forebears – behaviour which amounts to a refusal to 'pay back the labour of their rearing' (*apo threptêria doien*, 188). Again we encounter the spurious return of bad exchange (and notice that since the exchange is uneven Hesiod emphasizes the *unlikeness* of its two sides, whereas the good exchange engages like parties).[10]

So far I have given examples in which the good and bad exchange structures a developing social relationship (leading to replacement or usurpation of one person by another); but the two processes can be seen at work also in the maintenance of status and regular behaviour in society. Here good exchange consists in matching the other person, making yourself as he is, both positively and negatively. 'Give to one who gives, but do not give to one who does not give', is Hesiod's advice (*Op.* 354); and Theognis develops the pattern into a psychological ideal. Thus in the well-known analogy of the octopus (*Thgn.* 215–18) he praises as 'wisdom' (*sophiê*) that creature's ability to take on the colour of the rock upon which it sits (in contrast to 'intransigence', *atropiê*). It is a mistake, I think, to read such passages cynically. To be sure, a couplet such as 'among the wild I am wild, among the just I am the most just of all men' (313–14) can easily ring hollow in our ears, as if the poet were recommending insincere role-play as the model of social interaction; but it should be read alongside such sentiments as this: 'it is shameful to be drunk among the sober, and shameful if you stay sober among the drunk' (627–8); and this: 'but I would want my friend to be the kind of man who understands the moods of his companion, and can bear him, like a brother, even when he is a burden' (97–9). To see this ethic as a Goffmanesque donning and doffing of social masks would be to appeal to the concept of an authentic ego 'behind' the masks that seems to me simply not applicable here. The friend who can adapt to his fellow, who knows where he belongs, and who finds his values not within the closet of an authentic self but in the company of the noble – this is as good as it gets in Theognis' world. The 'changeable character' (*poikilon êthos*, 1,071) that he advises us to ply with our friends is not in itself a *deception*, or concealment of one's true thoughts and this despite the fact that he does indeed recommend that we should not tell all, even to our friends (73–4) – a wariness echoed by Hesiod, who warns us to get a witness even for dealings with a brother (*Op.* 371). For such discretion is made necessary only by the ever-present possibility of the corresponding *bad* exchange: the spurious return that takes place when friendly behaviour is met with the mere appearance of friendship – far harder to tell from the real thing than counterfeit gold from genuine (*Thgn.* 119–28; cf. 1,263). And only in the case of this sort of exchange does Theognis posit the existence of a hidden self behind the social mask: the boy with the character of a hawk beneath the appearance of beauty (1,259–62); the false friend who speaks soft words but thinks the opposite (96).[11] Moreover, despite his praise for the man who knows how to keep himself to himself in so dangerous a social environment, Theognis never recommends giving in to the ethical pressure and actually becoming a false friend oneself in order to get through life unscathed. He does not go further than advising discretion among one's friends; a discretion that does not actually present a false front, but simply does not show everything at once. On the other hand, with those whom you already know to be false friends, or open enemies, concealment (as at 579–80) may not be enough, and outright duplicity towards them is acceptable (as at 61–4); indeed, in a sense this is a part of good exchange, for it is to pay one's enemies back with like for like.[12]

Summing up, it should by now be apparent that the contrast and interaction between the two procedures of good and bad exchange is a consequence of that common archaic ethic against which Plato's Socrates takes his stand, for example in the *Crito* and in the first book of the *Republic*:[13] the ethic of being a friend to one's friends and an enemy to one's enemies, doing good to the former and bad to the latter.[14] Good exchange matches friends to friends and bonds the social group. It is not a process of imitation; at least, not one that remains *mere* imitation; for even if the young who are learning to be good or the son who emulates the father begin by imitating their model, they will end (if the exchange is indeed good) by instantiating it; and between peers the desire to be as others are leads you to become a genuine member of their group. But to bond the social group, in this world at least, is *eo ipso* to exclude others: to create outsiders, from whose ranks enemies will come. As Theognis says, you can't be friends with everyone (801–2); to be a friend to friends is also (on this line of thought) to be an enemy to enemies. And perhaps the most pernicious consequence of our time- and space-bound state is that even those with whom we bond in good exchange can become the outsiders, the people we seek to exclude: in land-starved Greece you will hope one day to buy the farm of the neighbour whom you emulate; the father who leads you into adulthood can become the obstacle you seek to remove in order to complete the journey (a preoccupation evinced in the violent and scheming succession of father by son among the gods of the *Theogony*).

Good exchange, then, is a coin with two sides; and from the

exclusion that is the obverse of its bonding arises the possibility of bad exchange. For bad exchange is simply what happens when the outsiders we inevitably exclude through good exchange will not *stay* excluded, but insert themselves where they do not belong, as a spurious presence. Perses, excluded from his brother's share by the rightful distribution of their father, imposes himself as a usurper; fathers and sons in the iron age Armageddon cannot see each other as anything but hostile competitors. Here the process of imitation finds its proper place; for the usurper has only a fake title to his position, and can never become what he seeks to be. And as we have just seen, there is little hope held out in these texts that one might escape bad exchange by attempting to live only by the good; for the temporal and spatial restrictions which they find to mark human life dictate that the very same people must be targets of both.

Thus, although the story I have told has the possibility of bad exchange 'arising' from good, one could as well take the sequence from the other end and analyse good exchange as the avoidance of bad – the attempt to set boundaries in its muddle. The two are mutually dependent, both historically and logically. That is why Hesiod can date the origin of 'hard toil (*ponos*)', which is an inescapable and praiseworthy sort of contention, and an example of good exchange, to the appearance among men of the first woman, Pandora (*Op.* 90–5), who is in many respects the very incarnation of bad exchange – this creature with the lying mind of a dog beneath her beauty (*Op.* 62–7; compare Theognis' beautiful boy with the mind of a hawk), who (like some gift-eating king) plunders the fruits of another's toil for her own belly (*Th.* 599), and whom (as has often been noted) the poet describes as the 'likeness' of a woman (*ikelon, Op.* 71; *Th.* 572) even though she is the original of the line. Yet Pandora also brings with her the possibility that a man can sire sons like their father to inherit his substance; a good exchange that no man now can turn his back on without miserable consequences – although he may equally be letting himself in for the pain of worthless progeny (*Th.* 602–12). Pandora, then, is not simply a bad exchange from Zeus (the gift that he gave to trick us, *Op.* 83–5); rather, she represents the indissoluble connection in our world of both good and bad exchange – a connection which is painful to look at whole, making the poet sigh for a golden age and take out his resentment on the hateful figure of woman. The blessed happiness that he imagines by contrast for the 'golden race of men', who 'lived like gods', is to exist free from exchange of either sort, whether good or bad (*Op.* 109–20). Not only did they live in peace and continual celebration (in which the usurpation of bad exchange has no part) but also felt no constrictions of time or space; for the earth bore sufficient fruit without toil, and they were not subject to old age, nor indeed to growth – their lives being as a single day (since they die 'as if taken by sleep'), and their 'hands and feet' being 'always alike (*aiei homoioi*)'. Here the mention of constant likeness is necessary only for us denizens of the iron age whose hands and feet will show their age; among the golden race there is no change against which the likeness would stand out. So too, the subsequent race of silver, which contrasts with them in every way (129), is marked not only by the bad exchange of internecine violence and a refusal to give the gods their due (134–6), but also by an exaggerated and distorted development of the good exchange between generations; for they spend a full one hundred years tied to their mother's apron strings, and then live only a brief span of maturity (130–3). Similarly in Theognis the uncomfortably close connection between good and bad exchange which we have just witnessed in the figure of Hesiod's Pandora emerges from his recognition, amounting at times to despair, of how hard it is to tell the true from the false friend (that is, how hard it is to know whether a person deserves your trust), despite the genuine distinction between the two.

Having sketched the broader ethical context, I come to the specifically linguistic issue: the fact that in Hesiod's couplet imitation is a feature of how lies signify, only, and not of true statements. The asymmetry is readily explicable as an instance of the contrast between bad and good exchange. A good exchange is even; one party is made like the other, not in the sense of becoming an imitation of the other, but in becoming what the other is; and this will entail the exclusion of a third party that does not belong to the group bonded by the exchange (a party which may or may not be identical with one of the parties to the exchange itself – in which case the exclusion amounts eventually to displacement). Such, I suggest, is Hesiod's model of truth. That is why the Muses do not mention 'likeness' when claiming the ability to 'speak true': because for Hesiod true assertions are not *like* the world to which they refer, in the sense in which 'like' implies 'and also therefore unlike, distorted, to some extent'; rather, they simply refer to it – correspond to or match it, without distortion. One of the most explicit texts on this point is a much-cited passage of the *Odyssey* (viii 487–98),[15] in which Odysseus praises the bard Demodocus for his account of the Achaean's fate. One would think, says Odysseus, that the singer had been there himself, or heard the tale from one who had; for his song is so very much 'in the proper order (*kata kosmon*)'. And he invites the bard to sing of the Trojan horse, promising to spread his reputation abroad if here too he can give an 'exact account, part for part (*kata moiran katalexêis*)'.[16] Here the criterion of truth is a matching of the details of the story to those of the event; a matching that involves 'likeness' only in the sense in which we have seen the term crop up in good exchange: as replication. We could say: Demodocus is telling it like it is (or was).[17] And as with good exchange in general, the bonding of the two parties (what the story says, and what it refers to) entails the exclusion of a third: in the case of poetic language, the workaday world of cares from which the story has the power to transport us. Hesiod devises a well-known oxymoron to fit this idea, announcing (later in the prologue to the *Theogony*, at 53–4) that the Muses were born of the union of Zeus and 'Memory' (*Mnêmosynê*) to be a 'forgetting (*lêsmosynê*) of evils and a respite from cares' (a theme reiterated at 98–103). Only Zeus, as Hesiod puts it (at *Op.* 267–8), 'sees everything, understands everything', can turn his attention to whatever he pleases, 'nor does it escape him' (*oude he lêthei*). Here Zeus' awareness of truth derives from the fact that he need never miss a trick; a point which seems to gain support (as is usually noted in this conneciton) from etymology; for *alêtheia*, 'truth', can be analysed as a compound of the negative prefix *a-* and the term for 'forgetting' or 'missing': *lêthê*. Mortals, however, locked in their zero-sum world, have no choice in the matter; we cannot be mindful of everything at once, either listening to song or in anything else.[18]

The point I wish to emphasize is that this symbiosis of 'truth' or 'mindfulness' and 'forgetting' or 'missing' is not being thought of as a special feature of language, poetic or otherwise, but is part and parcel of the broader ethic of good exchange that I have been examining. To be as mindful of as much as one can – as close to Zeus as possible – is Hesiod's general ideal: to watch for everything, and 'not to miss' (*oude se lêthoi*) either the coming of spring or the season of rain (*Op.* 49–2); to be the sort who 'understands everything on his own' (*panta noêsei*; cf. *panta noêsas* said of Zeus at *Op.* 267), or, second-best, who will listen to good advice (*Op.* 293–5). We must concentrate on the right things at the right time, know which days are good – days 'when people judge true (*alêtheiên . . . krinontes*)' (*Op.* 768) – and which are bad and should be sidestepped. This would be perfectly fine if we and the world were in synchrony, but unfortunately 'some think one day is good, some another, but few actually know' (*Op.* 824); and the mind of Zeus which sees everything goes 'sometimes one way, sometimes another, and is difficult for mortal men to understand' (*Op.* 483–4). As a result, the inevitable coupling of mindfulness and forgetting – the fact that by concentrating on one thing we must ignore another – can be pernicious; for we may choose to concentrate on the wrong thing, at the wrong time.

The good exchange of story-telling fits naturally into this scheme, and shares its disadvantages. From emulating their neighbours and being mindful of the seasons during the workday people turn their minds to the bard's story, following with their thoughts the path – the course of events or, more generally, the way of things – of which he sings. Here it is tempting for us, especially when we read, for example, of how the Phaeacians were held silent and 'spellbound' by the tale of Odysseus' adventures (*kêlêthmôi d'eskhonto*, *Od.* xi 334), to think in terms of 'fictionality'; as if the poetic power to which Hesiod and Homer refer is that of whisking the audience from the present, of replacing their world with a 'fictional' world which is there and yet not there. Thus, we might express the zero-sum of good exchange in this case by claiming that to gain the world to which the song permits us entry is, inevitably, to lose the world in which we hear its call; much as we cannot (to invoke a different art) see both the pigment on the canvas and what is depicted at the same time, but must concentrate on one or the other. But I think this would be an anachronistic mistake – untrue to the texts in question. What Hesiod says poetry can make us forget is not the present, or the world in which we now find ourselves – as if by super-imposing a veil – but rather our evils and cares; the tasks that have taken up most of our day. That was work, this is relaxation (which is not to say: trivial); and both are valid parts of this our one world. Odysseus laughs with the rest as Demodocus tells the story of Ares and Aphrodite, but weeps alone when he sings of the Trojan war (*Od.* viii 367–9 vs. 83–95, 521–34), because the bard is re-directing the hero's attention, precisely *not* to the present, but rather to the past and future cares of his life, to the origins of his still unfinished journey, rather than focusing it on the celebration at hand.[19] Similarly, the song of the Sirens (those emblems of dangerous speech) is not pernicious through duplicity or deception in its content – on the contrary, the Sirens are truth-tellers, who know everything and promise to tell all (*Od.* xii 184–91) – but rather because it would make Odysseus concentrate on the wrong thing at the wrong time. The danger is that Odysseus will be so soothed and delighted by their narration as to forget all about his journey home (37–46). The Sirens represent not the duplicity or fictionality of poetry, but its truth-telling power run amok; they are as much a part of Odysseus' journey as any other of its episodes – as listening to the bard is part of the daily or yearly round – but they threaten to become the whole.[20]

Thus we see why Hesiod does not dwell on the relation between truthful story-telling and the facts, but rather on the effects of poetic commemoration as an activity (the cares that it displaces): because that relation, taken just in itself, is as unproblematic for him as any other of the good exchanges that bond us; that is what comes to our notice through poetic memory comes as directly (*if* it comes) as any other of the things that we notice. It is what escapes our notice – whether as the obverse of good exchange (the background to memory) or as the deception of bad exchange (to which topic I shall turn in this paragraph) – that causes problems and gives food for thought. The power of poetry is still linked for him to a social context in which it has its proper time, the time of festivals and relaxation; and it is for its power in patterning our lives directly, in making our world for us as memory always does, and not for some mysterious capacity to reflect the whole of life through words (Pucci's 'magic mirror of *logos*', 11) – not, then, for its power of representation – that he recommends it. However, poetic commemoration is as open as any other good exchange to the danger that what is excluded will not remain in its place. The friend may be only a seeming friend; an enemy after all. The speaker, even a poet, may be misleading us, whether deliberately or not. (Have we not seen that many have their piece to say about good and bad days, but few know the truth?) And only in this case, because what the story says no longer simply refers, does it follow the model of bad exchange and become a spurious presence to be dwelt on in its own right, a 'false thing like the genuine' (similarly, only in the description of the false friend, we saw, does Theognis invoke the concept of a person behind the spurious mask).[21]

What is at issue here is not the relation between signifier and signified in general (*pace* Pucci 15), nor indeed a particular relation between signifier and signified. When Odysseus tells Penelope 'lies like the genuine' (*pseudea . . . etymoisin homoia. Od.* xix 203), it's not his *words* (signifiers) that resemble a genuine story; it's the story itself, which has no purchase on reality, but passes for (resembles) a true story. The signified is spurious, not the signifier. In the case of a genuine story, the distinction that I am marking by distinguishing the 'signified' (the content of the story) from the 'reality' on which it has purchase is simply not felt; that is why terms such as *alêthês* and *etymos* are ambivalent between our 'true', 'real' and 'genuine'. Whether any such distinction should be drawn in general, and how, precisely, to analyse what is meant by 'signified' and 'reality' in that case, are large metaphysical questions which I shall not broach. But it is clear – from the very fact that we cannot tell whether 'the genuine' in the phrase 'lies like the genuine' is to be glossed as genuine 'story' or 'truth' or just 'thing' – that the larger question is not broached even implicitly in our texts either. The problem they face up to is this: that good exchange is always open to the possibility of bad; that the power of speech can be used to lie (Penelope, after all, weeps as readily at Odysseus' lies, *Od.* xix 204, as Odysseus himself did at Demodocus' truth). Or, as Derrida likes to put it, that the iterable is always also imitable. But this fact does not have the consequences that either the Derridean classicists or Derrida himself attribute to it, as I shall now argue.[22]

iii

Some may feel that in the preceding section I have taken the very ideas of those whose interpretation I have declared myself to be resisting, and touted them as my own. This talk of good and bad exchange, of how the excluded or marginal will not stay marginal but infects the bonded group that seeks to exclude it – what is it but the very model of 'supplementarity' that Derrida has deployed in his deconstruction of western metaphysics? Yes, by all means. 'Supplementarity' is a powerful and useful notion; and I do not seek to avert my eyes entirely from the direction in which Pucci and Arthur want to pull Hesiod's text, but rather to plant my flag at a nearer horizon than the one they have in view. I mean this in two ways: I believe that the Derridean critique which they offer imports and relies upon a philosophic framework through which the most distinctive ideas in this and other archaic texts slip by unnoticed; and furthermore, that this framework is not in any case one that we should want to accept.

I promised earlier that I would not just parade Pucci's and Arthur's conclusions but would examine the argument by which they arrive at those conclusions. Their strategy is to look not just at what the Muses say, but at the effect of the content of what they say (in this couplet) on the stance we mortals are to take towards everything that they say (including the couplet). The Muses say that they can tell the truth when it pleases them to do so, but that they can also lie; and their lies look just like the truth. Surely this is the poet's way of declaring that he is cut off from the truth, 'alone, facing the precariousness of the *logos*' (Pucci 12)? If Hesiod believes that the Muses are telling *him* the truth, this can only be a matter of 'faith' (12); because since the Muses are 'the only witnesses of the past events whose narration they inspire in the poet' (13), since 'the simulation of identity may always go undetected' (14), and 'since the poet will forever be unable to compare their song with "the things as they are"' (13), there is no way for him to be sure that he is avoiding distortion; so that, indeed, 'with tremendous energy he denies the general demonstrability of truth' (12). This is the argument by which Pucci introduces the Derridean claim that 'the "original" signified is always absent' (13), and the sense in which he takes the Muses' message to be that all language, not just falsehood, imitates things with a measure of distortion; for the poet (as opposed to the Muses) is cut off from the truth in everything that they inspire him to say, whether it happens to be true or not. Furthermore, if we direct this line of reasoning more particularly to the Muses' couplet itself – something neither Pucci nor Arthur make a point of doing but a move which has been supplied for them by Ann Bergren – we can wonder whether their very claim to be able to tell truth and lies is not itself a lie; a thought Bergren compares with the notorious paradox of the liar.[23]

I will first examine whether this argument is sound, and then consider its conclusion as a philosophic thesis in its own right. It seems to me that the conclusion to which Pucci comes simply does not follow from the premises that he extracts from Hesiod's text. It is perfectly correct to reason that, if the Muses can tell the truth or lie at will, then anything they say to you may be a lie; but this is no reason at all to hold that, even if they are not actually lying, their words distort the world in the manner of lies (that is that 'the *logos* signifies things by *imitating* them with some obliquity, distortion, and addition', 12). In so far as a general thesis about language shows through Hesiod's couplet, it is the one seen in the previous section: that the power of speech can always be used to lie. Nothing in Pucci's argument rules out the thesis that when a person speaks true (even if we cannot *know* that he speaks true) his assertions match or correspond to the world directly, without distortion; and as we have seen, much in our sources can encourage us to believe that this is the model of truth with which they work. The worry to which Hesiod attests need only be the possible unreliability of the *users* of speech, as in Theognis, and not a worry about the relation of words to world in general. The burden of proof is on Pucci and Arthur to show how the latter follows from the former; and I find nothing in what they say that can bear this burden. Indeed, they seem not to appreciate the difference between the two positions. Thus Arthur, for example, cites Umberto Eco's contention that ' "every time there is signification there is the possibility of using it in order to lie" ' as just 'another way' of expressing Pucci's conclusion, which she herself, we recall, interprets as the notion 'that representation is always, in some sense, a "lie" ' (105–6). But Hesiod and Theognis could readily agree with Eco (for who can tell the false friend reliably? Even with your brother you should get a witness) while holding back from the thesis that signification in general operates in the manner of lies.[24]

Nor do I find it particularly helpful to correlate the Muses' couplet with the paradox of the liar. Bergren asks, 'Who except the Muses themselves can tell whether this very declaration is an instance of . . . their true or their apparently true speech?' She glosses her question as follows: 'Here the very utterance that proves the speaker's consummate knowledge of truth puts in question the truthfulness of that utterance'; and compares Sextus Empiricus' 'version of the "Cretan lie" '.[25] But the Muses' utterance does not 'prove' their knowledge of truth; that is just the problem. It only *claims* knowledge of truth. The problem is that words alone cannot guarantee truth or sincerity; saying 'believe me' in a passionate tone of voice does nothing to earn belief (though it might get you believed). Sextus' point is quite different. He shows that those who claim 'all things are false' refute themselves; for if the statement is true, then it is false; if it is false, it is false; so it's false. Thus, incidentally, his argument is a different animal from the Cretan lie (or paradox of the liar), which is not generated by the statement 'all things are false', but by the statement 'I am lying' (or 'all Cretans are liars', said by a Cretan), which is true if false and false if true. In either case, what follows from assuming the statement to be true (or false) is a categorical demonstration of falsity or truth or both, in strict logical fashion; whereas what follows from assuming the Muses' couplet to be true (as Bergren does) is the problem that, precisely, we can only *assume* it true, but cannot tell whether it is true or not. This is a social and psychological problem, not a logical one.

But to return to Pucci and Arthur. Having been saddled with the general problem that all language distorts the truth, Hesiod is allowed neatly to sidestep it by having the Muses claim to sing the truth; a statement about which Pucci has this to say: 'in view of line 27 [the claim that they can tell falsehoods like the genuine] we have to understand that the Muses sing a song without difference from truth and *identical* to it' (14); and he takes Hesiod to be suggesting that this is the kind of song the Muses choose to sing to him (13). Pucci is not very happy with Hesiod's response, calling it 'a solution of some sort' and judging that 'Hesiod . . . avoids the problems his text raises' (14).[26] But as we have seen, there is no reason to think that this is the problem he is confronting (or refusing to confront). It is not that all language signifies by means of some kind of distortion which in the case of Hesiod's language (lucky man) just happens to be zero; that *would* require some explaining. Rather, only in the case of falsehoods does the notion of distortion even come into play (and since Hesiod is our poet, and we are listening to him, we naturally give him the benefit of the doubt and hope he is not playing us false). We do not, after all, 'have to understand' the line about truth in the light of the line about falsehood; we can choose to give them their independent value.[27]

However, the reader might grant my rebuttal of this line of argument and yet remain dissatisfied. For one thing, why criticize the Derrideans for missing a pattern peculiar to archaic thought, when it is well known that deconstruction reveals the effects on its sources of problems that those sources are unable to look straight in the eye? Does not Pucci himself point out that 'though we cannot say to what extent Hesiod is aware of these problems, they are certainly raised by his text' (14)? And for another thing, surely the distinction that I stress between the use of language and its referential structure does not, pragmatically speaking, matter very much? That is, even granting that the true speech of the Muses refers directly, and not in the manner of falsehood, still, if we can never *know* whether what they say is true or false, from our perspective it might as well be the case, so to speak, that everything they say is lies.

These two complaints require a connected response, in which I must say a little about the Derridean thesis on language in its own right. Pucci's interpretation of Hesiod dips into a very deep issue in philosophy, with which I cannot hope to deal adequately here. Briefly, it seems to me that in order for Pucci to propound Hesiod's problem (the problem that I have argued is not Hesiod's) he must himself espouse a theory of 'metaphysical realism'; and that this a theory we should resist. The metaphysical realist, in the sense in which I am using the term, believes not just that true statements correspond to the way the world is, but that their truth must somehow be 'grounded' in this correspondence; that is, that they can be known to be true only by *verifying* their correspondence to the way the world is.[28] It is this second belief that generates the problem, and allows Pucci to claim that 'since the poet will forever be unable to compare [the Muses'] song with "the things as they are", he *cannot* be aware of the distortions, deflections, and inventions that draw the poetic discourse into falsehood and fiction' (13). Pucci must be making this proposal in his own name, for it underlies what we have seen him refer to as 'Derrida's insight' that 'the "original" signified is always absent'. Only those who believe that we have a genuine need for an act of 'comparison' between our true statements and the way the world is can dwell on the difficulty or impossibility of so doing, as Pucci and Derrida do, in such a way as to make it seem a genuine problem. But there is a strong move in current philosophy to see this as not a genuine problem at all, and as a line of thought that leads swiftly to the Kantian invocation of a 'noumenal' realm – understood as the realm of the 'always absent', that to which we can have no access in thought but which is the limiting condition of our thought.[29] This is a notion that others have argued we would be better off without; I shall limit myself to the point that we should appreciate that not only archaic but also later Greek philosophic thought manages to live without it. Hesiod has no thought of comparing the truth about the world with the way the world is, because the need for comparison is imported only by lies which are *like* the genuine. And even Plato, whom we might think generalizes such a need when he insists that particulars have a share in reality or truth only to the extent that they are like the corresponding Form, is better understood, I suggest, as generalizing the Hesiodic model of the spurious to cover the entire 'realm of becoming' (and that would be why he can envisage direct awareness of the Forms; because to them he assigns the immediacy of Hesiodic truth).[30] My overall point here can be closely correlated with what I take Myles Burnyeat to have shown: that 'Greek philosophy does not know the problem of proving in a general way the existence of an external world', a problem that Descartes can be seen as inaugurating, and that 'the characteristic worry ... is not how the mind can be in touch with anything at all, but how it can fail to be' (as our archaic texts worry about lies, not truth).[31]

I hope I have said enough to indicate, if not fully to demonstrate, why it matters to keep the view about the referentiality of language that emerges from Hesiod's couplet distinct from his worry about the deceptive use of language, and not to allow consideration of the pragmatic consequences of the latter to twist our thoughts about the former until we have it matching the Derridean view of referentiality. It matters because these are, metaphysically speaking, very different views, and have very different philosophic consequences. This is my response to the second of the two complaints which I supplied as devil's advocate; but it is surely also a response to the first. That is, even granting that the problems of metaphysical realism can indeed be seen as developing out of or in reaction to a Greek tradition to which they were foreign, and so in that minimal sense can be said to be 'raised by Hesiod's text',[32] we shall better understand what it is that Hesiod and others are *not* confronting (for whatever reason, whether due to some necessary 'inscription' of the *logos* or because he is blessedly free of an unnecessary philosophic problem) if we first take the proper measure of their difference, and temper our eagerness to make them fit a modern mould.

iv

I often hear it said that Derrida should not be held responsible for the excesses of Derrideans. But in this case it strikes me that Pucci and Arthur are following to the letter at least one facet of the example that Derrida has set; for in his now classic debate with John Searle on the topic of intentionality, Derrida makes a move of just the same sort as the one I have criticized in the Derridean classicists' interpretation of Hesiod. This is a point worth establishing in its own right, and because the parallel with the work of the classicists is instructive.

The pattern of debate between Searle and Derrida can be set out as follows. Searle reads Derrida as attempting to undermine or do away with a notion that he holds dear, namely that 'intention is the heart of meaning and communication'. Derrida would be achieving this goal in two stages: first by showing that 'intentionality is absent from written communication', and then by extending this conclusion to apply to all forms of communication.[33] And if intentionality is universally absent from communication, not only will it fail to be the heart of communication, but also the very distinction between presence and absence of intentionality will have collapsed. Intentionality will no longer be a workable concept in the philosophy of language.

Derrida responds to Searle with the claim that he was not out to show, simply, that intentionality is never present, whether in written or spoken language, but rather that in both cases intentionality is never simply present. Not that he would exclude the possibility of what he calls an 'effect' of simple intentionality, as seen for example in the contrast between spoken and written language. What he maintains is that no (performative) utterance would succeed, whether spoken or written, delivered in real life or in a contrasting context (in the course of a theatrical play, perhaps), unless it were 'identifiable in some way as a "citation" ',[34] that is, unless even the spoken or real-life utterance were somehow a reproduction or imitation in the sense thought peculiar to the written, the dramatic, the fictional. This claim, however, is not meant to undermine outright the distinction between the real-life and the staged or fictional utterance: 'Not that citationality in this case is of the same sort as in a theatrical play, a philosophic reference, or the recitation of a poem'.[35] Compare the inquiry into signatures that stands as an *envoi* to 'Signature événement contexte' – a part of that essay which Searle chooses not to discuss (but which I shall presently make the focus of my criticism). There Derrida quizzes the dependence of signatures on the intentions of signatories, but carefully distinguishes such probing from a straight denial of common sense: 'Are there signatures? Yes, of course, every day. Effects of signature are the most common thing in the world'.[36]

Much hangs, then, on the persuasiveness of Derrida's reasons for not simply accepting the simple distinction between the presence and absence of intentionality (but keeping it at arm's length with his deliberately coy talk of 'effects' of intentionality and of signature). He reasons in the following way. He fastens on the fact that since any signifier, just in order to function as a signifier, must be repeatable, it is also, and necessarily, open to various special possibilities of 'parasitic' repetition: imitation, citation, writing, use on stage or in the course of fictional language. In each of these cases the signifier continues to function even though divorced from the signifying intention of its original user or creator. Derrida begins by agreeing that these parasites are indeed special; that not every actual instance of iteration is parasitic. But he next points out that the possibility of parasitism is a 'structural' or 'necessary' possibility. In other words, the fact that parasitism is possible follows necessarily from the fact that iterability is an essential or defining property of the signifier. Therefore, claims Derrida, the divorce from signifying intention that brands the parasitic cases is also to some extent, and necessarily, a mark of the signifier as such. To what extent? To an extent sufficient, it would seem, to bar the signifying intention from being ever 'fully present to itself' ('pleinement présente à soi'; compare Pucci's mention of the 'original' that is 'always absent'). The result is that, if a speech act is an intentional event, it is an event that never quite happens. The structural possibility of parasitism prevents any 'actual event (in the standard sense) . . . from ever entirely, fully taking place (in the standard sense)'.[37]

This is the point at which Searle quite rightly balks. In the 'standard sense' Derrida has given no reason for doubting that the intentional event which is the speech act takes place 'entirely' and 'fully'. In order to express signifying intentions we use linguistic tokens that are iterable, and therefore also imitable, open to parasitism. When Searle talks of the occurrence of speech acts and the presence of intentions, he means to invoke nothing more than this mundane phenomenon. If Derrida, despite his awareness of the distinction between iterability and imitability, wishes nevertheless to insist that the peculiarities of the latter are also ('to some extent') the peculiarities of the former, Searle is free simply to deny it. On the other hand, to the extent that Derrida means such phrases as 'the full presence of intention' to carry more metaphysical baggage than this, neither Searle nor Austin (whose analysis of speech acts is of course the topic of Derrida's critique in Signature, événement, contexte) show any inclination to haul the load. Derrida seems to feel that Searle's philosophic assumptions leave him no right to disavow the burden; but the particular line of argument being considered is inadequate to substantiate this feeling.

Indeed, it is rather Derrida who ends up saddling himself with the metaphysical baggage. In order to convince us that even when uttered in non-parasitic contexts a performative statement is identifiable in some way as a 'citation', he points out that such utterances could not be made unless they were 'identifiable as *conforming* to an iterable model'.[38] He emphasizes the word 'conforming', as if to make it bear the weight of his argument; but it juggles its burden shakily. If he means no more by the phrase 'conforming with an iterable model' than that each time I open the meeting, marry the couple, or christen the liner I produce an instance of the appropriate formula, Searle can understand this in terms of the logician's type-token distinction, which he readily accepts as applying generally to any signifying system,[39] and which he has been given no reason to conflate with the parasitic cases of imitation, citation and their fellows. Hence Searle can declare himself unimpressed. If on the other hand my utterances are to conform to the model in the more zesty sense that they *imitate* the model, then Derrida will have bought Searle's attention at the cost of indiscriminately accepting the very pattern of thought that he is usually taken to be putting in question.

I can explain this point by turning to Derrida's discussion of signatures – which also makes it clear that the zestier sense of 'conforming' is indeed the one that operates in his argument. At the outset of 'Limited inc. a.b.c. . . .' he recalls the fact that 'Signature, événement, contexte' bears on its closing page a printed reproduction of his handwritten signature – of what is, in effect, a scriptural performative. Concerning this signature (the purportedly original, handwritten one rather than the printed reproduction) he roguishly declares himself ready to swear that it 'is not from *my hand*' ('n'est pas de *ma main*'). Why not? Because, if the printed version can be declared a reproduction or imitation of the handwritten signature, then for similar reasons the handwritten version is no less a reproduction: 'For I imitate and reproduce my "own" signature incessantly. This signature is imitable in its essence'.[40] Here the excesses of Derrida's ploy reach their starkest expression. The two sentences in this quotation are presented as equivalent; but they are not equivalent. When I sign cheque no. 100 I don't produce an imitation of the signature on cheque no. 99, nor indeed of that on cheque no. 1; and still less do I produce an imitation of some archetypal model of my signature. What I produce is an instance of my signature. Being repeatable, my signature is also (and this is the claim made in the second sentence) essentially imitable; but that is no reason to consider it an actual imitation.

The unremarked shift between these two sentences seems to me exactly analogous to that which we saw Arthur make when she glossed Eco's point that all signification can be used to lie by insisting that all language is, in some sense, a lie. In just the same way that Pucci and Arthur generalize the parasitic imitation characteristic of lies to cover all cases of language use, so Derrida here universalizes the imitation or citationality of a broader range of parasitic cases, and on the strength of an equally unsatisfactory argument.[41] And just as Pucci and Arthur have to accept metaphysical realism in order then to show how very disturbing it is to be a metaphysical realist, so Derrida can justify the apparent paradox that he 'counterfeits' his own signature[42] only through the sceptical implication that no signature of mine is ever genuine, that rather the real signature is an archetype, of which I can produce only imitations (as when Pucci insisted that Hesiod could never compare the Muses' words with things as they are) – an implication with a most un-Derridean ring.[43] But this is because Derrida's well-known 'questioning' of 'western metaphysics' (that is, of metaphysical realism) takes place very much from inside the scheme of thought that it questions; in fact, it does not seem to me to question the scheme of thought as such, but only to attempt to stir from their complacency those fellow metaphysical realists who, so to speak, think that being a metaphysical realist is easy (and the ambition is fair enough, if such opponents can be found). But for those who actually try to work outside the metaphysical realist framework, such as Searle, or who never even entered it, as I contend is the case with archaic and even later Greek thought, this whole line of questioning misses the mark.[44]

Derrida is perhaps somewhat 'pushed' here into such spectacular but dubious claims as that about signatures; pushed by the apparent exasperation that he allows to show (however rhetorically) in a passage like this one from 'Limited inc. a.b.c . . .' on Searle's attitude to 'real life', that

'real life' about which he is so certain, so inimitably (almost, not quite) confident of knowing what it is, where it begins and where it ends; as though the meaning of those words ('real life') could immediately be a subject of unanimity, without the slightest risk of parasitism; as though literature, theatre, deceit, infidelity, hypocrisy, infelicity, parasitism, and simulation of real life were not part of real life![45]

Derrida is bothered by what he thinks of as complacency on the part of Searle and his ilk. It is as if he is determined (again, I speak of what need be only a rhetorical attitude) to grab the fellow by the lapels and shake him into taking notice; something which only daring assertions of the 'counterfeit – signature' sort can be expected to achieve. But clearly the problem to which Derrida alludes in the long quotation just given is the old friend that Eco encapsulated: that signification can be used to lie, that the iterable is always also imitable, that the bad exchange of simulation cannot be barred from the good exchanges by which we constitute 'the normal case'. This is a genuine problem about the use of language, and Searle can accept it as such without being inclined to swallow the model of signification which Derrida unnecessarily (and I think, wrongly) derives from it; for the problem that Derrida spins from that general model is a pseudo-problem – a merely technical philosopher's problem, drawing strength from a doctrine of metaphysical realism that we have no good reason to accept. This is a bad exchange that, for once, we can avoid with impunity, and without complacency. Unfortunately, as we have seen, it is the very heart of what the Derridean classicists considered in this chapter have taken from Derrida.

v

I have selected these examples from the work of Derrida and of Derridean classicists in order to urge caution (at the very least) in the use of their metaphysical presuppositions and of the blunt instrument they provide for the analysis of Greek thought. Readers looking for a positive message in what I have to say will have had to settle for my sketch of good and bad exchange in the second section of this chapter. However, I do not want to leave the impression that I consider the Derridean strategy here criticized (and its associated thesis about language) to be the whole Derrida;[46] and I shall conclude with some brief (and therefore rather allusive) remarks, commensurate with the goals of this volume, about what stimulates me in his work.

Derrida's writing tends to focus upon or take its start from particular texts rather than develop general theses in a more free-standing manner; and he chooses his texts, both ancient and modern, with care. He likes to home in on those points where an author is pulling himself up by his own bootstraps; where the author engages his authority; where what is being said exhibits or alludes to or even attempts to capture the very conditions that make such saying possible.[47] He seems to love the vertigo that arises from such moments; and who cannot feel its thrill? And certainly, when we are all of us, to adapt the famous image, in a boat being built at sea, there is much to be said for those who sit in the crow's nest and wonder – articulately wonder – over how the feat is done down below; since the builders on deck (such as Plato, such as Searle, to use the examples in this chapter; those who replace and construct, whether adding whole planks or tightening a

few rivets) may become so engaged in their task as to lose sight of
the horizon. But notice two things. One is that it does not matter
much whether the author is himself conscious of this vertigo or
not – although on a popular (and not wholly unjustified) view the
great trick of deconstruction is to turn the author's own words
against himself and show he never knew what he was getting into.
Thus, for example, to the extent that the prologue to Hesiod's
Theogony displays such an effect of bootstrapping (and I believe
it does; of which a little more presently), I would judge from the
rest of his poetry that the author is not firmly in control of this
effect; whereas when a similar question arises in the case of Plato's
Phaedrus, to which Derrida devoted perhaps his best-known study
of an ancient text,[48] I have no doubt that the author was fully aware
of the implications of his gesture. But the philosophic problems
that underpin this gesture seem to me independent of authorial
awareness. The second point to notice is that 'Derrida's insight'
that 'the original signified is always absent', when understood as
the model of signification criticized in the previous two sections,
has only a restricted application and a particular historical domain
within the broader inquiry into the effects of bootstrapping to
which I have alluded. That is, the assumptions of metaphysical
realism which hamper the Derridean examples I have discussed
can be seen as deriving from the fact that Derrida so often finds
the bootstraps pulled tautest in metaphysical realist texts (or texts
that he deems metaphysical realist, such as Plato's). But this would
represent just one particular way in which philosophers have
attempted to capture the conditions which make knowledge possible (hence also the knowledge and articulation of the conditions
that make knowledge possible), and its assumptions need not be
applied to the vertigo induced also by texts that are not metaphysical realist – ancient texts.

But I find that Derridean classicists are eager to adopt that
restricted and dubious 'model of signification' for the analysis of
their own favoured texts, and indeed to think of the model as
applying to all texts, to the 'textuality' of texts. I urge them at least
to pause and consider whether what Derrida exhibits here is not
rather an interest in a quite particular philosophic theme, one
which appears, admittedly, in a broad range of texts, and which
has similar consequences for those texts that play with it, but which
does not in any sense constitute or entail a theory of textual

interpretation that should be brought to bear on all texts.[49] If anything is to be vivified in general by Derrida's stimulus (as opposed to particular insights gleaned from particular studies), I think it more likely to be a theory of myth than of textual interpretation; for just as Derrida concentrates on the attempts of others (whether philosophers or not) to capture, as if from without, the very system of understanding in which they find themselves, so the category of myth is invoked whenever we can see both the limitations of a system (from without) and appreciate how it sustains the social life that goes on within. (I shall perhaps be told that all texts are myths. Well, ultimately, maybe. But it's what happens on the way to that ultimate place that matters.)[50]

Despite the fact that I have built this piece around the couplet spoken by Hesiod's Muses, I have had very little to say about what I take the significance of the couplet to be in its context in the prologue to the *Theogony*. The reader need not fear that I am about to lose my reticence now. As I have mentioned, these are harried lines, and a proper attempt to establish my own interpretation of them in Hesiodic terms (rather than for the model of thought that shows through them) would have to take into account a great wealth of scholarship (somewhere in the recesses of which it has perhaps already been established) and would require a paper to itself. I will simply end by agreeing that the prologue is indeed striking in its treatment of the poet's authority (as the Derridean critics have sensed); but I suggest that what is striking emerges most clearly, not when we ask whether the Muses are lying to Hesiod (and pose a logical conundrum) but if we ask whether Hesiod is lying to us (and pose a question of the social relation between poet and audience).[51] In other words: there we are, at line 22 of the *Theogony*, secure in the knowledge that the poet is launched on a conventional hymn to the Muses in preface to his larger song when all of a sudden the poet is no longer describing the Muses as they sing of the other gods, but describing how they came and sang to *him*, a poor shepherd on Helicon. No longer are they talking the poet's poetry for him (through him); they are talking to the poet himself. He becomes a part of their larger narrative. And if we ask (as the suddenness of the poet's appearance will prompt us to ask): did this epiphany actually happen?[52] — there is only Hesiod's word to go on. He *shows* us, then, that he has indeed been given that sceptre of authority, the conferral of which is narrated in the prologue itself; for he makes us conscious of the authority that, while listening to the first twenty-two lines of the prologue, we had quite unthinkingly accepted. He has been given the power of truth and lies, and for so long as we consent to listen to him, he can dispose of us as he will. Would we continue to listen to him if we knew he was misleading us? No; no more than he would expect Perses to.[53] Can we know that he is not misleading us? No; at least, it is difficult. Hesiod is asking for – and showing he considers himself quite worthy of – our trust.

Notes

1 'Signature, événement, contexte' and its companion piece 'Limited, inc. a.b.c . . .' which I come to in the fourth section.

2 The use of polar opposition to express a god's power is frequent in archaic texts. A famous example is that of the two jars of Zeus at *Iliad* xxiv 527, one containing good, the other bad fortune; so too in Hesiod's *Works and Days* we read that a safe time for sailing is fifty days after the summer solstice, unless Poseidon or Zeus are set against it, 'for in them lies the determination of both good and evil' (669); and cf. *Theognidea* 157–8 (West – to whose edition of the work I refer throughout this paper). These examples set a positive against a negative value; but this is not invariably the case: e.g. *Odyssey* v 47–8 (Hermes uses his staff both to put mortals to sleep and to wake them from sleep, as he chooses); and x 22 (Aelus has the power to calm and to stir the winds, whichever he wishes). Thus we cannot tell simply from their use of the motif whether Hesiod's Muses in the *Theogony*, by setting lies against truth, are opposing something bad to something good. I have tried to make my translation of their words broad enough to reflect the fact that the Greek terms rendered as 'true', 'false', 'genuine' do not distinguish 'truth' – a linguistic property applicable only to propositions – from 'reality', said of things in general.

3 The quotations are from P. Pucci, *Hesiod and the Language of Poetry*, Baltimore, Md, Johns Hopkins University Press, 1977, pp. 12, 13 and 13–14 respectively.

4 I take the quotations from M. Arthur, 'The dream of a world without women: poetics and the circles of order in the *Theogony* prooemium', *Arethusa* xvi 1, 2, p. 105 (citing Pucci, op. cit., p. 16) and p. 106. Henceforth in this chapter I will refer to these two articles simply by author's name and page number.

5 The variety of non-Derridean interpretations of the Muses' message is considerable, and beyond my brief to consider here. A good conspectus of the range can be extracted from the following sources: W. Stroh,

'Hesiods lügende Musen', in H. Gorgemanns and E. A. Schmidt (eds) *Studien zum antiken Epos*, Meisenheim am Glan, Anton Hain, 1976; H. Neitzel, 'Hesiod und die Lügenden Musen', *Hermes* cviii, 5, 1980, pp. 387–401; G. Nagy, 'Hesiod', in T. J. Luce (ed.) *Ancient Writers*, vol. i, New York, Scribner's, 1982, pp. 43–73; E. Belfiore, ' "Lies unlike the truth": Plato on Hesiod, *Theogony* 27', *Transactions of the American Philosophical Association* cxv, 1985, pp. 47–57.

6 I am aware that this is too slim a base on which to establish my claim that the pattern of thought to be presented in this section is widespread in archaic culture; but for my purposes in this paper it would indeed be sufficient to establish its presence in Hesiod alone. One of the best indications of its pervasive grip is the fact that this is the model on which Plato builds and against which he reacts; a topic I hope to treat elsewhere.

7 'Good exchange' and 'bad exchange' are working terms; I do not set great store by them. That is they do not structure a preconceived theory that I am anxious to find at work in archaic Greek thought; rather, it seems to me that certain cardinal facets of that thought can be readily gathered under the rubric of this contrast, and that the pigeon-holing is not just convenient but instructive.

8 This is not to say that Hesiod thinks it a worthy ambition to covet even one's brother's land (as opposed to one's neighbour's); but the fact remains that the focus of his criticism is not Perses' ambition as such, but the means by which he attained it.

9 See M. L. West, *Hesiod: Works and Days*, Oxford, Clarendon Press, 1978, for this translation.

10 The notion of 'likeness' eats from both tables, that of good as well as that of bad exchange, as we shall see later in this section.

11 Compare Achilles' vituperation in *Iliad* ix 312–13 of the man 'who hides one thing in his mind, and says something different'.

12 W. Donlan, in his article 'Pistos Philos hetairos' (in *Theognis of Megara: Poetry and the Polis*, T. J. Figueira and G. Nagy (eds.) Baltimore, Md, Johns Hopkins University Press, 1985, pp. 223–4) lists a number of Theognidean passages under the rubric 'poet advises to be a duplicitous friend'; advice which I have claimed is not to be found in this text. All of the passages Donlan cites seem to me understandable in the three ways I have indicated: as recommending the positive (and not duplicitous) adaptability of the octopus, or the discretion made necessary by the possible duplicity of others, or duplicity towards one's enemies. In this last case, admittedly, we could indeed say that the poet advises us to be a duplicitous friend; but Theognis makes a point – as Donlan does not – of specifying that we should be dupli- citous friends only to known enemies (thus the context of 63–5, advising Cyrnus to be only a seeming friend to all, is the extreme declaration that *everyone* in town has become a crook, 53–62). What

he never does, so far as I can tell, is advise us to pre-empt even possible duplicity in others with a stance of false friendship.

13 See esp. *Rp.* i 331d–332b and the ensuing discussion with Polemarchus.

14 The sentiment is found in many writers other than Hesiod and Theognis: for example, Solon xiii 5; Pindar *Pyth.* ii 83–5; Aeschylus *P.V.* 1,040–2 (references which I gratefully take from Adam's commentary on the *Republic*).

15 Truly explicit texts are hard to come by, however, precisely because the matching of true assertions to the world is thought of as direct and not *in itself* problematic (the problems derive from the possibility of lying, as we are about to see); hence I must argue from the very absence of attention to this relationship, as in Hesiod's couplet.

16 *Moira* is one's 'share', hence also 'lot' or 'fate'; and the phrase *kata moiran* can be more generally translated as 'according to what is due'; but here too there is the notion of even exchange – of getting what you have coming to you (as at *Iliad* i 286 and xvi 367). It is interesting that Odysseus' invitation to Demodocus also includes a use of the term *kosmos* not in the sense of a good exchange that matches the 'order' of the tale to that of the event (the example I have cited) but referring to that decidedly bad (deceptive) exchange, the 'fashion [or perhaps 'fashioning'] of the wooden horse (*hippou kosmon . . . dourateou*)' (492–3).

17 Charles Kahn is fond of bringing up this colloquialism when expounding notions of truth among the Greeks; and my account is in debt at this point to his article, 'The Greek verb "to be" and the concept of being', *Foundations of Language* ii, 1966, pp. 245–65.

18 Of course, Zeus is too anthropomorphically represented to conform rigorously to the condition that nothing escapes him. The Muses sing to soothe their father as much as they cause their servants to soothe mortal audiences (*Th.* 51); and Pindar has Zeus' eagle lulled to sleep by the golden lyre (in the opening lines of *Pyth.* i). Xenophanes (DK 21 B 23–6) testifies to this particular path towards the problem of ineffability.

19 Despite his reaction, Odysseus himself is the one who asks to hear the story of the wooden horse. Indeed; for it is his fate to be caught in a limbo of expectancy, unable to relax as ordinary people do, until he can get back home.

20 Notice too that Odysseus explicitly denies that there was any deceptive malice in the Lotus-eaters' gesture of offering his scouts the drug that will make them 'forget their return' (*Od.* ix 91–5). On the other hand, Calypso does use 'crooked words' to soothe Odysseus into remaining on her island (*Od.* i 56–7). This seems to be required by his unwillingness to remain (v 155), by contrast with his willingness to hear the Sirens' song, or of his scouts to eat the lotus, or of an audience to

listen to a bard. Deception and distortion is an additional recourse for inducing forgetfulness, not the standard pattern.

21 The relevant opposition is no longer that between *alêtheia* and *lêthê* but that between *alêtheia* and *pseudos*.

22 It should be obvious how much the preceding sketch owes (no less than does the work of Pucci and Arthur) to the seminal account of these issues offered in M. Detienne, *Les Maitres de vérité dans la Grèce archaïque*, Paris, Maspéro, 1967, especially ch. 4. My contrast between good and bad exchange in the sphere of language can be closely correlated with Detienne's distinction between 'parole' as 'puissance efficace orientée vers la réalité' and as 'séduction' (see his p. 79). I do have a reservation about his account, however: namely, that he does not keep the negative aspect of good exchange (*lêthê*) sufficiently distinct from the negativity of bad exchange (*pseudos, apatê*), but hastens to show how they infect each other, thus eliding the importance of the distinction (see e.g. his p. 72).

23 See A. Bergren, 'Language and the female in early Greek thought', *Arethusa* xvi 1, 2, 1983, pp. 70, 87 n. 3 and 89 n. 17.

24 With this assimilation of all speech to the model of lying we can compare in general the readiness with which Pucci and others detect traces of devious and deceptive behaviour in the agents described in these texts. Thus according to Pucci (18) the statement in the *Theogony* that the just king persuades his citizens with soft words 'hints at some softening of the truth' (and he compares how the Muses' gift of song distracts mortals from their cares), and the idea that Zeus' mind goes now one way, now another he sees as an expression not just of 'inscrutability' but of 'inconsistency', and compares Zeus' and the Muses' capacity for deception (8, with n. 2). But this is to conflate the negative side of good exchange – that from which one's attention is diverted – with the negativity of bad exchange (the presence of something spurious, in this case deceptive). Yet Hesiod says nothing at all about the just king's using *deception* to calm his subjects (Bergren, in a review of Pucci, op. cit. (*Modern Language Note* Comparative Literature xciii, 1977, pp. 1,059–65) goes so far as to assert (p. 1,063) that 'the *logos* of the straight and just king speaks crookedly and unjustly'); nor are we deceived when we listen to the bard and forget our cares (although, as the Sirens demonstrate, we must carefully choose our time for forgetting); rather, both king and Muses use a rhetorical tool that has the *potential* to divorce itself from truth. And to compare Zeus' changeability with his power to deceive is to make an analogous move to that of reading the adaptability of Theognis' octopus in what I argued to be an unnecessarily cynical manner. As this last point shows (for its target was Donlan op. cit.), the tendency is not confined to those who claim the influence of Derrida. I find it also in the analysis of the deviousness of *mêtis* – the mobile and

74

adaptable intelligence of the hunter, the fox, the navigator, the octopus – in Detienne and Vernant, *Les Ruses de l'intelligence: la mètis des Grecs*, Paris, Flammarion, 1974 (*Cunning Intelligence in Greek Culture and Society*, trans. J. Lloyd, Brighton, Harvester, 1978); see also n. 22.

25 The quotations are from Bergren, 'Language and the female in early Greek thought', pp. 70 and 89 n. 17. Bergren gives to John Peradotto the credit for noticing this connection.

26 Similarly Arthur, having decided that 'the *logos* which the Muses offer ... is a self-conscious re-presentation of the ambiguity which constitutes it' then sees this act as one by which it 'transcends the ambiguity which it represents ' (op. cit., p. 106); but how?

27 In her review of Pucci, Bergren seems to misunderstand him on this point. She thinks he has Hesiod divide poetic language into two categories, one in which 'there is no difference between language and truth' and one in which 'language is identical *or* similar to truth' (Bergren, review, p. 1,060) – a position which would come somewhat closer (barring that 'identical or ...') to the more straightforward and, I believe, correct reading of the couplet. She then becomes puzzled as to whether Pucci is urging the validity of these two categories in his own name (which he seems clearly to do with the second), and what Derrida would make of the first category in that case (p. 1,061). But in fact Pucci only ever works with the second category, of language as 'identical or similar' (his idiosyncratic translation of *homoios*) to truth (after all, the first category collapses into the option of 'identity' contained in the second). Imitation is the underlying operator in all language, from which he then derives the 'identity' operative in true discourse, as is clear from the following: 'the concept of false discourse derives from the idea of imitation as *difference* from things, *simulation* of identity with things; the concept of true discourse also derives from the idea of imitation, but in this case the imitation should involve no difference' (p. 16).

28 The label is a convenient one, but I use it gingerly, aware of the vast debate that has grown around it in current philosophy, and also that I am giving it a rather stronger sense than that in which it is sometimes used. Let me only mention, for those unfamiliar with this debate, the discussion in chapter 3 of H. Putnam, *Reason, Truth and History*, Cambridge, Cambridge University Press, 1981 (a mention which should not be taken as an endorsement of his views).

29 Many less negative and more sympathetic interpretations of Kant have been propounded, of course, some of which would make him an enemy of metaphysical realism. I use his name as a label only, without making any interpretative claims. My general point here has been well made in J. R. Searle, 'The world turned upside down', *New York Review of Books*, 27 October 1983.

30 Thus Plato's Forms are quite unlike Kant's 'noumenal realm' but, if anything, more like Kantian 'categories'; but in fact, since the categories and the noumenal are correlative notions, importantly different from both. Indeed, Plato is not a 'classical metaphysician' (not a 'metaphysical realist') in the sense that allows Searle to lump him together with that tradition in modern philosophy 'from Descartes to Husserl' (in Searle, 'The world turned upside down').

31 M. F. Burnyeat, 'Idealism and Greek philosophy: what Descartes saw and Berkeley missed', *Philosophical Review* xci, 1, p. 19. Compare also this from R. Rorty, 'The world well lost', in *Consequences of Pragmatism*, Minneapolis, University of Minnesota Press, 1982, p. 15: 'If we no longer have a view about knowledge as the result of manipulating *Vorstellungen* then I think we can return to the simple Aristotelian notion of truth as correspondence with reality with a clear conscience – for it will now appear as the uncontroversial triviality that it is'.

32 After all, I could say this much of practically any association I care to make with the content of his text, however tenuous.

33 The quotations are from J. R. Searle, 'Reiterating the differences: a reply to Derrida', *Glyph* i, pp. 207 and 201 respectively.

34 'Identifiable en quelque sorte comme "citation" ', J. Derrida, 'Limited, inc. a b c . . .' Supplement to *Glyph* ii, Baltimore, Md, Johns Hopkins University Press, 1977, p. 30.

35 'Non que la citationnalité soit ici de même type que dans une pièce de théâtre, une référence philosophique ou la récitation d'un poème', ibid.

36 'Y a-t-il des signatures? Oui, bien sûr, tous les jours. Les effets de signature sont la chose la plus courante du monde', Derrida, 'Signature, événement, contexte', in *Marges de la Philosophie*, Paris, Editions de Minuit, p. 391.

37 'Empêche tout événement plein (au sens courant) d'arriver pleinement, purement et simplement', Derrida, 'Limited inc. a b c ', p. 29 – also the source of the argument and the other quotation in this paragraph.

38 'identifiable comme *conforme* à un modèle itérable', Derrida, 'Signature, evenement, contexte', p. 389.

39 See Searle, 'Reiterating the differences', p. 199.

40 'Car j' imite et reproduis sans cesse ma "propre" signature. Celle-ci est essentiellement "imitable" ', Derrida, 'Limited inc. a b c ', p. 167 (from which the other quotation in this paragraph is also taken).

41 Notice also that the ambivalence to which I pointed in his use of the term 'conforming' is just that of the term 'like' in the contrast between the different kinds of 'likeness' involved in good and bad exchange (likeness as matching, and likeness as imitating, hence being also significantly *un*like).

42 See Derrida, 'Signature, événement, contexte', p. 393.

43 Indeed, when I questioned him on this point at a public discussion (held at Yale in April 1984) he explained that he had not meant to suggest that to write one's signature is actually to imitate it, and that if the relevant sentence seemed to say otherwise the larger context made clear what was intended. Derrida can see as well as anyone how implausible (quite apart from its un-Derridean ring) the claim about signatures is when taken at full strength. What he is unwilling to acknowledge is how nothing but a full-strength interpretation of his argument gives it even the possibility of bite against Searle. (Also, I think we have seen enough to appreciate that the assumptions behind the statement 'I imitate and reproduce my "own" signature incessantly' cannot be simply dismissed as the result of a momentary rhetorical enthusiasm, but that the statement could indeed stand as an emblem for the entire argumentative strategy of 'Signature, événement, contexte' and 'Limited inc. a b c . . .' together.)

44 As I have mentioned already, and as those familiar with these controversies will have recognized, Searle himself, in a subsequent piece for the *New York Review of Books*, has clearly voiced what he intends as the criticism – for some might not think it a criticism, after all – that Derrida should himself be ranked among the classical metaphysicians whom he claims to deconstruct (see Searle, 'The world turned upside down'). I have nevertheless delved into my example in this section at some length both in order to provide additional and more detailed support for Searle's contention, and because it is so clear a model for the strategy of Pucci's and Arthur's interpretation.

45 'Cette "real life" dont il est si assuré . . . de savoir ce qu' elle est . . . comme si le sens de ces mots ("real life") pouvait immédiatement faire l'unanimité, sans le moindre risque de parasitage, comme si la littérature, le théâtre, le mensonge, l'infidélité, l'hypocrisie, le malheur (infelicity), le parasitage, la simulation de la real life ne faisaient pas partie de la real life!', Derrida, 'Limited inc., a b c', p. 62.

46 My major reservation about Searle's criticism of Derrida in Searle 'The world turned upside down' is that it tends to do exactly this. Nevertheless, I do consider the inadequate position to be the only thing on show in the argument of 'Signature, événement, contexte' and 'Limited inc. a b c . . .' as also in the Hesiodic interpretations.

47 This is not my own attempt to sum up 'the whole Derrida' in a sentence; but I think it undeniable that the tendency I refer to here makes up a very important strand of Derrida's work.

48 Derrida, 'La Pharmacie de platon' in *La Dissemination*, Paris, Seuil (1968) 1972, pp. 71–97.

49 Of course, Derrida is not the only influence on those 'Derridean classicists' – whom I ask to forgive the simplified label. And some of these other influences, such as Barthes, do indeed propound explicit theories of textual interpretation, which I have not directly considered here.

50 I have something more precise to say on this point, in connection with Derrida's *La Pharmacie de platon*, in the final chapter of my *Listening to the Cicadas: A Study of Plato's Phaedrus* (forthcoming from Cambridge University Press).

51 If my memory is correct, this question was asked also by Diana Browning in her comments on a paper of Pucci's delivered at a conference on 'Truth and Reality in the Ancient World' held at Brown University in November 1983.

52 I do not mean this as a question sceptical of supernatural occurrences, but rather of the poet's claims about himself. Nagy 1982, p. 53, correctly notes that Archilochus also was said to have been visited by the Muses while tending his herd, and that in the *Homeric Hymn to Apollo*, 165–78, the poet addresses the Muses and asks to be remembered by them in his own name. But neither of these comparisons fully match (and so downplay) what is striking in Hesiod's prologue (as Nagy imagines): the fact that the poet inserts a narrative of the Muses' visit, and therefore himself as a character in that narrative, into the hymn itself.

53 See e.g. *Op.* 10; 27; 293–300.

· 4 ·

Desire and the figure of fun: glossing Theocritus 11

SIMON GOLDHILL

The picture overleaf is an advertisement from the classy US magazine, the *New Yorker*. It is a picture which exudes class. The well-dressed model by the exclusive shop front looks out of the frame towards us, but despite her glasses, briefcase (almost concealed in her left hand) and the severe cut of her suit, hers is not the uncompromising look of the mass-media depiction of the business woman. Compromised, then? Well, her smile is certainly a bit crooked, her look indirect. Her arms are set behind her, exposing the full front of her suit, and, at the same time, suggesting a 'suggestive' submission to parallel the lack of uncompromising stare. In the coded world of the photographic advertisement, if a woman wears glasses — except and especially in a spectacles' advertisement — it is a special cultural sign that puts the woman in a different class. A female doctor — or even academic — will have glasses to emphasize (constitute) her status as the one-who-knows; the business woman wears glasses to create her status as the not-just-a-beautiful-woman figure: the model who offers . . . another model. 'The glass of fashion'? What's behind the smile and the glasses here, then? How do we read her body language? What does she know in her glasses? (Be careful in your answer. Remember Molly Bloom's smile — read by Bloom as a mark of love and a remembered scene of pleasure — for Molly meant the worry of menstruation. The smile is also the sign of the inscrutable, the mark or mask of irony.)

Behind the smiling woman there is, of course, a man. Here the

'A good style must, first of all, be clear. It must be appropriate.' –
Aristotle

man, delicately faded into a more generalizable presence and shaded by an umbrella, can be seen to stare at the woman. He's reflected in the glassy shop front but he does not look at himself as if in a mirror. Both he and his reflection are looking at the woman who looks towards us. Perhaps what the woman knows is that she is being looked at – as Lacan, following Sartre, puts it, what she sees is herself being seen.[1]

> *The arrested gaze, looking back over the shoulder*
>   *as the man passes*
> *Does not merely double our gaze*
>   *at the woman in glasses.*

It is not merely that looking at the woman is built into the photograph with that *mise-en-abîme* effect we may recognize from discussions of Great Art.[2] Rather, in the world of desire and desiring conjured by the glossy advertisement, it is the desirability of the woman – what she is selling – that is confirmed by the gaze of the onlooker. Caught between the gaze of the man under the umbrella and the gaze of the reader, the woman is the focus of attention, watched and watching. In one guise, what is to be sold is the expectation of seeing oneself being seen.

Not really. One can be too serious or sophisticated about this. What is to be sold is the woman's clothes. A suit by Corbin Ltd. Though perhaps it would not be too pretentious to say that the message of the photograph, the medium of the sale, could be construed to say that in possession of such an outfit one will possess the knowledge of seeing oneself being seen, seeing oneself as desirable in or through the eyes of others. Even if one does not look precisely like the model.

Although the picture is reproduced here simply as a picture, that is not how it appeared in the magazine, of course. In the classic style of advertising technique, there is a catchy message on top of the picture and below there is the small (but not suspiciously small) print leading to a final heavy type message. The picture is framed by a text. If we want to read the image we have to read the words.

The catchy phrase set above this picture is 'A good style must, first of all, be clear. It must be appropriate.' This dictum is attributed very properly with quotation marks and name to Aristotle. The classy picture has a classical tag to direct our reading. It is under Aristotle's aegis that this model stands. Like a caryatid, a sculptured prop to support a pediment of wisdom.[3] 'Classic styling'. How does this dictum affect our reading, then? It might be possible to suppose a supremely naive reader for whom the name Aristotle meant nothing – or rather for whom the authority supposed by the attribution of the dictum to a name 'Aristotle' brought no special connotations of authority. Perhaps an executive of Corbin Ltd? A celebrity? Didn't he marry Jackie Kennedy? She's got style! But not really. This is not any magazine and it is not selling any sort of item to any sort of person. The supremely naive reader is a figure of fun against whom the more or less confidently sophisticated readers are to constitute themselves. The woman in the picture after all wears glasses and she may be expected to smile at the thought of herself standing under Aristotle as an epigraph. She at least knows that there is something to smile at.

But it is a double-edged joke. At least, the more or less confidently sophisticated reader is faced with a more or less uncertain, indeterminate reading. It is, first of all, a question of 'style'. 'Style' is a standard translation of *lexis* in Aristotle; it is also often translated 'diction' and it is a key term both in the *Poetics* and in the *Rhetoric* to express the way things are expressed, how an argument is put together.[4] The joke is a fairly simple one, then? Is it merely the appropriation of Aristotle's rhetorical vocabulary for a skirt and jacket that constitutes the irony? (As Aristotle says, 'We should give style a foreign air.')[5] Not really; not totally. I think there's more to be said, and in particular there are two lines of analysis I want to trace here. First, there is the continuing question of the frame (which will be an important topic for all the readings in this chapter). I asserted before that the picture is framed by texts which are to direct and guide our reading of the picture (as well as providing the essential information of what's being sold). Now we can see rather that it is the content of the picture which provides the context – the frame of reference – necessary for properly understanding the text. The frame is framed by its content. A formal(ist) model of image and explanation, or generalization and example is inverted by the *interplay* of difference, the ironical slippage or disjunction between the appropriateness and clarity of the quotation and the appropriateness and clarity of the picture and its dress code. The terms of 'style', despite the apparent attribution to an authoritative context by the name 'Aristotle', are resited by the picture. The authority of Aristotle is turned to a joke by the picture's re-citation of the vocabulary of style.

Moreover, this is a very particular witty or poignant joke for the more or less confidently sophisticated Aristotelian reader. 'Clarity' and 'appropriateness' are terms essential to Aristotle's philosophy of language; and his critique of metaphor for example stresses the dangers of inappropriate excess, obscurity and unbounded uncertainty of meaning that are inherent in metaphoricity.[6] Even (or especially) metaphors with their shifting of semantic boundaries must be comprehended within the criteria of clarity and appropriateness. Here, however, it is precisely a statement culled from Aristotle's argument on the dangers of metaphorical excess that is itself turned to dangerous metaphor by this appropriation to the advertisement's discourse. And such appropriation is scarcely appropriate. For the sophisticated Aristotelian reader, it is a special irony that it should be 'style', 'clear' and 'appropriate' which are the terms to be semantically, metaphorically shifted by their re-citation, their repetition in another's discourse. Maybe, it is this irony that the woman is smiling at . . .

The question can be reframed: my second line of analysis, then. To what degree are we to press this witty use of Aristotle's words as a context in our view of this advertisement, how 'sophisticated' a reading should we provide? How seriously should we read the joke? Under the picture the first two lines of the blurb read 'Classic styling. Exquisitely loomed fabric. Elegant tailoring. Together, they make a statement about the woman.' 'Classic styling' is, of course, a standard fashion term – but it also points up the joke of using the classic Aristotle and his 'style'. But what then about 'Together, they make a statement about the woman.' If I were selling to a 'modern woman', particularly one in glasses, I might consider it a risky policy to do so under the aegis of Aristotle, especially with such an expression as 'Together, they make a statement about the woman.' What if she remembers the sort of statement about the woman Aristotle was rather fond of making. Like, 'the female is a natural deformity'.[7] (The business woman is a . . .) No wonder the woman's smile is a little crooked. Selling *woman's* clothes through *Aristotle*? Seriously?

There is in other words a surplus of meaning, a dangerous excess produced in the interplay of image and text here. The relation of generalization and picture does not lead immediately and certainly to the closure of explanation or proof, but to the openness of (playful) misappropriation.

But the question is not simply how seriously to take the joke of using Aristotle's expression in an advertisement. (After all, who *would* buy clothes on Aristotle's word?) Rather it is a question of how far to read the *rhetoric* of an advertisement which quotes from a rhetorical textbook, how far to concentrate on its *style*. 'Together, they make a statement about the woman.' How far should we dwell on the process of *'making a statement'*? About the woman. Which is also around – above and below – the woman (the topography of rhetoric, its *lay-out*). How does the rhetoric work if we study it as rhetoric, if we are conscious and reflective on its *topoi* and technique? Should our eye rest on it or pass through? As Aristotle says,

Those who practise artifice must conceal it and avoid the appearance of speaking artificially instead of naturally; for that which is natural persuades and the artificial does not. For men become suspicious of one whom they think to be laying a trap for them, as they are with mixed wines.[8]

How suspicious should a reader be of an advertisement that proclaims so clearly its 'styling'? The final heavy type remark of the advertisement is indeed a further pun on the shared vocabulary of dress and rhetoric. 'Great statements in style.' Is rhetoric clear and appropriate if it is recognized as rhetoric? Or is the flaunting of rhetoric just a different ploy? Should we be afraid of a rhetorical frame up? It would seem that if this advertisement is to be a successful advertisement on its own terms it needs to be carefully framed, carefully restricted in its reading. To boundary the excess. To make sure we don't take it too seriously. The picture and its framing text need to be further framed by the sort of device one reads often in a newspaper where a framed-in text or picture is headed by the word 'Advertisement' in a different type, marking the genre, making sure it is separated from the business of the news and stories, making sure we take it only just seriously enough. There must be a further frame to delimit and control the picture's reading, if its text is not to deviate seriously from its business of selling, if we are not to read it otherwise. The worry of taking the joke too seriously, of being too sophisticated, is the worry of transgressing the advertisement's self-proclaimed requirement of limited reading. The woman from the USA should smile towards us, but not at us . . .?

One cannot read without such framing of genre, without what might be called a 'code of restricted practice'. Could there be comprehending, otherwise? Yet the frame itself is not constituted like a mathematical line with no breadth. Nor can even the word 'advertisement' be read without *its* frame of reference, be it Marxist, feminist, semiotic, economic, lexical. Each frame becomes framed. Like the picture and its text. The lines of context shift. Can there ever be a position outside this recession of frames? Beyond the margins? Not really, not seriously.

This example of advertising from the *New Yorker* will function as a general opening discussion for my main text, Theocritus' eleventh Idyll (See Appendix for a text). Theocritus is one of the most influential of the Hellenistic poets in particular through the development of what becomes known as pastoral or bucolic poetry.[9] And with pastoral poetry and particularly with *Idyll* 11, the questions of sophisticated and naive readings, of desire, and also of the frame, will be seen to be essential topics of discussion. *Idyll* 11 is a particularly delightful work. The central section and main claim to the status of pastoral poem is the love song of the love-sick Cyclops, Polyphemus. The brutal monster of the *Odyssey* is taken back to his green youth, and the song itself is an amusing fantasy of what happens to the standard *topoi* of love poetry in the mouth of such a bucolic grotesque. 'Whiter than cream cheese', the Cyclops begins his wooing compliments to Galatea, and with the classic line of the ugly but wealthy, he attempts to bribe her with the promise of his rustic riches of a cave and unlimited cheese. There are numerous lovely touches: the monster's desire to have been born with gills, for example – a charming addition to his list of physical attributes – or his fussy pedantry about winter and summer flowers explaining why he can't bring lilies and poppies in the same bouquet. In particular, his hopes and aspirations are set against the *Odyssey*'s depiction of the monster. 'If only a stranger would come', he muses, 'to teach me how to swim', then he would reach his love who may 'burn even his soul and his one eye, dearer to him than anything'. The stranger – a key term in the Cyclops episode in the *Odyssey* – is Odysseus and he will not teach the Cyclops how to swim. Rather, the metaphor of the burning of love, or the rhetorical exaggeration of Polyphemus' extreme willingness to suffer, will be horribly literalized in the putting out of the Cyclops' one eye.

This song of the Cyclops is set within a frame of the poet's address to Nikias, a doctor and a friend, for whom Polyphemus' love song is offered as an example of the power of poetry with regard to desire, *Erōs*. The poem opens with a statement of the potency of the Muses as opposed to drugs and ends with a dig at Nikias' profession with the reprise that Polyphemus fared more easily in this way than if he'd paid for medical treatment.

This poem has been extensively discussed in terms of its relation to Hellenistic poetry. The playful metamorphosis of the Homeric monster to a love-sick youth, the discussion of the value of poetry itself, as well as the highly self-conscious parody of the love song genre, the detailed manipulation of earlier, particularly Homeric, language, have all been seen as typically Hellenistic strategies.[10] The device of setting a song within a song – the frame – itself has been described[11] as a reaction to the questionable status of writing and the writer typical of the Hellenistic poet's awareness of what Walter Jackson Bate has termed 'the burden of the past'[12] – or, to use Bloom's phrase, the 'anxiety of influence'.[13] But in general this device of the framed song within a song has been treated by critics as a formal strategy which makes the meaning of the poem clear. 'First the moral of the poem is set out quite explicitly: the only cure for love is song. This vital clue to the meaning of the poem is picked up in the last lines' (Du Quesnay).[14] 'Theocritus is very explicit . . . Polyphemus composed a song . . . and this song cured him' (Walker).[15] 'He organizes the poem as a miniature treatise, complete with thesis (1–6), demonstration (7–79) and recapitulation (80–1)' (Brooke).[16] Francis Cairns's influential reading marks the steps of the argument clearly enough:

At the end of the song (80–1), we are told that by singing it Polyphemus cured himself. Theocritus must therefore show the cure occurring in the song. Had Polyphemus behaved like a normal komast, Nikias might well have been unable to see how the Cyclops was helped by singing. The change of mind is therefore both required and guaranteed by the use to which Theocritus puts the story of Polyphemus.[17]

As I will demonstrate, at each step this argument begs the question.

The frame, indeed, rather than establishing a closed structure of generalization and example, may be seen as the source and site of the poem's most interesting complexities. For the frame is not merely composed in order to constitute the ironic distance between the world of the sophisticated Nikias and Theocritus and the world of the naive Polyphemus (despite their similar afflictions of desire). Other Idylls, such as *Idyll* 3, where a naive and buffoonish goatherd sings a love song outside his beloved's cave – a further parody of the traditions of Hellenistic love poetry – could have been introduced by such a framing narrative, but the poem stands simply as a dramatic monologue.[18] None the less, it is precisely the implied presence of the sophisticated audience that is essential for the humorous effect of that parody, too. So, in *Idyll* 11 it is not sufficient to see the marking of Nikias' talent in all nine Muses (5–6) merely as introducing the need for a close, sophisticated reading of the rapid shifts of tone and the subtle or more obvious jokes of Polyphemus' song. Nor is the frame simply in order to tie the poem to the circumstances of contemporary social life – although the relation between Polyphemus and Nikias will remain important. There is more at stake in the frame.

Gow, justifiably the most influential editor of Theocritus,[19] points to a primary crux of interpretation. He focuses his reading on the last word of line 13 *aeidon* 'singing'. Here is his analysis:

Song, says T., is the only cure for love as Polyphemus found when in love with Galatea. He was distraught with passion and neglected all his affairs, but he discovered the remedy and thus would hymn his love. T. is here describing the symptoms of Polyphemus' affliction and if one of them is singing, his whole paragraph which asserts that it is not a symptom but a cure, falls to pieces.[20]

Can song be a symptom as well as a cure for desire? Dover tries to find his way round the apparent impasse by glossing the phrase as 'by *persisting* in singing he *eventually* found a remedy he could not have found any other way'.[21] However, neither of the words that Dover needs to emphasize 'persisting', 'eventually' are in the Greek, or even hinted at (unless he is commenting on Theocritus' remark that the cure isn't easy to find: 4–5). This solution, however, is worked out in more detail by Holtsmark and Erbse,[22] who see this poem as a sort of 'talking cure' – a catharsis for

Polyphemus who reaches self-knowledge and self-enlightenment finally through his poetry.

Much depends in Erbse's and Holtsmark's readings – as for Cairns, Du Quesnay and Dover – on the final lines of Polyphemus' song 72–9.

Ah, Cyclops, Cyclops, where have your wits flown? You would show more sense if you'd go and plait cheese-baskets and gather greenery for your lambs. Milk the ewe that's by. Why pursue one who flees? Another and a fairer Galatea you will find, maybe. Many a maiden bids me spend the night in sport with her, and they all titter when I hearken to them. It is plain that on land I too am a somebody.

The Cyclops rhetorically questions his sanity and explains in a potential clause that he *would* be more sensible *if he were to* go and plait cheese-baskets. There is no sign he actually does leave or that his question 'Where have your wits flown?' is anything but a rhetorical expression of misery.[23] The lover as madman. A *change* of mind, then? It would seem a strangely indirect way of expressing it. 'Why pursue one who flees?' is a sensible enough question — were it not that Greek love poetry constantly turns to precisely such unfulfilled and unfulfillable desire as the basis of the erotic encounter, from Odysseus' string of deserted females,[24] through Sappho's first ode which revolves around such vocabulary of the repeated pursuit and flight of desire,[25] to tragedy's depiction of the horrors of transgressive desire for the forbidden and, typically, fleeing object.[26] It is a constitutive factor in the rhetoric of desire that pursuit is precisely for the one who flees. In general, 'love poetry' in Greek is poetry of the *sickness* of *Erōs*, poetry of unfulfilled desire. The Cyclops' question marks the continuation of a generic expectation as much as any change of mind. The suggested answer to his questions (finding another and prettier Galatea) – is not only undercut by the addition of 'maybe' or 'perhaps' – which may be hopeful, or perhaps is despairing or a threat, or just plain doubtful – but also by the proposed flight from one Galatea to the next. The cure for desire seems to be . . . another desire. But not quite: because Polyphemus goes on to explain the basis of his hope for a more successful pursuit this time. Lots of girls call him out to play in the night; *sumpaisdein*, 'to play together', 'to disport' is a word whose erotic connotations are common;[27] so too is the giggling with which they greet his attempt to obey them; *kikhli-zonti*, 'they titter' is a verb used of seductive, lewd or lascivious laughter in particular.[28] Does it follow, however, as Du Quesnay thinks, that 'the giggling of the girls should be understood as genuine enticement: it is sexual laughter not mockery'.[29] Is Polyphemus' understanding of an erotic encounter, (presumably as yet unfulfilled) to be trusted? *He* may describe their laughter as wanton and lascivious, and regard it as genuine enticement, but is there no possibility that he may have misread (with his one eye) the girls' expressions – especially when we recall his misunderstanding of Odysseus? He sees himself as being seen as an object of desire, but how does he seem in the girls' eyes? One must be more careful perhaps than Du Quesnay or the Cyclops about reading the significance of a woman's smile or laugh. As the scholion on this passage comments, 'Perhaps they are laughing at him'.[30] Indeed. Perhaps they are. There may, then, be thought to be something of an irony in Polyphemus' use of their giggling to show that he is a somebody on land at any rate. The irony of this final assertion to seem to be a somebody, however, is not merely because of the character he has displayed throughout the song, but also because of the echo of the famous joke in the *Odyssey*'s Cyclops episode – perhaps the most famous joke in Greek literature.[31] For Polyphemus will be blinded in the Homeric epic and reduced to violent impotence by Odysseus' deceit and an essential part of that deceit is Odysseus' trick of calling himself 'nobody' (*outis*) – which by a further pun is called the wile (*mētis*) of Odysseus of the many wiles (*polumētis Odusseus*). Polyphemus may use the girls' laughter here to prove that he seems a somebody: but it will be Odysseus' joke on the difference between being a somebody and a nobody which will finally make him a laughing stock. The Cyclops' mention of his assumed status ironically looks forward to his future humiliation at the hands (or words) of Odysseus.

So, then, can we be sure that we are seeing a development of cathartic self-awareness through song in these final lines? Is this song really a serious proof of the eventual healing powers of song? What sort of an example is the Cyclops for the efficacy of love poetry? Indeed, Horstman and Brooke suggest in different ways that the song demonstrates rather a necessary self-illusion or self-delusion (that saves the Cyclops from the *despair* of thwarted passion).[32] Not so much a cure, as a necessary deceit. To keep going. Is the Cyclops approaching desire with open eye(s) now, or with careful averting of the gaze of truth? Turning a blind eye? Through a glass . . . darkly? Perhaps the problem stems from critics taking a parodic love song too seriously as proof of the nature of poetry with regard to desire. Perhaps it stems from not taking it seriously enough.

It is interesting at this point to return to Gow who pointed out the problem that song appeared to be a symptom of what it was meant to cure. He goes on to suggest that if we delete lines 1–7, 17–18, 80–81, then there is nothing in the poem to 'provoke suspicion'.[33] Gow's bizarrely Draconian solution to his critical problem – simply cut out a seventh of the poem[34] – develops a fundamentally different line from the critics on whom I have been focusing so far. For by removing these particular lines, Gow removes any hint that the poem is about the *cure* for desire at all. For him, Polyphemus' song is a sign and symptom of desire: 'The whole content of the song . . . shows Polyphemus very far from cured'.[35] We would seem to be, then, in a situation where the exemplum is taken by critics as certain and explicit proof of mutually exclusive and contradictory generalizations. There is certainly something more to be said here.

But too fast. Surely the frame in which Theocritus explains the point of the poem makes all clear? How perversely must we read against the grain of the poem to see the song as anything but a demonstration of the efficacy of poetry against desire? The final two lines of the poem are taken as a statement of the opening expression of song as the only cure for love. So Cairns, 'We are told that by singing it Polyphemus cured himself'.[36] So, too, Du Quesnay, who writes that the conclusion of the poem allows 'the reader no room to doubt that the Cyclops has been successfully cured'.[37] *No* room? Certainly the end of the poem echoes the beginning: *erōta* (80) 'desire' echoes *erōta* (1) 'desire'; *rhāon de diāg* (81), 'fared easier', echoes *rhāsta diāg* (7), 'fared most easily'; and *mousisdōn* (81) 'singing and playing' (root *mous-*), picks up *Moisais* (6) 'Muses' (root *mous-*), as well as the sense of *Pierides* (3) 'Muses', *aeidōn* (13), 'singing', *aeide* (18) 'he sang'. So, too, the mention of spending gold (81) may be thought to relate to the rejected use of unguents and salves in the first two lines. But the first main verb of the final couplet contains a notable ambiguity which is repressed by most critics in order to maintain their position of certainty: *epoimainen ton erōta*. 'He *shepherded* his love'. Polyphemus is doing to his desire what he is not doing to his sheep. In 65 the same verb is used in the expected context of a shepherd and his flock, and, indeed, when *poimanien*, 'shepherd', is used in a metaphorical manner elsewhere it is generally taken as implying 'tend', 'care for', 'nourish'.[38] Agamemnon is the shepherd of his people[39] – the lord is my shepherd. Can we really see this verb here as implying simply and explicitly the removal, destruction or even cure of 'desire? Theocritus' witty final use of *poimanien* scarcely resolves any uncertainty whether the love-poem really demonstrates the shepherd's cure. As Alpers writes, 'The wit largely involves the opacity of shepherded (*epoimainen*) which suspends divergent interpretations by saying in effect "saw it through by behaving like the herdsman he was".'[40] The conclusion of Theocritus' moral tale, then, scarcely reduces the problematic nature of the exemplum. What sort of cure is poetry if by singing it Polyphemus is said to 'shepherd his desire'?

Let's return, then, to the beginning of the poem where the problem was first diagnosed by Gow in the form of the awkwardness that both the symptom and the cure for desire seemed to be writing or singing poetry. Perhaps now that doubleness is beginning to take on a more significant guise. 'Is poetry to be taken as a symptom or cure for desire?' may be more of a question than critics have allowed for. The key word that occurs in 1 and 17, framing by its repetition the argument which Gow found disturbing, is *pharmakon*. 'There is no other *pharmakon* for love than the Muses' . . . 'but he found the *pharmakon*', and sat and sang. So far we have muddled along with the translation 'remedy' or 'cure' for *pharmakon*, but it is time to mark the doubleness of this key term also. *Pharmakon* means not merely remedy but also poison, not merely cure but also harmful drug. Especially with regard to desire. Phaedra's nurse in Euripides' *Hippolytus* promises her a *pharmakon* for her desire for Hippolytus, but it turns out to be a fatal advancement of the tragic chain of events that destroys Phaedra – through *Erōs*.[41] So Deianeira in Sophocles' *Trachiniae* smears a *pharmakon* on a robe to win back her husband's love.[42] It proves, however, to be the destruction of Herakles, who cannot escape the poison. One should be careful about taking a *pharmakon* for love in a naively straightforward way as a cure. It turns quickly to a curse. To disaster. When Odysseus smears a *pharmakon* on his arrows[43] – the only time in Homer that *pharmakon* is used with *khriesthai*, 'smear', the verb from which *engkhriston* (2) 'unguent' is derived – it is a poison and method of attack that no upright, decent man would adopt.[44] What, then, about Aphrodite's weapons fixed in the heart of Polyphemus? Is poetry a love philtre or love cure, then? Read the poem and see . . . And the systematic uncertainty we traced particularly at the end of the poem mirrors the doubleness we are finding in the opening statement of poetry as a *pharmakon*.

Perhaps a closer look at the opening lines of the Idyll is now called for. There is no other *pharmakon* for desire, Nikias, no drug but the Muses. This is something light and sweet for mortals but hard to find (1–3). Indeed, the poem-as-cure that we are reading is 'light' and 'sweet' – both terms, especially *hādu*, 'sweet', can be seen as descriptions especially applicable to Hellenistic, and especially Theocritean, poetics which reject the grandeur and heaviness of the epic and tragic poetry of the past[45] – but it is also proving, as Theocritus says, 'not easy to find' – as we try to specify the relation between desire and writing in this text. The warning's there. This will not be easy. Nikias should be able to recognize the truth of Theocritus' statement because he's a doctor and especially beloved of all nine Muses. Nikias' status as doctor and poet makes him especially capable of recognizing the interplay of the disease of desire and the *pharmakon* that is poetry. The double status of Nikias makes him a perfect recipient of the demonstration of the *pharmakon*. So at any rate the Cyclops, ancient Polyphemus – whose name means both 'much talked of' and 'of many voices', 'many auguries' – the one from down the road (Gow's translation 'our countryman' is perhaps a shade too formal for *Ho par'hamin*), spent his time most easily, when he loved Galatea. Poetry is 'not easy' to get hold of, but the Cyclops fared 'most easily' singing it. He loved, too, not with apples or roses or ringlets, but with real frenzy. The apples and roses mark the tradition of the narrative of *Erōs* in erotic poetry. The loved one is attracted by tossing an apple towards him or her, and the rose as a gift or sign of love may be because it is a flower said to be sacred to Aphrodite and to have sprung from the blood of Adonis or to have been turned red by Aphrodite's blood.[46] But for the Cyclops it is not a question of such signs and demonstrations of love according to the narratives of love poetry. For him, it is the real thing: *orthais maniais*:

real, genuine fits of madness; *orthos*, the adjective in this phrase (whence 'orthodoxy', 'orthopaedics', and so on) is a central term of fifth- and fourth-century intellectual discourse. It connotes in linguistics and literary criticism the proper and certain connection of signifier and signified – the etymological, phonetic or semantic 'rightness' that guarantees the proper use of language.[47] In political language, it implies the right and proper organization of (the laws of) the state. In philosophical debate it implies the proper or correct organization of a discussion towards truth, the proper aim and method of an epistemological enterprise. In less specific terms, it can imply simply 'right', 'correct'. Perhaps most importantly for my discussion here, *orthos* is a term that can authorize the poet's voice as the voice of truth, that can authorize the poet to speak publicly to the citizens as educator, adviser, seer.[48] It is, however, typical of the third-century Hellenistic poet's reaction to the past and to his status as poet that such protestations of truth, such self-authorizations of poetic discourse, are fenced and framed with irony.[49] Here Theocritus prefaces his parodic love song, which draws precisely on the *topoi* of love poetry for its humorous effect, with a denial that Polyphemus' love was just love-token, love-song desire, and with the claim that it was the real, proper madness of desire. The parodic – typically enough for the Hellenistic writer – is introduced by the claim of the genuine and real. What's more, the Cyclops may not deal in apples and roses and kiss curls, but he does offer cheese and the fruit of the vine, and lilies and poppies, and he discusses his facial hair at some length. The 'real thing' is not as far removed from the devices of love poetry as it may at first seem. It is not a straightforward thing to relate the song of Polyphemus to its explanatory frame in terms of the genre of love songs, or to relate *parōdiā* to *ōdē*. The sense of *orthais maniais* rather than explaining the song to come is set in an ironic tension with it. The frame again finds itself framed by its content.

At first sight, this Idyll may seem to demonstrate the simple form critics have assumed, that is generalization followed by example; a truth followed by its proof. A thus-we-have-seen conclusion to seal the exchange. On this reading, the joke, I suppose, is primarily in the grotesque inappropriateness of making a bestial monster the example of the curing power of poetry in matters of love, and in the parodic nature of the song itself (both of which have rarely seemed to critics to set at risk the possibility of any too serious point about the nature of poetry in this poem). Let's return briefly to see how Cairns frames his argument for this reading: 'At the end of the song (80–1) we are told again that by singing it Polyphemus cured himself'. This represses any suggestion of doubt in the phrase 'shepherded his love', or any sense of development through the poem which might change our sense of the repeated phrases. 'Theocritus must therefore show the cure occurring within the poem.' Despite the 'must' and the 'therefore' this statement does not necessarily follow from the first remark; it ignores any possibility of tension between frame and song, and fails to consider any ambiguity or irony in the final lines in which the cure is supposed to be demonstrated. 'Had Polyphemus behaved like a normal komast' (difficult to imagine, especially if introduced by *orthais maniais*, 'real madness', and a rejection of normal love tokens), 'Nikias might well have been unable to see how the Cyclops was helped by singing'. It is important for Cairns that there should be no hint of uncertainty in anyone's reading of this poem. 'The change of mind is therefore both required and guaranteed by the use to which Theocritus puts the story of Polyphemus.' Because he thinks it *should* be there, Cairns claims a change of mind *must* be there. But the 'use to which Theocritus puts the story of Polyphemus' is what we may hope to discover by reading the poem not that by which a reading of the poem may be judged or authorized. In other words, it can be shown that in order to develop this reading, at each step of the argument Cairns must carefully frame from his view a series of what are seen from my view as worrying doubts and questions.

What we may term the naive reading of the poem, then, can be maintained only by a systematic glossing over of a certain doubleness in the text. In one guise, it is the doubleness of song as both symptom and cure, song as *pharmakon*. It is the uncertainty whether the song shows the Cyclops cured or maintaining, even creating, his love. This makes the poem's joke neatly double-edged, particularly if we care to assume the Idyll to be written for a love-sick Nikias, as most critics do. The figure of fun in the poem is not merely Polyphemus, but also Nikias, the reader. Not merely in the unflattering comparison with Polyphemus as a lover, but also and more precisely in the suggestion that in performing love poetry – like this Idyll – the love-sick reader is fostering his love even if he approaches the text as an attempt to cure his desire. The general frame of reference implied by 'among mortals' (4), or by placing Cyclops among us as our countryman is relevant. We – the sophisticated Nikias and us – may read *Idyll* 11 for an expression and example of the cure for desire. What we get also, however, if we do not adopt the blinkered naivety of a Cyclopean reading, is the surprising suggestion that in the very act of singing or reading the poem, we, like Polyphemus, are actually fostering and helping to maintain our desire. It is not only Polyphemus who is framed by Theocritus' poem. The joke, then, is not on the naive reader – finally – but on the sophisticated. As we perform by singing a poem which professes to tell us what happens to those who perform poems, the superiority of the sophisticated reader to the naive is twisted to mark the uncertainty of even the sophisticated control over the poem and over desire. As Wright puts it, in another context, 'Instead of the reader getting hold of the story . . . the reading effect is that of the story getting hold of the readers, catching them out in a fiction of mastery'.[50] It is the canny, intelligent reader who finds himself for all his suspicion repeating the passage of the text. The screw is turned . . . and the figure of fun is inverted. The smile is aimed in more than one direction.

In a further guise, the doubleness can be expressed as the double, enfolded relation of Polyphemus' song to the frame. Critics take the song as proving without doubt the cure of Polyphemus, or showing him clearly to be uncured. The more general but unasked question skirted in such analyses is, 'Does not the structure of frame and framed, generalization and exemplary tale always produce such a doubling, such a surplus of evidence, such a supplement in the interplay of difference?' It is not simply a question of the appropriateness, the fittingness of a moral exemplum to the moral; it is rather a question of what Derrida calls the '*logic of the parergon*'.[51]

And I suppose that if this chapter were to have any claim to stand under the aegis of philosophy and literature, or classics and post-structuralism, it would be in the methods and attitudes of reading implied by such an allusion to the 'logic of the parergon'.

For my most general point could be regarded as exemplifying the paradoxes of parergonal logic which

prove that the structure of framing effects is such that no totalization of the border is even possible. The frames are always framed; thus, by some of their content. Pieces without a whole, 'division' without a totality – this is what thwarts the dream of a letter without division.[52]

Or as Ulmer concludes simply and directly,[53] 'The logic of the parergon, then, defeats conceptual closure'. The frame in *Idyll* 11, in other words, cannot be treated as Polyphemus treated all his work, as a *parergon* to the *ergon* of the love song, at least it cannot be considered as an explanatory preface and summing up conclusion, as if it were somehow outside the poem, as if Theocritus' explanation, his signature, *in* the poem were not *part* of the poem. And/or as if there could be an explanation outside the poem that did not partake in the same game of framing, the same glossing contagion of text on text, frame on frame. The frame cannot be treated as if it were a figure of clarification, control and order (through the rigid delimitation of inside and outside, argument and exemplum); rather the frame, as the source and site of difference, is the figure which always already undermines the rigid determination of the boundaries of sense, the sense of boundaries.

The total inclusion of the frame is both mandatory and impossible. The frame thus becomes not the borderline between the inside and the outside, but precisely what subverts the applicability of the inside/outside polarity to the act of interpretation.[54]

There is, then, a certain interplay between the naive and sophisticated readings of this poem which cannot be regarded simply in terms of a hierarchical opposition. The sophisticated reading finds itself framed, entrapped as does the naive. It is not simply a question of ambiguity, but rather an ambiguity about how ambiguously the poem should be read. As Barbara Johnson writes in 'The Frame of Reference',

The 'undeterminable' is not opposed to the determinable; 'dissemination' is not opposed to repetition. If we could be sure of the difference between the determinable and the undeterminable, the undeterminable would be comprehended within the determinable. What is undecidable is whether a thing is decidable or not.[55]

How serious an example is Polyphemus' song, then?

The interplay, the *oscillation*, between naive and sophisticated readings – how serious a reading to offer, how far to go – seems a constant outcome of the framing inherent in pastoral poetry (dramatized forcibly in the framing opposition of the world of Nikias and Theocritus and the world of Polyphemus). The attempt to comprehend the naivety of bucolic life within the textual artifice of poetry or painting not only requires a framing gesture but also replays again and again the divisions and divisiveness set in motion by the logic of the frame. The bucolic masque (mask) always divides us from the picture it invites us to see ourselves in: a never-never or always-already land of sameness *and* difference in which the Cyclops has to be *ho par-hamin*, one who is *para* to us, for us, who parodies, is a parody, who parades the paradoxical parergonal logic of the frame. Of being relative. (Relatively sophisticated. More or less wealthy.) Of what the frame is . . . about. Or (to put it otherwise) there is always a *pharmakon* in the green cabinet.

To conclude, let me return to the glossy ad from the classy *New Yorker*. the lines of the blurb that I have not yet quoted (continuing from 'Together, they make a statement about the woman') are as follows:

Corbin fashions for women are uncompromisingly made by American craftsmen the careful, caring family business way. And because there's always been a Corbin behind every Corbin, one of the many special things we do is to precisely match our plaids in nine different areas for that custom-tailored look. This takes more fabric and more work. But the result is the reward. We've always been very, very fussy.

The text-ile carefully woven: uncompromisingly. Behind every Corbin, a Corbin. That custom-tailored look. The value of being very, very fussy. I'm sure after what I have just been saying, it will be completely clear how appropriate this advertisement has been. And why the woman in glasses is smiling.

Notes

1 J. Lacan, *The Four Fundamental Concepts of Psychoanalysis*, trans. A. Sheridan, Harmondsworth, Hogarth Press, 1979, pp. 67–119.
2 See N. Bryson, *Tradition and Desire. From David to Delacroix*,

Cambridge, Cambridge University Press, 1984; M. Foucault, *The Order of Things*, London, Tavistock, 1970, pp. 3–16.

3 A phrase culled from discussion with John Henderson, to whom as ever my thanks are due.

4 See *Poet.* 1456b1.18 ff; *Rhet.* 1403b2 ff.

5 *Rhet.* 1404b3 1–3: *dio dei poiein xenēn tēn dialektēn.*

6 See e.g. P. Ricoeur, *The Rule of Metaphor*, trans. R. Czerny, with K. McLaughlin and J. Costello, London, Routledge & Kegan Paul, 1978; J. Derrida, 'White mythology: metaphor in the text of philosophy', *New Literary History* 6, 1974, pp. 5–74. Both oversimplify the *development* of Aristotle's thought on the question of focal meaning and ambiguity (despite the apparent certainty of e.g. *Topics* 139b34–5 *pan gar asaphes to kata metaphorān legomenon*; 'For everything expressed through metaphor is unclear'); cf. *Soph. El.* 76b21–5, *Post. An* 97b33). As Owen comments,

In the earlier ethics a word such as 'good' which is used in different categories is ambiguous and the analysis of such ambiguities falls to dialectic. In the later ethics the ambiguity is circumvented and this circumvention is the work of metaphysics.

('Logic and metaphysics in some earlier works of Aristotle', in J. Barnes, M. Schofield and R. Sorabji (eds) *Articles on Aristotle* vol. iii, London, Duckworth, 1979, p. 16.)

7 See e.g. *Gen. Anim.* 716a17 ff, 716 a 18 ff, etc. For discussion, further references and bibliography, see G. E. R. Lloyd, *Science, Folklore and Ideology*, Cambridge, Cambridge University Press, 1983, pp. 58–111, especially 94 ff.

8 Aris. *Rhet.* 1404b4–5.

9 There is a vast bibliography on the development of pastoral. See, for example, T. Rosenmeyer, *The Green Cabinet*, Berkeley and Los Angeles, University of California Press, 1969; R. Poggioli, *The Oaten Flute*, Cambridge, Mass., Harvard University Press, 1975; W. Empson, *Some Versions of Pastoral*, London, Chatto & Windus, 1935. For the much discussed question of the specific early development of Greek Pastoral, see D. Halperin, *Before Pastoral*, New Haven, Conn., Yale University Press, 1983; J. Van Sickle, 'Theocritus and the development of the conception of bucolic genre', *Ramus* 5, 1976, pp. 18–44; H. Berger, jnr, 'The origins of bucolic representation: disenchantment and revision in Theocritus' seventh Idyll', *Classical Antiquity* 3, 1984, pp. 1–39.

10 On this metamorphosis, see S. D. Goldhill, 'Framing and polyphony: readings in Hellenistic poetry', *Proceedings of the Cambridge Philological Society* ns 32, 1986. On the discussion of the value of poetry, see, for example, H. Erbse, 'Dichtkunst und Medizin in Theokrits' 11. Idyll', *Museum Helveticum* 22, 1965, pp. 232–6; E. Holtsmark,

'Poetry as self-enlightenment; Theocritus 11', *Transactions of the American Philological Association* 97, 1966, pp. 253–9; C. P. Segal, *Poetry and Myth in Ancient Pastoral*, Princeton, NJ, Princeton University Press, 1981, pp. 224–9; A. Brooke, 'Theocritus' *Idyll* 11: a study in pastoral', *Arethusa* 4, 1971, pp. 73–81; A. Horstman, *Ironie und Humor bei Theokrit*, Meisenheim am Glan, Verlag Anton Hain, 1976, pp. 85–110.

On parody and genre, see Ph. -E. Legrande, *Etude sur Theocrite*, Paris, Albert Fontemoing, 1898, pp. 111–13; and especially F. Cairns, *Generic Composition in Greek and Roman Poetry*, Edinburgh, Edinburgh University Press, 1972, pp. 143–7 (criticized below) and I. Du Quesnay, 'From Polyphemus to Corydon: Virgil *Eclogue* 2 and the *Idylls* of Theocritus', in D. West and T. Woodman(eds) *Creative Imitation and Latin Literature*, Cambridge, Cambridge University Press, 1979, criticized in S. Goldhill, op. cit.

11 See G. Seeck, 'Dichterische Technik in Theokrits "Thalysien" und die Theorie der Hirtendichtung', in *ΔΩ PHMA Hans Diller*, Athens, Griechische Humanishische Gesellschaft, 1975.

12 W. J. Bate, *The Burden of the Past and the English Poet*, London, Chatto & Windus, 1970.

13 H. Bloom, *The Anxiety of Influence*, London, Oxford University Press, 1973. I have discussed this aspect of Hellenistic poetry at greater length with further bibliography in my article, op. cit. (n. 10).

14 Du Quesnay op. cit. (n. 10) p. 45.

15 S. Walker, *Theocritus*, Boston, Mass., 1980, p. 41.

16 Brooke op. cit. (n. 10) p. 73.

17 Cairns op. cit. (n. 10) p. 147. I have chosen Cairns's reading both because it has been especially influential and because his argument seems paradigmatic of a range of approaches to the poem.

18 The first five lines with the address to Tityrus function as an introduction however to the *kōmos* to Amaryllis.

19 A. F. S. Gow, *Theocritus*, Cambridge, Cambridge University Press, 1952, 2 vols. All further references are to the second volume.

20 Gow op. cit. (n. 19) ad 13.

21 K. Dover, *Theocritus*, London, Macmillan, 1971, p. 174.

22 Holtsmark op. cit. (n. 10) passim; Erbse op. cit. (n. 10) passim.

23 The same phrase occurs at *Idyll* 2, 19, where Simaetha upbraids her servant with the same question: 'Are you mad?' The perfect tense implies continuation in Greek, not completion.

24 On the *Odyssey's* narrative of sexuality, see S. D. Goldhill, *Language, Sexuality, Narrative; The Orestia*, Cambridge, Cambridge University Press, 1984, pp. 184–95.

25 See especially 21 *kai qar ai pheugei, takheōs diōxei* ('For if s/he is fleeing, s/he soon will pursue').

26 Tragedy often revolves around the *destructive* force of *Erōs*. One

example from each of the major tragedians will suffice: Aesch. *Cho* 586–681; Soph. *Ant* 781–801; Eur. *Hipp* 525–64.

27 See S. D. Goldhill, 'Praying to Dionysus: Re-reading Anacreon fr 2 (301 Page)', *LCM* 9.6, 1984, p. 86.

28 See Gow op. cit. (n. 19) ad loc.

29 op. cit. (n. 10) 213.

30 *isōs de katagelōsin autou.*

31 *Od.* IX 364–414.

32 Brooke op. cit. (n. 10) passim; Horstman op. cit. (n. 10) pp. 95–110.

33 Gow op. cit. (n. 19) ad 13.

34 He does not print this suggestion in his text, of course.

35 Gow op. cit. (n. 19) ad 13.

36 Cairns op. cit. (n. 10) p. 147.

37 Du Quesnay op. cit. (n. 10) p. 47.

38 See LSJ *poimainein* II.1.

39 A common Homeric expression: *Agamemnona poimena laōn.* The relation between a shepherd and his flock is discussed differently at Plato *Rep.* 343a1 ff.

40 *The Singer of the Eclogues*, Berkeley and Los Angeles, University of California Press, 1979, p. 123.

41 Eur. *Hipp.* 516.

42 Soph. *Trach.* 685.

43 *Od.* I. 262.

44 Homer also provides the *locus classicus* for the expression of the doubleness of pharmaka: *Od.* IV 230 *pharmaka, polla men esthla, polla de lugra* ('Drugs, many good . . . but many harmful').

45 On *hādu*, see especially H. Edquist, 'Aspects of Theocritean Otium', *Ramus* 4, 1974, pp. 104–14. On rejection of Homeric grandeur in Theocritus, see especially *Idyll* 7 43–51, lines which have been extensively commented on; see for bibliography and discussion e.g. Segal op. cit. (n. 10) pp. 110–66. Although I have found no other example of *kouphos* used for poetics, the Latin *levis* and *mitis* by which it may be translated are common terms for poetics in those poets affiliating themselves to a Callimachean and Theocritean tradition.

46 See Gow op. cit. (n. 19) ad loc.

47 See e.g. R. Pfeiffer, *History of Classical Scholarship*, Oxford, Clarendon Press, 1968, pp. 39–40, 74–5; W. Guthrie, *A History of Greek Philosophy*, Cambridge, 1969, vol. III, pp. 205–25.

48 See P. Pucci, *Hesiod and the Language of Poetry*, Baltimore, Md, Johns Hopkins University Press, 1977; C. Calame, *Les Choeurs de jeunes filles en Grece archaique*, Rome, Edizioni dell-Ateneo e Bizzarri, 2 vols, esp. p. 399; M. Detienne, *Les Maitres de vérité dans Grece archaique*, Paris, Gallimard, 1967. I have discussed this material extensively in *Reading Greek Tragedy*, Cambridge, Cambridge University Press, chs 6, 9, 10, 11.

49 I have discussed this further in my article op. cit. (n. 10).

50 E. Wright, *Psychoanalytic Criticism*, London, Methuen, 1984, p. 131. I have purloined this quotation from J. G. W. Henderson's forthcoming article on Penelope (*LCM* 11, 1986).

51 See *La Vérité en peinture*, Paris, Flammarion, 1978, pp. 21–168; 'The purveyor of truth', *Yale French Studies*, 52, 1975, p. 99.

52 J. Derrida, 'The purveyor of truth', p. 99.

53 G. Ulmer, *Applied Grammatology*, Baltimore, Md, Johns Hopkins University Press, 1984, p. 102.

54 B. Johnson, *The Critical Difference*, Baltimore, Md, Johns Hopkins University Press, 1980, p. 128.

55 Johnson, op. cit., p. 146.

Appendix

No other remedy is there for love, Nicias, neither unguent, methinks, nor salve, save only the Muses; and this remedy is painless for mortals and pleasant, but hard to find – as well, I trow, thou knowest, who art a physician, and loved exceedingly withal by all the nine Muses. So at least my countryman the Cyclops fared most easily – even Polyphemus of old, when, with the down new on his lips and temples, he was in love with Galatea. And he loved not with apples, or roses, or ringlets, but with downright frenzy, counting all else but trifles. Many a time would his sheep come of their own accord back from the green pastures to his fold, while he, alone upon the wrack-strewn shore, would waste away with love as he sang of Galatea from dawn of day, having deep beneath his breast an angry wound which the shaft of the mighty Cyprian goddess had planted in his heart. Yet the remedy he found, and seated on some high rock would gaze seaward and sing thus:

O white Galatea, why dost thou repulse thy lover – whiter than curd to look on, softer than the lamb, more skittish than the calf, sleeker than the unripe grape – why thus, when sweet sleep holds me, dost thou straight approach, and when sweet sleep leaves me, art gone forthwith, flying, as the ewe flies when she sees the grey wolf? I fell in love with thee, maiden, when first thou camest with my mother to gather hyacinth-flowers on the hill, and I showed the way. And having seen thee, from that day forth even until now I cannot cease; but naught thou carest, nay, naught at all.

I know, fair maid, why thou fliest. It is because a shaggy brow stretches over all my forehead – one long and single brow from ear to ear; and single is the eye beneath, and broad the nostril above my lip. Yet, though such I be, I tend a thousand head of cattle, and draw and drink from them the finest milk. Cheese I lack not, neither in summer, nor autumn nor in the depth of winter, and my racks are ever heavy. And I can pipe as none other Cyclops here, as often in the depths of night I sing of thee, my sweet honey-apple, and of myself. And for thee I rear eleven fawns with collars all, and four bear-cubs.

Nay, come to me, and thou shalt fare well enough. Leave the green sea to pulse upon the shore; thou wilt pass the night more pleasantly in the cave with me. There are bays and slender cypresses; there is dark ivy, and the sweet-fruited vine, and water cold, which wooded Etna puts forth for me from her white snow-fields, a draught divine. Who would rather choose the sea and its waves than these?

But if it is I myself that seem too shaggy to thee, oak-logs I have, and fire undying beneath the ash, and thou mayest burn my soul, and my one eye too, than which nothing is dearer to me.

Alack that my mother bore me not with gills, that so I might have dived down to thee and kissed thy hand, if thou wilt not let me kiss thy mouth; and might have brought thee snowdrops white, or the soft poppy with its scarlet petals. But one in summer grows, the other in winter, so that both together I could not bring. Now, maiden, even now, will I learn at least to swim, if but some stranger sail hither in his ship, that I may know what pleasure it is to you to dwell in the depths.

Come forth, Galatea; and coming, forget, as I do now sitting here, to go home again. Consent to shepherd with me, and to milk, and to set cheese with drops of acid rennet.

My mother alone it is who wrongs me, and her I blame; for never once has she spoken a kindly word for me to thee, though she sees me growing thinner day by day. I will tell her my head throbs, and both my feet, that she may suffer since I too suffer.

O Cyclops, Cyclops, whither have thy wits wandered? Thou wouldst show more sense if thou wouldst go and plait cheese-crates, and gather greenery for thy lambs. Milk the ewe that's by; why pursue him that flees? another and a fairer Galatea wilt thou find, maybe. Many a maiden bids me spend the night in sport with her, and they titter all when I give ear to them. 'Tis plain that on land I too am somebody.

Thus did Polyphemus shepherd his love with minstrelsy, and fared easier than if he had spent gold.

Θεοκρίτου Κύκλωψ

Οὐδὲν ποττὸν ἔρωτα πεφύκει φάρμακον ἄλλο,
Νικία, οὔτ' ἔγχριστον, ἐμὶν δοκεῖ, οὔτ' ἐπίπαστον,
ἢ ταὶ Πιερίδες· κοῦφον δέ τι τοῦτο καὶ ἁδύ
γίνετ' ἐπ' ἀνθρώποις, εὑρεῖν δ' οὐ ῥᾴδιόν ἐστι.
5 γινώσκειν δ' οἶμαί τυ καλῶς ἰατρὸν ἐόντα
καὶ ταῖς ἐννέα δὴ πεφιλημένον ἔξοχα Μοίσαις.
οὕτω γοῦν ῥάιστα διᾶγ' ὁ Κύκλωψ ὁ παρ' ἁμῖν,
ὡρχαῖος Πολύφαμος, ὅκ' ἤρατο τᾶς Γαλατείας,
ἄρτι γενειάσδων περὶ τὸ στόμα τὼς κροτάφως τε.
10 ἤρατο δ' οὐ μάλοις οὐδὲ ῥόδῳ οὐδὲ κικίννοις,
ἀλλ' ὀρθαῖς μανίαις, ἁγεῖτο δὲ πάντα πάρεργα.
πολλάκι ταὶ ὄιες ποτὶ τωὔλιον αὐταὶ ἀπῆνθον
χλωρᾶς ἐκ βοτάνας· ὁ δὲ τὰν Γαλάτειαν ἀείδων
αὐτὸς ἐπ' αἰόνος κατετάκετο φυκιοέσσας
15 ἐξ ἀοῦς, ἔχθιστον ἔχων ὑποκάρδιον ἕλκος,
Κύπριδος ἐκ μεγάλας τό οἱ ἥπατι πᾶξε βέλεμνον.
ἀλλὰ τὸ φάρμακον εὗρε, καθεζόμενος δ' ἐπὶ πέτρας
ὑψηλᾶς ἐς πόντον ὁρῶν ἄειδε τοιαῦτα·

    ᾿Ω λευκὰ Γαλάτεια, τί τὸν φιλέοντ' ἀποβάλλῃ,
20 λευκοτέρα πακτᾶς ποτιδεῖν, ἁπαλωτέρα ἀρνός,
μόσχω γαυροτέρα, φιαρωτέρα ὄμφακος ὠμᾶς;
φοιτῇς δ' αὖθ' οὕτως ὅκκα γλυκὺς ὕπνος ἔχῃ με,
οἴχῃ δ' εὐθὺς ἰοῖσ' ὅκκα γλυκὺς ὕπνος ἀνῇ με,
φεύγεις δ' ὥσπερ ὄις πολιὸν λύκον ἀθρήσασα;
25 ἠράσθην μὲν ἔγωγε τεοῦς, κόρα, ἁνίκα πρᾶτον
ἦνθες ἐμᾷ σὺν ματρὶ θέλοισ' ὑακίνθινα φύλλα
ἐξ ὄρεος δρέψασθαι, ἐγὼ δ' ὁδὸν ἁγεμόνευον.
παύσασθαι δ' ἐσιδών τυ καὶ ὕστερον οὐδ' ἔτι πᾳ νῦν
ἐκ τήνω δύναμαι· τὶν δ' οὐ μέλει, οὐ μὰ Δί' οὐδέν.

30 γινώσκω, χαρίεσσα κόρα, τίνος οὕνεκα φεύγεις·
    οὕνεκά μοι λασία μὲν ὀφρὺς ἐπὶ παντὶ μετώπῳ
    ἐξ ὠτὸς τέταται ποτὶ θώτερον ὡς μία μακρά,
    εἷς δ' ὀφθαλμὸς ὕπεστι, πλατεῖα δὲ ῥὶς ἐπὶ χείλει.
    ἀλλ' οὗτος τοιοῦτος ἐὼν βοτὰ χίλια βόσκω,
35 κἠκ τούτων τὸ κράτιστον ἀμελγόμενος γάλα πίνω·
    τυρὸς δ' οὐ λείπει μ' οὔτ' ἐν θέρει οὔτ' ἐν ὀπώρᾳ,
    οὐ χειμῶνος ἄκρω· ταρσοὶ δ' ὑπεραχθέες αἰεί.
    συρίσδεν δ' ὡς οὔτις ἐπίσταμαι ὧδε Κυκλώπων,
    τίν, τὸ φίλον γλυκύμαλον, ἁμᾷ κἠμαυτὸν ἀείδων
40 πολλάκι νυκτὸς ἀωρί. τράφω δέ τοι ἕνδεκα νεβρώς,
    πάσας μαννοφόρως, καὶ σκύμνως τέσσαρας ἄρκτων.
    ἀλλ' ἀφίκευσο ποθ' ἁμέ, καὶ ἐξεῖς οὐδὲν ἔλασσον,
    τὰν γλαυκὰν δὲ θάλασσαν ἔα ποτὶ χέρσον ὀρεχθεῖν·
    ἅδιον ἐν τὤντρῳ παρ' ἐμὶν τὰν νύκτα διαξεῖς.
45 ἐντὶ δάφναι τηνεί, ἐντὶ ῥαδιναὶ κυπάρισσοι,
    ἔστι μέλας κισσός, ἔστ' ἄμπελος ἁ γλυκύκαρπος,
    ἔστι ψυχρὸν ὕδωρ, τό μοι ἁ πολυδένδρεος Αἴτνα
    λευκᾶς ἐκ χιόνος ποτὸν ἀμβρόσιον προΐητι.
    τίς κα τῶνδε θάλασσαν ἔχειν καὶ κύμαθ' ἕλοιτο;
50 αἰ δέ τοι αὐτὸς ἐγὼν δοκέω λασιώτερος ἦμεν,
    ἐντὶ δρυὸς ξύλα μοι καὶ ὑπὸ σποδῷ ἀκάματον πῦρ·
    καιόμενος δ' ὑπὸ τεῦς καὶ τὰν ψυχὰν ἀνεχοίμαν
    καὶ τὸν ἕν' ὀφθαλμόν, τῶ μοι γλυκερώτερον οὐδέν.
    ὤμοι, ὅτ' οὐκ ἔτεκέν μ' ἁ μάτηρ βράγχι' ἔχοντα,
55 ὡς κατέδυν ποτὶ τὶν καὶ τὰν χέρα τεῦς ἐφίλησα,
    αἰ μὴ τὸ στόμα λῇς, ἔφερον δέ τοι ἢ κρίνα λευκά
    ἢ μάκων' ἁπαλὰν ἐρυθρὰ πλαταγώνι' ἔχοισαν·
    ἀλλὰ τὰ μὲν θέρεος, τὰ δὲ γίνεται ἐν χειμῶνι,
    ὥστ' οὐ κά τοι ταῦτα φέρειν ἅμα πάντ' ἐδυνάθην.
60 νῦν μάν, ὦ κόριον, νῦν αὐτίκα νεῖν γε μαθεῦμαι,
    αἴ κά τις σὺν ναΐ πλέων ξένος ὧδ' ἀφίκηται,
    ὡς εἰδῶ τί ποχ' ἁδὺ κατοικεῖν τὸν βυθὸν ὕμμιν.
    ἐξένθοις, Γαλάτεια, καὶ ἐξενθοῖσα λάθοιο,
    ὥσπερ ἐγὼ νῦν ὧδε καθήμενος, οἴκαδ' ἀπενθεῖν·
65 ποιμαίνειν δ' ἐθέλοις σὺν ἐμὶν ἅμα καὶ γάλ' ἀμέλγειν
    καὶ τυρὸν πᾶξαι τάμισον δριμεῖαν ἐνεῖσα.
    ἁ μάτηρ ἀδικεῖ με μόνα, καὶ μέμφομαι αὐτᾷ·
    οὐδὲν πήποχ' ὅλως ποτὶ τὶν φίλον εἶπεν ὑπέρ μευ,
    καὶ ταῦτ' ἆμαρ ἐπ' ἆμαρ ὁρεῦσά με λεπτύνοντα.

70 φασῶ τὰν κεφαλὰν καὶ τὼς πόδας ἀμφοτέρως μευ
   σφύσδειν, ὡς ἀνιαθῇ, ἐπεὶ κἠγὼν ἀνιῶμαι.
   ὦ Κύκλωψ Κύκλωψ, πᾷ τὰς φρένας ἐκπεπότασαι;
   αἴ κ᾽ ἐνθὼν ταλάρως τε πλέκοις καὶ θαλλὸν ἀμάσας
   ταῖς ἄρνεσσι φέροις, τάχα κα πολὺ μᾶλλον ἔχοις νῶν
75 τὰν παρεοῖσαν ἄμελγε· τί τὸν φεύγοντα διώκεις;
   εὑρησεῖς Γαλάτειαν ἴσως καὶ καλλίον᾽ ἄλλαν.
   πολλαὶ συμπαίσδεν με κόραι τὰν νύκτα κέλονται,
   κιχλίζοντι δὲ πᾶσαι, ἐπεί κ᾽ αὐταῖς ὑπακούσω.
   δῆλον ὅτ᾽ ἐν τᾷ γᾷ κἠγών τις φαίνομαι ἦμεν.
80   Οὕτω τοι Πολύφαμος ἐποίμαινεν τὸν ἔρωτα
   μουσίσδων, ῥᾷον δὲ διᾶγ᾽ ἢ εἰ χρυσὸν ἔδωκεν.

· 5 ·

Time and interpretation in Heraclitus

ANDREW BENJAMIN

Reading the Heraclitean fragments after Heidegger is a daunting if perhaps impossible task. Furthermore the complexity of Heidegger's repeated return to Heraclitus, almost independently of its forming a fundamental part of the development of his own philosophy, poses the problem of how to take a stand in relation to it. Perhaps a way into the problem could start from a consideration of the conception of language Heidegger deploys in his reading. I must indicate that in order to give this chapter a specific focus I have limited myself to a discussion of his 1953 text *An Introduction to Metaphysics*.[1] Heidegger emerges as an important detour on the way to developing an interpretation of Heraclitus. It is however a detour that must be made.

In a sense it is important to keep returning to the question of a beginning, not to forestall or put off the actual encounter but to underline and underscore the real problems posed by interpreting Heidegger and Heraclitus. It would for example be all too easy to take Heidegger's translation of 'physis' and try and argue that it is incorrect. That he is wrong in thinking that

> 'physis' is being itself, by virtue of
> which entities become and remain
> observable.[2]

It is initially hard to know what an objection to this translation would be like except via an historical excursus involving a detailed consideration of the Milesian roots of this particular term. Even then it would be unclear what would have been shown. A more fruitful approach would be to stay with Heidegger and attempt to unpick what guides his interpretation and translation of the fragments. It is at this stage, therefore, unnecessary to depart from Heidegger's text.

The guide I have in mind is provided by the conception of language and translation deployed in his interpretation of Heraclitus. Early in the text he advances a particular definition of 'physis'; not the one that has already been cited but a more deliberate and careful definition. However, the question is, how is it to be understood? Prior to stating and discussing the definition it is vital to answer this preliminary question; its answer provides, in part, the ground for understanding the definition itself.

The definition is advanced after a brief discussion of the problems involved in translation of 'physis' by 'natura'. The major problem that Heidegger isolates is that this translation involves a thrusting aside of 'der ursprungliche Gehalt' of 'physis'.[3] In his excellent translation of *An Introduction to Metaphysics* Manheim renders this expression as 'the original meaning'. There is a sense in which this translation is accurate. However, it needs to be explained. The two words in German that are usually used to translate meaning are 'Sinn' and 'Bedeutung'. 'Gehalt', on the other hand, has a range of meanings, of which 'content' and 'capacity' are the most apposite in this instance. Why, then, would Heidegger have used the expression 'der ursprungliche Gehalt' when the more usual expression would have been 'die ursprungliche Bedeutung'? The most straightforward answer is that Heidegger wants to distinguish between a simple sense of meaning and the attribution of actual content to the word.[4] Meaning refers out while the identification of content refers to that which is contained within the word. Meaning is but a short slide from meanings and hence polysemy, while content and the identification of content involves a semantics that is not simply in line with, but could even have been sanctioned by, the implicit conception of interpretation within Heidegger's works, already discussed in the first chapter. Consequently, 'der ursprungliche Gehalt' can be translated as 'original meaning' if it is recognized that 'meaning' in this instance refers to the essential content of the word. Having made these points it is now possible to see the import of Heidegger's charge that the translation of 'physis' involved a casting aside of the 'original meaning' of the 'physis'. In a sense, however, it is always possible to argue this position in that it is likely, if only for historical reasons, that a translation may betray an originally held meaning. However, this is not Heidegger's position, nor is it that translation must transform an originally held meaning because, it is argued, translation does not involve the substitution of one word for another word (or series of words) where the accuracy of the translation would depend upon the extent to which the word in the second language captured the sense of and hence could substitute for the word in the original language. Nor, finally, does he argue that in order for translation to take place, what is inevitably lost in the act of translation is the polysemy inherent in the original term and therefore any translation must involve a denial of possible meanings.[5] Rather, his point is far stronger because he is claiming that this particular translation involves the transgression of an originally held meaning because there is a single original meaning. There is, therefore, a commitment to the existence of an initial act of pure signification in which the original and essential meaning (or content) was revealed. The sign of the original – the original signification – may become distorted, indeed it may even be complicit in its own distortion; none the less, there is an original, unified site to meaning. There must be the additional point that the meaning of the original site must have been apparent and hence be able to be cited. Furthermore, its identification must not result from or be the consequence of an interpretation because the need for interpretation entails that the meaning is not apparent. Moreover, interpretation always involves the possibility if not potentiality of duplicity. To the extent that a meaning is not apparent or self-evident, the determination of meaning is only ever approximate and therefore the subject of debate if not dispute. If it is possible to claim that an original meaning has been transgressed or betrayed then it must have been unified and exact if only in order to pinpoint both what was betrayed and the betrayal itself. An original meaning must not have been concealed but rather must have been stated or declared. The text that demands interpretation could not reveal its original meaning, for an interpretation can only ever be justified by the claim that it was providing the original meaning. Meaning as the consequence of interpretation is always, and of necessity, one step removed from apparent meaning.

This particular stance which, while not explicit in Heidegger's text, though one which is demanded by the reference to an original meaning, is linked to an intriguing series of claims about sloppy language.

But now let us skip over this whole process of defamation and decay and attempt to regain the unimpaired strength of language and words; for words and language are not wrappings in which things are packed for the commerce of those who write and speak. It is in language that things first come into being and are. For this reason the misuse of language in idle talk, in slogans and phrases destroys our authentic relation to things (un den echten Bezug zu den Dingen).⁶

It is only after having made these claims that Heidegger then asks, 'What does the word physis denote?' The answer to the question, indeed the strategy deployed in order to answer it, is structured first by the idea that a term has a single and original meaning; and second that between subjects, language and things there can be an authentic relation; and finally that the misuse of language can destroy this relation. However, it is essential to be very careful here for both Locke and Hobbes could be seen as arguing a similar position given that they both held that unless language or signs were used methodically the nature of things (or objects) would be betrayed. For Hobbes there is, of course, the additional point that the misuse of language and the subsequent deception to which it would give rise could have disastrous political results. Consequently more needs to be said both in order to distinguish Heidegger's position from the well-known Lockean and Hobbesian arguments, as well as to establish what for Heidegger is involved in the thrusting aside of an original meaning.

It is fortunate that Heidegger provides examples of a distinction between, on the one hand, words understood as having a single and essential meaning, and their being 'mere' words on the other. Furthermore, and in part because the major concern of Heidegger's text is the question of Being, the discussion of language is joined to the continual elucidation of this important question. An instance of the above-mentioned distinction is advanced in the following question:

Is Being a mere word and its meaning a vapour (*Ist das Sein ein blosses Wort und seine Bedeutung ein Dunst*), or does what is designated by the word Being hold within it the historical destiny of the West (*das geistige Schicksal das Abendlands*).[7]

Prior to discussing this question it is important to link the distinction drawn within it between two conceptions of meaning, to the connection that Heidegger establishes between uses of language, the question of Being and the destiny of a nation.

The organizations for the purification of the language and defence against its progressive barbarization are deserving of respect. But such efforts merely demonstrate all the more clearly that we no longer know what is at stake in language. Because the destiny of language is grounded in a nation's relation to Being, the question of Being will involve us deeply in the question of language.[8]

The positions, both implicit and explicit, which are advanced here provide a way into examining the problem of what is involved in claiming that physis has an 'original meaning'. The major preparatory problem that must be confronted is the nature of the distinction between 'vapour' and 'historical destiny'.

It is, of course, important to realize that the 'mere word' in question is Being and therefore what is at issue is the meaning of Being. However, while Heidegger's discussion of Being cannot be too quickly generalized to cover all words, the fact that he states elsewhere in the text that, 'language is the original poetry in which a people speaks being',[9] indicates that the link between language and Being does not simply concern the word Being. The consequence of this is that what is true for the word Being is going to be true for language in general (without necessarily of course being true for every word). This is the reason why, as will be seen, the meaning of a word or words cannot be a simple 'vapour'; and that is especially true for the word 'Being'.

It should not be forgotten that 'vapour' is opposed to 'historical destiny' (das geistige Schicksal). It is perhaps advisable to sketch part of the interplay between 'vapour' and 'destiny' prior to linking this distinction to Heidegger's concern with purity and a 'nation's relation to Being'. A 'mere word' is a word that is not implicated in the fulfilment of destiny. Its meaning therefore neither endures nor perdures but vanishes in the moment of its utterance. The meaning of a 'mere word' involves a continual vanishing and hence for such a word there is no larger process in which it plays a role and therefore which it enacts. A continual and returning vanishing stands opposed to destiny. Destiny is either inherent in something and therefore comes to be realized or destiny, while inherent, is realized only in action and therefore certain actions are engendered and justified because they intend to realize historical destiny. Consequently, because of the inherently actative dimension within destiny, no matter how destiny is construed, it involves teleology. A further reason for holding to a link between destiny and teleology resides in the capacity of destiny to be thwarted. The teleological process, which can be defined simply as a process demanding either self-realization or realization through actions, can be perverted. The way of destiny can become lost. Destiny therefore is inevitably linked to a strategy of loss and recovery. A strategy which must involve an original moment whose direction-giving capacity may have become lost or perverted and thus must be recovered or retrieved. The acting out of destiny – the process of realization – regardless of whether this takes place actively or passively involves three elements. First, the identification of the original, second the experience of the original as the original, and finally the recognition of the teleological process in which destiny is articulated and which articulates destiny. 'Vapour' therefore stands opposed to the unity of an original destiny and the process whereby it is fulfilled. Unity, the origin and teleology are the terms inextricably linked to the recognition and the realization of destiny and therefore all are at play in the claim that the word Being 'holds within it the historical destiny of the West'. It should also be noted that destiny gives rise to a specific structure of temporality. While time is one of Heidegger's major philosophical concerns the problem of the temporality of destiny does not fall within his considerations, if only because this temporal structure is implicit within the conceptual framework within which destiny plays a fundamental role. If destiny can be understood as taking place within a teleological process, and it can be argued that this is still at play in his later writings when Being becomes *Geshick*,[10] then language itself can be understood as involving the same temporal framework. In fact, it is not difficult to see that this is the case. If the temporality proper to teleology is sequential continuity, this must be the only temporal framework within which it is possible to retrieve a lost meaning. It is only within this framework therefore that it is possible, in Heidegger's words, 'to regain the unimpaired strength of language and words'.

Heidegger's conception of language and hence interpretation, coupled to the destiny of Being, must exclude a conception of time that involves discontinuity, for the simple reason that discontinuity involves a change and hence the inability to return. This does not mean that within a conception of interpretation connected to the temporality of discontinuity it is impossible to understand the historical; it is rather that it casts doubt upon the possibility of breaking through all 'dialogical interpretations' of a text and return to its original saying. The question of the origin is not simply a problem within interpretation; it is also one for a philosophy of time. Without wanting to trace all the connections between Being, destiny, language, and so on, what emerges as of great importance is the singularity and unity at play in meaning and destiny. This point is made in Heidegger's formulation: 'The West has an historical destiny'. The west should be one with its destiny and its destiny won for it. Each has a specific identity.

The dominance of unity and identity is also apparent in Heidegger's claim that 'the destiny of language is grounded in a nation's relation to Being' (*das Schicksal der Sprache ist dem jeweiligen Bezug eines Volkes zum Sein ge grundet ist*). At this stage the attribution of destiny to language is not at issue (though perhaps it should be noted in passing that it serves to reinforce some of the points made above concerning the temporal framework of interpretation); what must be discussed is the nation. Despite Heidegger having described German, as 'along with Greek . . . the most powerful and spiritual of all languages',[11] and the identification of the primitive – or rather a conception of the primitive – as a 'higher type of Hottentot',[12] it should not be automatically assumed that nation is coextensive with the German nation and thereby other nations are excluded. The question that must be answered is what is at stake in a nation?

A nation is at once singular, for it can be distinguished from other nations, and plural because it contains a plurality. However, for Heidegger that plurality is unified by the existence of a 'relation to Being' and it is that relation that grounds the destiny of a language. The plurality of language is limited by its having a destiny in the same way as the plurality of a nation is limited by its having a 'relation to Being'. It is precisely in terms of a limiting function that mediates plurality redefining it in terms of unity that both the nation and the semantics of Being should be understood. Nation and Being are interrelated by their both having a destiny. The difficulty is in determining what type of unity is presupposed by such a conception of nation. Clearly, of course, this question works the other way around; namely what type of nation is presupposed by such a conception of unity?

There are two different though related conceptions of unity that will serve as answers to these questions. The first conception of unity is one that excludes difference and, therefore, the act of exclusion is fundamental to the construction of unity, and hence the exclusion of difference. The second conception is one that attempts to explain difference either in terms of an initial unity that sanctions apparent differences or as a transcendental unity that incorporates difference. It is this latter conception of unity which is the most important because the consequences of such a conception of unity (or identity) always amount to more than the belonging-together of difference and in its being named (as for example a nation or people) it comes to have a life of its own that transcends difference and as such works to efface difference by demanding or giving homogeneity. This latter point is extremely important as well as being very complex; it can, however, be elucidated in relation to certain Platonic considerations of naming.

If unity or totality can be understood as the belonging-together of differences, then the important question is what is involved in its being named and therefore what is presupposed in the act of naming? In the *Theaetetus*,[13] Plato discusses his task of determining what knowledge (*episteme*) is in relation to naming. This occurs at two specific moments in the dialogue. The first at 147b, 2–3:

Do you suppose that anyone has any understanding of the name of something, when he does not know what the thing is?

The second occurs at 147b, 10–147c1:

it is ridiculous to answer the question, what is knowledge? (*episteme ti estin*) by giving the name of some type of knowledge (*techne*) because we give in such an answer something that knowledge belongs to and we were not asked to provide this.

The important element in these passages is, as was indicated, that the term 'name' plays a central role in determining an answer to the question 'what is knowledge'. What needs to be understood is why it is ridiculous to answer the question 'what is knowledge' by giving an instance of knowledge. It is clear that there are two different types of questions being alluded to here. The first one concerns first what something is (what it essentially is) and second what can be said of it (in the sense of being able to give attributes of it). These two types of questions are suggested in the following important passage from the *Euthyphro*:

It seems Euthyphro that when you were asked what piety is you were unwilling to reveal its essential being (*ten ousian*) and only stated one of its attributes (*pathos*) namely that piety is loved by the Gods. (11a, 6–9)

This section ends with Socrates asking Euthyphro to tell him what piety itself is (*ti esti to hosion*). What underlies the importance of this passage is not simply the distinction between *ousis* and *pathos* (to which we shall return) but the fundamental role the distinction plays in the text itself. In sum, it can be argued that Socrates is attempting to bring Euthyphro to the position from which he will be able to see that in order to answer the first question – *ti esti to hosion* – he has to reveal its *ousin* or essential being. Even after stating at 11b, 6–9 that this is the aim, Euthyphro still fails to grasp Socrates' point and thus the dialogue continues as though what were at issue was giving the answer to the question concerning attributes. The two types of question that emerge both from the *Theaetetus* and the *Euthyphro*, though their existence cannot be limited to these two dialogues, can, following Dodds,[14] be called ti-questions and poion-questions. The latter form of question concerns what it is that can be said of a thing, for example of piety it can be said that it is loved by the Gods. Ti-questions, on the other hand, are concerned with what it is that something is. The answer to a ti-question can be given only by providing the *ousia* of that which is in question. Therefore, the answer to the question 'what is knowledge' can be answered only by giving the *ousia* of knowledge. Consequently when the name 'episteme' or 'hosion' is used correctly it names the respective 'ousia'. This point is made in the Cratylus in the suggestion that 'the essential being of the thing is shown in the name' (*he ousia tou pragmatos delou-mene en to onomati*) 393d, 4–5. However, the essential being of a thing is not simply an element; it forms one of the three aspects fundamental to it. A point made clearly in the Laws; the three aspects are:

One is the essential being, one the definition of the essential being and the other the name. (895d, 4–6)

Ti-questions and poion-questions not only demand different answers, but also the answers involve different ontological and temporal frameworks. The *ousia* of a given thing must be permanent and enduring, therefore, even if the object in which the *ousia* is present is neither permanent nor enduring, the name must none the less name the essential in the object. The consequence is that the essential, to use another formulation provided by the Cratylus, must be 'always the same as itself' (*aei estin oion estin*) (439d, 5). That which is named must be a single essential unity. Indeed Plato goes so far as to suggest that if the essential changed, then there would be no one thing to name and hence, by implication, naming would be impossible.

As is well known, within Platonism a beautiful vase is beautiful if it partakes (*metechein*) of the form Beauty. The name 'beauty' does not name the particular qua particular but the essential in the particular. While there are a potentially infinite number of beautiful things, in order that they be named the totality of beautiful things must be both different in relation to each other and the same in so far as they are beautiful. Within Platonism there is only one way in which a thing is named as beautiful. Consequently it is possible to describe the totality of beautiful things as a belonging-together of differences in so far as the contents differ (for example a vase in relation to a painting) and yet their differences – except perhaps on the rather banal level of purely physical description – are effaced in order that they all be named as beautiful. Presupposed in the act of naming, therefore, is that not only must the essential being of what is named be unified and the same as itself but also what is named in the particulars is the presence of the essential in each. A homogeneity amongst the particulars is demanded in order that they be named and therefore in being named they become homogeneous. This structure allows for Beauty to be an object in itself. This would not be the case in Aristotle, when in the *Eudemian Ethics* he argues contra Plato that there is no one way in which things are either good or exist but rather there are numerous types of goodness and types of existence.[15]

Put in the same way therefore that Being is not one in the categories just enumerated, and just as the good is not one – there is not a unique science of either Being or the good. (1217b)

(The latter of course is to be explained via the categories.) There is, therefore, no way to make either the Good or Being, and by implication Beauty, and so on, into a transcendental object, and thus for it to have an existence independently of what is named. To the extent, therefore, that a name can be made transcendental, it is either the case that it is the consequence of homogeneity among the named, or it demands homogeneity among the named. In both instances, if the name has an independent existence, then, moving to a more general level, it either sanctions or demands actions in relation to that name such that if the actions differ or are not homogeneous, then they are no longer done in the name of the originator of the actions. This latter point is easy to see in relation to the nation (and even that matter in relation to a 'people', recognizing the ambiguity of the German word 'Volkes').

If nation is understood within the context outlined above, it is not simply a term descriptive of a diverse collective, that is a pure belonging together of differences, but a transcendental term (which may have destiny) because it gives identity as members of the nation to each individual member of the totality. The nation becomes a unified totality. To contrast this with an implicitly Aristotelian conception[16] in which nation would be no more than the collectivity, a Platonic conception of nation (or people) would involve the identity of the members of the nation being determined by nation understood as a transcendental term. An individual became a member of the nation in so far, and only in so far, as they identified or came to identify with what in Heideggerian terms could be described as the nation's destiny. It has already been observed that an important part of Heidegger's description of nation and the west, as well as of language, is that each was attributed a single destiny and each were themselves expressed as unified totalities. When it was suggested that a nation has a relation to Being, or that the west has a destiny, the singularity of these terms is not chance. It is, in fact, part of a tradition that stems from Plato. The emergence of language, the west and the nation as transcendental categories entails that the belonging together of the differences that they name, in order to maintain their identity each element of the difference must re-present, and hence present, that which is essential to either language, the west or a nation. Unity or totality therefore, whether in the sense of naming the belonging together of differences and thereby effacing them or, as was discussed earlier, as locked into a theological process marked by the presence of the word 'destiny', involves the eventual and necessary subordination of difference.

The task now is to link the subordination of difference to the semantics of Being since the initial question that these deliberations is trying to answer is how to understand the basis of Heidegger's translation of the word 'physis'. All of the problems considered thus far have been preparatory, preparing the way, not for a discussion of the definition, but of what is presupposed in it.

The distinction between 'vapour' and 'historical destiny' should now be understood in terms of unity, identity and difference. 'Vapour' as the continual vanishing, as the refusal of teleology, gives rise to a semantics not of an original meaning inscribed within the temporality of stasis but of dissemination inscribed within the temporality of becoming. 'Historical destiny' on the other hand depends upon the effacing of difference coupled to the dominance of unity and identity. Both are necessary in order that destiny be fulfilled. Without dwelling further on the distinction between them it is evident that it involves a moral if not political dimension. To see the word 'Being' as a 'mere word' is not simply a mistake about language, it is rather to fail to comprehend the destiny of the west and of a nation's place within it. 'Vapour' vanishes betraying the way of the west. The irony is that vapour appears in a Heraclitean fragment in which not only does it play a positive and pivotal role, but also it opens up the possibility of investigating the conception of interpretation advanced by the fragments. The fragment in question is Kahn CXIII:[17]

The soul (*psychen*) is an exhalation (*or vapour*) (*anathymiasis*) that perceives, it is different from the body and continually flowing (*kai asoma-totaton te kai reon aei*).

This particular claim is in fact made in two fragments, Kahn

CXIIIA and CXIIIB. I want to focus on the latter, for Aristotle has included some additional material. The full quotation from the *De Anima* (1.2, 405a 25) is:

Many thinkers, above all those who consider the cognitive powers of the soul identified it with their first principles (*tas archas*). And Heraclitus too says that the *arché* being (the same as) the soul (*ten archen einai* . . . *psychen*) since he identified with exhalation (or vapour) (*anathymiasin*) from which he produces all the rest. And it is both incorporeal and always flowing (*kai asomatotaton te kai reon aei*).

There is a minor philological problem associated with Aristotle's description, namely that the term 'arche' comes from Aristotle and not from Heraclitus. Consequently Heraclitus would not have said that the soul was an 'arché' and nor would he have identified 'arché' with 'anathymiasin'. However, what is important is that the concept designated by Aristotle with the word 'arché' is not absent from Heraclitus.

For Aristotle what distinguishes an 'arché' from similar terms, for example 'aitia', is a lack of causal necessity. It is precisely this lack that is identified in the definition of 'arché' offered in the *Poetics*:

An arché is that which does not of itself follow anything by causal necessity (*anagkes*) but after which something is or comes to be. (1450b, pp. 28–9)

An 'arché' as opposed to an 'aitia' is defined outside of teleological progression. Furthermore, even though an 'arché' is in some sense a first principle it is not in any obvious sense an origin. It is precisely this point that is being made in the identification of the soul and what could be called the concept of 'arché'. What must be determined is what is at play in and what is the nature of the identification of 'psyche' and the concept of 'arché'. The suggestion in the Heraclitean fragment is not that they are identical in so far as they are one and the same; it is rather that through their exhalation all other things are produced; both are 'incorporeal' (*asomatotaton*) and both are always flowing (*reon aei*). That they are both 'incorporeal' is the least problematic element and is clearly true by definition. It is the other two elements that are difficult and need to be explained.

What is common to both 'psyche' and the concept of 'arché' is 'anathymiasis'. How therefore is Heraclitean vapour to be understood? Kahn quite rightly suggests that, 'the anathymiasis referred to by Aristotle is clearly cosmic or elemental'. It is the reference to the cosmological that must be pursued. However, prior to doing this what must be noted is the link established in the fragment between ontological, cosmological and temporal concerns. The ontological and the temporal are in fact co-joined in the description of the soul as 'reon aei'. Understanding this fragment, indeed understanding Heraclitus in general depends upon developing an understanding of the Heraclitean 'aei'.

It is fortunate that Heraclitus joins the discussion of time and an implicit critique, or at least distancing from teleology, to a description of the cosmos in fragment, Kahn XXXVII.

The cosmos the same for all, neither God nor man has made, but it ever was and is and will be (*all'en aei kai estin kai estai*): fire everliving (*aei-zoon*) kindled in measures and in measures going out.

The cosmos is not a creation. It is not the result of action. The cosmos is not a 'poiéma'. The claim is made while dismissing the two possible creators, namely 'theos' and 'anthropos'. What must be understood is that there is a temporality proper to the 'poiéma'. It is of course the temporality of creation and destruction in which the created product defines the before and after and thereby has what may be called an existence of de-limited duration. It is clear that Heraclitus is aware of the importance of teleology and the link between it and temporality. The 'poiéma' has a cause that accounts for its coming to be and it has a duration in which it is what it is. The description of the temporality of the cosmos is radically different from the temporality of the 'poiéma'.

The Greek verb 'to be' has three tenses, the imperfect, the present and the future. The fascinating thing about the description of the 'cosmos' is that Heraclitus uses all three tenses to describe its temporal mode of being. The immediate consequence of this description is that the temporality of the 'cosmos' is not only incommensurable with the temporality of the 'poiéma' but also placed beyond teleologically based concerns. To say of the 'cosmos' that it 'ever was and is and will be' is to render impossible the attribution to it of an historical destiny. The mode of being of the 'cosmos' is pure becoming in which man and Gods may act but which itself has neither a telos nor a destiny.

However, the fragment suggests more than this for the second half meets the obvious objection raised by Plato to the doctrine of becoming. Namely that if everything changes, then what existed at one moment could not be said to exist at the next and consequently there would be nothing at all. Plato's point has a particular formulation that indicates his misconstrual – ironic or otherwise – of the Heraclitean position. In the *Cratylus* he makes the characteristic move:

If the form of knowledge (*to eidos . . . tes gnoses*) changes at the moment of change there would be no knowledge, and if it is always changing, there will be no knowledge. (440b)

Without entering into the debate as to whether 'to eidos' means form or essence Plato's position is still clear. The identity of knowledge depends upon the presence of the 'eidos' in each instance of knowledge. The consequence being that while acts of cognition begin and end what must endure beyond the instant is the 'eidos' since it provides and guarantees the identity of the act of cognition. To argue therefore that everything is in flux, in Plato's sense, would be to deny the endurance of 'eidos', and consequently because the particular is dependent for its identity on the presence of the 'eidos' then knowledge would indeed be impossible. Plato's position is dependent upon an interrelated temporal distinction between the actual and the eternal. The 'eidos' of knowledge must be eternal while a particular knowledge claim comes into existence and passes away. It is important to note that these two temporal realms are interdependent. It is not only that they are absent from Heraclitus's description of the 'cosmos', but also the case that the identity of particulars for Heraclitus is not dependent upon the presence of an 'eidos'. Plato's point would still have some force if the temporality of becoming denied or rendered impossible existence of a finite duration. However, existence coming to presence and passing away is precisely what is alluded to in the description of 'fire' as 'kindled in measure and in measures going out'.

An ontology of de-limited existence is signalled in these words and yet for Heraclitus it neither falsifies nor negates the other description of fire as 'ever-living' (*aei-zoon*). It is in terms of the distinction between Plato and Heraclitus in regards to temporality that the Heraclitean 'aei' can be explained.

In the *Cratylus* after the purported critique of Heraclitus Plato describes the essential being of beauty, the good, and so on, as '*aei estin oion estin*' (439d). In other words it must always be the same as itself. The Platonic *aei* takes place therefore within the interrelated, and of necessity interrelated, temporal structure of the eternal and the actual. The *aei* must always be removed from the domain of the actual. Within Platonism these two realms while functionally interrelated in so far as the eternal functions to guarantee the identity of particulars, must themselves be incommensurable. Their intermingling would involve their mutual negation. The Platonic 'aei' signals therefore the temporality of the eternal coupled to an ontology of stasis.

It is not just chronology that distances the Heraclitean 'aei' from the Platonic. It is also the presence of a radically different conception of temporality and hence of ontology. It should always be remembered that within Greek philosophy – and perhaps within philosophy in general – temporality and ontology are interarticulated. The Heraclitean 'aei' rather than marking the existence of a transcendental realm signals the existence of the temporal realm which is neither transcendental nor empirical. Understood both ontologically and temporally this third domain (or realm) I would like to call the primordial. It indicates a conception of presence which while not at hand and hence not empirical is equally not transcendental in the sense that the transcendental inevitably functions as that in which the identity of the empirical is grounded. It is furthermore a presence that is neither reducible to nor exhausted by its contextualization.

The primordial opens up a way of thinking philosophy that involves a departure from Platonic-based thinking. A mode of thought which is characterized, first by the interrelated distinction between the transcendental and the actual and second by a commitment to the position that the existence of determinant being(s) entails the existence of indeterminant being. In the case of Heraclitus the primordial forms an integral part of the conception of interpretation suggested by the fragments. Before discussing Heraclitean interpretation the link between Heraclitus's vapour and the description of the soul as 'always flowing' needs to be clarified. The task of clarifying this link can be only begun.

Leaving aside the perceptive quality of the soul the similarity of soul and the concept of 'arché' is that they are both cosmic forces implicated in an explanation of what there is. However, to attribute to the soul the function of an origin is made impossible by the description of it as 'always flowing'. In light of what has already been noted about the Heraclitean 'aei', it should be clear that the soul is primordially present. It is neither empirical nor transcendental but 'reon aei'. It should not be thought that Heraclitus dismisses the empirical; indeed it is the problems posed by the empirical, by 'manifest things' (*ton phaneros*) that will serve as a point of entry into a discussion of a Heraclitean conception of interpretation and understanding.

In the famous first fragment the incomprehension before the 'logos' is defined in relation to the experience of the empirical. Both in the specific sense of hearing and in the general sense of 'being awake'. It is this general sense that is the most interesting for it shows that despite the full presence of all the senses 'anthropos' remains uncomprehending. Comprehending the 'logos' is not of the same status as the experience of sense-data. The nature of the object demands a different type of understanding. The object of interpretation, that is that which must be both comprehended and known, is the relationship existing between what is and the 'logos' such that it is possible to know and understand what is meant by the claim *ginomenon gar panton kata ton logon* (all happens comes to pass) in accordance with the 'logos'. Without wanting at this stage to define or elucidate what is intended by 'logos' it is clear that the object of interpretation is not the 'logos' itself nor is it the empirical but the relation between them. However, at the moment what must be pursued is deception; the state of uncomprehending.

In this regard fragment Kahn XXII is of great interest for it makes a general claim about deception and then goes on to give a specific example of the general claim. The general claim is that Men are deceived in the cognition (*ten gnosin*) of the obvious/or manifest (*ton phaneron*). The specific example is:

like Homer who was the wisest of all the Greeks. For he was deceived by boys killing lice who said, what we see and catch we leave behind; what we neither see nor catch we carry away.

This fragment has been the object of detailed and careful consideration. Perhaps the most interesting interpretation is offered by Bollack and Wismann, who argue that understanding the riddle depends upon understanding an etymological word play. The word for lice 'phtheir' is contained in the word 'phtherio' meaning to kill or destroy. Homer fails to grasp this play. The riddle as Kahn has pointed out in his commentary is couched in the form of a paradox. However, the important point that is evident in both Kahn and Bollack and Wismann's interpretation is that a literal understanding of the fragment is impossible. What rules out an obvious or literal interpretation is the nature of the object itself. If therefore the obvious is understood as what is manifest, that is the empirical, then the claim is that the empirical cannot be understood as an end-in-itself. The additional point is of course that the senses which are the organs that understand the empirical or obvious as an end-in-itself are on their own inadequate for understanding the nature of things. The limit of the senses is advanced in Kahn XVI:

Eyes and ears are poor witnesses for men with barbarian souls.

It is clear that 'eyes and ears' stand for the senses and therefore it is the senses that are poor witnesses. Before inquiring why it is perhaps best to ask of what are they poor witnesses. Presumably the answer cannot be of empirical entities for 'eyes and ears' are precisely the right organs to perceive and know the empirical. The object of the senses is the empirical *tout court*. In order to understand the nature of the object the rest of the fragment must be brought into play.

The senses as 'poor witnesses' for what there is, is limited to people with 'barbarian souls'. This is not helpful for the expression 'barbarian souls' is a direct translation of *'barbarous pyschai'*, which, as is well known, is an idiomatic expression for a person (a soul) who does not speak Greek. However, recognizing the expression as idiomatic does not display all that the expression involves. The fragment is far more complex, for here speaking Greek is itself a metaphor for understanding the nature of things. A soul that is not barbarian, whether it is Greek or not, is one that knows what is involved in things (manifest things) coming to pass in accordance with the 'logos'. Consequently the senses are deceived if on the one hand the relationship between things and 'logos' is neither known nor understood, and on the other if there is no awareness that understanding the nature of things involved recognizing that presence is not reducible to empirical presence but that empirical presence also involves the primordially present, for example 'fire', 'psyche', 'logos'.

In developing an interpretation of the fragment it was essential that it was not taken literally, but rather it involved recognizing the existence of a complex structure involving, at the minimum, literal usage, idiomatic usage and metaphor. It is for this reason that it is possible to draw an analogy between interpreting the fragments and the problems involved in understanding the empirical. Neither a particular fragment nor the empirical can be understood literally, that is as an end-in-itself, rather both demand the recognition that understanding is never immediate but is the result of the process of interpretation. Crude empiricism on the level of understanding 'manifest things' has its analogue in regards to the interpretation of the fragments. It is this latter point that must be developed and there are two fragments that are central to this task, Kahn X and Kahn XXXIII.

It is in fragment Kahn X that we confront 'physis' as a general term. The fragment states:

physis kruptesthai philei (the nature of things is accustomed to hiding itself)

The immediate problem is how to understand 'physis'. A way towards it is suggested in fragment 1, for here it is claimed that of the 'all' (panton) that comes to pass in accordance with the 'logos' each thing has a 'physis'. The consequence is that the term has at least two meanings or uses. One in relation to specific things and the other as a general 'covering' term for a totality. The totality must however be understood in terms of the Heraclitean 'aei', namely as a dynamic, primordially present totality. It is both the totality and the 'physis' particular to each thing that are neither at hand, nor empirical, nor manifest. Both are therefore concealed and hence both are accustomed to concealing themselves. However, what does 'kruptesthai' – to conceal, to hide – mean in this instance?

The imperative here is not to take 'kruptesthai' literally but rather to see it as a term demanding interpretation. There is no mystery attached to it but rather it suggests that the reality of things is not empirical and therefore cannot be interpreted as such. 'Physis' is not hidden in the sense that it cannot be found but rather part of the sense of its being hidden is that it is to be elicited by interpretation. This further reinforces the analogy drawn between literal interpretation and the work of the senses. The senses take as their object sense-data, and the Heraclitean position is that an understanding based simply on the relationship between the senses and sense-data will not yield an understanding of that which is primordially present, for example 'physis'. In the same way to interpret the fragments literally will fail to confront the meanings inherent in the fragments themselves.

Fragment Kahn XXXIII presents another important development of the presentation of the conception of interpretation at play in the fragments:

The God whose oracle is in Delphi neither states (*legei*) nor conceals (*kruptei*) but signifies (*semainei*).

The theme of the fragment should now be familiar. That which is said by the God is neither literally true nor is the meaning hidden forever but rather it must be interpreted. Kahn makes the following important point about the meaning of the term 'semainei':

[it] means uttering one thing in turn signifies another – what Greeks call *hyponoia*, a 'hint' or allegory. The sign may be of different types: image, ambiguous wording, or the like. The Delphic mode of utterance presents a plurality or complexity of meaning, so that reflection is required, an unusual insight, if the proper interpretation is to be discovered.[18]

The important question is of course whether or not his description is true merely of the 'Delphic mode of utterance' or if it can be generalized to cover all objects of interpretation. The major reason for thinking that it can be is that the threefold semantic distinction at play in the fragment, and in which signifying emerges as a third possibility, not only is compatible with the structure of interpretation that has emerged thus far, but also is, I shall argue, a semantic possibility that is compatible with, if not engendered by, the idea of primordiality.

Our first concern must be the threefold semantic distinction.

The three elements are, stating/declaring, hiding, signifying. Each element is of course linked to a specific structure of temporality. 'Legei' (stating/declaring) is literal meaning. An utterance that does not seem to need interpretation. Its meaning is instantaneous and present. Though it is an obvious trap it is essential to note the distinction between the 'logos' of fragment 1 and 'legei'. 'Logos' involves a primordial presence and thus of necessity a temporality that is distinguished from one incorporating the instant, that is the temporality of de-limited existence. The literal, therefore, like the empirical when taken simply on its own and when viewed as an end-in-itself, has an ontology of de-limited existence and the temporality proper to that existence.

What Heraclitus intends by 'kruptei' in the fragment is less clear. However, if the hidden or concealed is taken in its strongest sense then it denotes the existence of that which is never present as itself. A modern analogy may be the God of Descartes' *Meditations* who is by definition unknowable as himself. The impossibility of the presence of the hidden when taken as a semantic term would mean that the Delphic utterance could never be understood. The meaning would never be manifest. It is uncertain what type of temporal scheme would be proper to such a semantics. However, it is tempting to describe it in terms of the temporality proper to the transcendental in so far as the transcendental can never be manifest.

Signifying (*semainei*) is of course the most important semantic term for our concern. It has already been noted that if the manifest or empirical is viewed as an end-in-itself then its nature (physis) remains uncomprehended. This means that the meaning of the manifest is not exhausted by a description of the manifest itself. Present in the manifest is the 'more' which, while not manifest, is fundamental to the meaning of the manifest. Understanding the manifestation of the non-manifest is grasping primordial presence, for example 'fire', 'logos', 'physis', and so on. Finally there is the problem of describing this potential meaning. If the meaning of the utterance is not obvious – is not stated (*oute legei*) – then it is present 'in' the utterance but not manifest. It is the unstated in the stated. It is a meaning therefore that is not reducible to either the literal meaning of the utterance or even to the symbolism deployed in it. It is a continually restatable and hence inexhaustible meaning that is primordially present in the utterance. Both the nature of the meaning itself and of its presence entail that there can be no 'ursprungliche Gehalt'. Primordial presence is ontologically similar to the Heraclitean vapour. The important point to realize is of course that the description of the primordial as the 'unstated in the stated' does not mean as it would within Platonism that the unstated determines the meaning of the stated. But rather that part of the meaning of the stated involves the recognition of the presence of the unstated. This intermingling is, as has been mentioned before, alluded to by Heraclitus in his discussion of 'fire' in fragment Kahn XXXVII.

There is one final subject or term that needs to be discussed in order to elucidate further the idea of the primordial. The term is 'harmonia'. Once again my discussion can be only cursory. The importance of this term is that it provides ways of understanding the concept of difference at play in the fragments. It has already been seen in our discussion of 'physis' that if one were to speak of a Heraclitean conception of unity then it would have to be understood in terms of the Heraclitean 'aei', that is 'reon aei': the unity of pure becoming. How then within this conception of unity is difference to be understood? This question is extremely difficult to answer for any answer depends upon the recognition that the distinction between determinant and indeterminant being is absent from the fragments. Consequently differences cannot be explained in terms of an identity either sanctioning, generating or accounting for difference. And yet it is precisely 'harmonia' understood as primordially present that provides an account of difference. The most interesting fragment for our concerns is Kahn LXXXIA:

Homer was wrong when he said 'would that conflict (eris) might vanish from among the Gods and men'. For there would be no attunement (*armonoian*) without high and low notes nor any animals without male and female, both of which are opposites.

On the surface Heraclitus' rebuke of Homer may seem very odd for would it not be a good thing if conflict were abolished? The rebuke is of course based on the consequences, rather than the simple absence, of conflict (or discord). For Homer such an absence would mean that everything accorded. However, Homeric accord would entail the subordination of difference. For Heraclitus it is the belonging-together of difference – of the discordant – which results in accord; in 'harmonia'. Conflict (*eris*) is the belonging-together in 'harmonia' of the discordant. 'Harmonia' therefore is the belonging-together of the different in which difference is not effaced. 'Harmonia' is not a specific identity. It is not part of a teleology and finally it has no destiny. There is, however, a recognition in the fragments that identity and destiny can be attributed to a belonging-together, to do so would mean that 'harmonia' was no longer primordially present but would have to be manifest. This is exactly the point that is made in fragment Kahn LXXX:

armonie aphanes phaneres kpeitton (Hidden harmony is better than obvious harmony.)

The obvious harmony – the manifest belonging-together – involves a subordination to that external element that provides unity. The 'hidden harmony' on the other hand is the primordially present belonging-together in which the human continually confronts itself, and which it can be argued provides the locus of the ethical.

Having made these tentative steps towards developing an interpretation of Heraclitus perhaps it is now possible to move back through the Heraclitean vapour towards Heidegger's vapour. The difficulty is of course that 'vapour' for Heidegger would be the meaning of the word 'Being' were it thought to be a 'mere word'. For Heraclitus, however, it would be virtually impossible for a word ever to be simply a 'mere word'; that is for it to be restricted to the 'legei' of fragment Kahn XXXIII. It is precisely in these terms that there emerges the split in their philosophical concerns.

It has already been argued that there are three consequences to Heidegger's claim that the interrelationship between language, being and destiny coupled to the position that the word 'being' has an original meaning (or value) are inherent in a semantics of being. They are first that there is an obvious need to retrieve a lost manifest meaning. Second that teleology forms a fundamental part of such a semantics. Finally the existence of an identity (or unity) that necessitates, in order that the identity be both maintained and its destiny realized, the subordination of difference and plurality. Heidegger's semantics of being stands in sharp contradistinction to both the semantics and theory of interpretation and understanding suggested by the fragments.

It is now possible to return to Heidegger's initial translation or explication of 'physis'. I said that I wanted to discuss another description that Heidegger provides, however, before doing that I want to repeat the initial one:

Physis is being itself (*Die Physis ist das Sein selbts*) by virtue of which entities (*das Seinde*) become and remain observable.[19]

The second definition is:

Physis originally encompassed heaven as well as earth, the stone as well as the plant, the animal as well as man and it encompassed human history as a work of men and Gods; and ultimately and first of all it meant the Gods themselves as subordinated to destiny (*Geschick*). Physis means the power that emerges and the enduring realm under its sway . . . . Physis is the process of arising from the hidden, whereby the hidden is first made to stand.[20]

There are clearly a number of elements in Heidegger's formulation that are in agreement with some of the conclusions reached in our discussion of the fragments. However, the moments of disagreement are the points at which the concerns of the fragments can be recuperated by Heidegger only if the specific ontological and temporal positions advanced by them are themselves denied. Perhaps the two most obvious examples of this are, first the claim that 'Physis is Being itself' and second the description of the Gods as subordinate to 'destiny'.

To say that 'physis' is Being is not incorrect in the sense that 'physis' is something else, it is rather that there is no space within the Heraclitean cosmology for Being. In fact the distinction between 'Sein' and 'seindes' and especially the type of argument used to establish this distinction in the opening pages of *Being and Time* are, as is implicit in what I have tried to argue, impossible with Heraclitean terms. 'Physis', 'cosmos', 'harmonia', 'Fire', and so on, are all to be explained in terms of the Heraclitean 'aei'. Each involves what has been called primordial presence. Physis is not Being itself because there is no independent realm of naming that sanctions the naming of 'physis' as being.

Finally it has already been argued that man and God act within the 'cosmos'. However, there is nothing outside these actions except of course the primordially present 'Cosmos' within which they take place, consequently there is no position that 'destiny' can occupy, let alone be that to which the Gods are subordinate. On a large level to incorporate history and destiny within the concerns of Heraclitus is to intrude a structure of temporality and the onto-logical dimension compatible with it, that is not simply absent from the fragments in any positive sense, it is precisely a structure recognized by Heraclitus and from which he attempts to establish a critical distance.

I do not wish to try and conclude for I have simply tried to offer some introductory thoughts about Heraclitus and Heidegger,[21] none the less I would add that the return to Heraclitus is not fuelled by nostalgia but rather is concerned with a philosophical thinking in which difference is never subordinate or subordinated to identity. This perhaps marks the first and last break between Heidegger and Heraclitus.

Notes

1 Martin Heidegger, *An Introduction to Metaphysics*, trans. Ralph Manheim, New Haven, Conn., Yale University Press, 1959. The German edition is M. Heidegger, *Einfuhrung in die Metaphysik*, Gesamtausgabe Band 40, Frankfurt am Main, Vittoroi Klostermann, 1983. I have used Manheim's translation with occasional modifi-cations. All references are to the English edition, except in special circumstances.

2 Heidegger, ibid., p. 14.

3 Heidegger, *Einfuhrung in die Metaphysik*, p. 15.

4 This interpretation is reinforced by the following claim about language made by Heidegger in his study of Nietzsche, (M. Heidegger, *Nietz-sche*, vol. IV, Nihilism, trans. Frank A. Capuzzi, San Francisco, Calif., Harper & Row, 1982). The German text is M. Heidegger, *Nietzsche, Zwester Band*, Pfullingen, Neske, 1961. 'Language demands not only that we correctly comprehend mere words (der Blosses Wortes) as lexical artifacts but that we heed the matter expressed in and with the word'.

5 For an important discussion of this point see J. Derrida, 'Letter to a Japanese friend', trans. A. Benjamin and D. Wood, in R. Bernasconi and D. Wood (eds) *Derrida and Difference*, Warwick, Parousia Press, 1985.

6 Heidegger, *An Introduction to Metaphysics*, p. 14.

7 Heidegger, ibid., p. 42.

8 Heidegger, ibid., p. 51.

9 Heidegger, ibid., p. 171.
10 This occurs especially in *On Time and Being*, trans. Joan Strambough, New York, Harper & Row, 1972.
11 Heidegger, *An Introduction to Metaphysics*, p. 14.
12 Heidegger, ibid., p. 15.
13 I have used McDowell's translation of the *Theaetetus* which I have occasionally modified. *Plato, Theaetetus*, trans. with notes by J. McDowell, Oxford, Clarendon Plato Series, 1983. In the case of other texts by Plato and Aristotle, I have used a combination of the Loeb Editions, the Oxford Classical Texts, and the standard Oxford translations.
14 Dodds draws this distinction in his edition of *Georgias*, Oxford, Oxford University Press, 1979, p. 193. I have made far more use of it than perhaps Dodds ever intended.
15 This passage needs to be read in conjunction with Metaphysics, Zeta 1028a 10–15.
16 The point must be made that I am not claiming that this is Aristotle's own position, but rather one that could be arrived at via a specific reading of Aristotle and hence via a specific use of Aristotelian concepts.
17 I have used Charles Kahn's edition of the fragments, *The Art and Thought of Heraclitus*, Cambridge, Cambridge University Press, 1981.
18 Kahn, ibid., p. 208.
19 Heidegger, ibid., p. 14.
20 Heidegger, ibid., pp. 14–15.
21 My reluctance to offer a more sweeping conclusion is based on the fact that this chapter became the basis of a recently completed book-length study of Heraclitus, (*Time, Being and Interpretation: A Reading of Heraclitus*, forthcoming). Part of the object of the book was to develop the critique of Heidegger that I began in this chapter, as well as developing a more integrated study of the fragments.

· 6 ·

Banter and banquets for heroic death

PIETRO PUCCI

Pulchrumque mori succurrit in armis (Verg. *Aen* 2. 317)

Among the many passages in the *Iliad* that represent a hero's decision and a motivation in favour of a glorious course of action, those which state the hero's reasons for accepting his death are memorable and exemplary. They are also psychologically difficult and morally enigmatic. First, all subjective motivation in Homer raises the thorny questions of the subject, of its will, and of its autonomy from the theological forces – with which the text is identified – under whose laws the hero operates. But in the specific case of an heroic *prohairesis*, when the king decides to take his stand and to stake his life, his motivations reflect more than ever the text's *raison d'être*, and therefore its theological and edifying purposes. In those passages the Iliadic metaphysics rises to its most sublime, as it upholds the glamorous portrait of the king, his inflexible will to obtain imperishable glory (*aphthiton kleos*), and it develops the great consolatory themes that make death acceptable and even freely chosen.[1] The monumental funeral oration that the *Iliad* utters through its doomed heroes contains many of these edifying passages.[2] I choose Sarpedon's speech in *Il* 12. 310–28 in which he impresses on himself the necessity of staking his life. It is exemplary in many ways: the king has no private reasons to fight in Troy and therefore he grounds his decision on general arguments, that evoke his exalted position, his royal portrait and his human mortal destiny.[3] The text therefore exposes here in the most vivid fashion its large concerns and its most far-reaching consolatory themes: it erects what for us is the first edifying oration that affected generations of readers and still has a tremendous power. For these very reasons, however, the passage also unveils the paradoxical aspects of the Iliadic metaphysics, and it displays what it is my goal here to demonstrate, the desultory discontinuities of the text, the supplementarity of the Iliadic writing, the occasional opacities in the reading that it offers of itself.

310 Glaukos, why in fact are we honoured (*tetimemestha*) so greatly
311 by a (distinctive) seat (*edre*) and meat and full cups,
312 in Lycia, and all people look at us as at gods?
313 And why are we granted a domain (temenos) by the bank of Xanthos,
314 a fair domain with orchard and wheat bearing arable land?
315 Therefore now we must stand among the foremost
316 and face the fiery battle
317 so that some of the well-corseleted Lycians may say:
318 'Truly our kings are not without glory (*ou . . .akleees*), as they rule over Lycia
319 and eat fat sheep and choice wine sweet like honey,
320 but they have also excellent might,
321 since they fight in the foremost ranks of the Lycians'
322 O friend! If we could escape from this war
323 and if we would live forever ageless and immortal,
324 then myself I would not fight in the front rank
325 nor would I send you into the battle that gives glory to men (*machen es kudianeiran*);
326 but now – for all the same countless fates of death stand upon us
327 and it is not possible for a mortal to escape or to avoid them –
328 let us go: either we shall give the boast (*eukhos*) to others or others to us. (*Il.* 12. 310–28)

This passage has always been admired,[4] but as far as I know, never extensively commented,[5] though as my analysis shows, it requires attention and explanations. The first part of Sarpedon's speech (310–21) is unanimously considered today as a statement of *noblesse oblige*, and the second (322–8) as a paradoxical and moving argument of existential order.[6] And yet there is much more and much less in Sarpedon's episode than the sober and coherent line of thought critics describe. Much more: the 'portrait' of the king is huge and has a supernatural glow, a divine and bestial beyondness; his decision to stake his life is sublime since it is almost gratuitous; in fact, he accepts immediate death in order to uphold the truth of his (supernatural) portrait . . . Much less: his royal portrait crumbles in ruin and the image of his frailty takes its place; the truth of his epic portrait is doubtful; the gain of an imperishable glory, uncertain . . .

The superimposition of these features endows the text with the desultory, discontinuous movement which I shall analyse as the trace of Iliadic 'writing'.

The frame: the mane in the royal figure

Sarpedon begins to speak *suddenly* (*autika* 309). Before this moment he is described as a lion in one of the longest and more elaborated lion similes in the *Iliad* (12. 299–308).[7] The suddenness of his words corresponds to the suddenness of his return to humanity. For, as a lion, he was fighting, of course without a word just like Sarpedon, the king; even in the details he was engaged in the same sort of attack that he launches as a hero. For as a lion, a 'valiant heart' (*thymos agenor* 300) incited him to attack a well-built stable (*pykinon domon* 301) just as the king's heart excites him to attack the Achaean wall; as a lion, he was willing to be wounded in the front ranks (*en protoisi* 306), just as he is ready to do now (*meta protoisi*(n) 315, 321, 324); as a lion, he was needing meat, just as he, as a king, consumes abundant meat (*kreion* 300, *kreasin* 311). Though the lion and the king have different sources of provision, they have the same requirement of rich, bloody food for their meals.[8]

Because of this thorough assimilation, the *simile* confuses the identification of the comparing entity and of the compared one, so that it is no longer clear who is compared to whom. The mere ornamental function of the simile should be seriously doubted, and the leonine features of Sarpedon's portrait should be seriously considered.

The king's portrait, however, while showing some fierce traits of the lion, encompasses a larger set of features. He is represented as being human and godlike. The text combines the animal traits with the human and the godlike ones in the concluding lines of the simile (*Il.* 12. 307–10)

So then his heart incited the God-like *(antitheon)* Sarpedon to attack the wall and to break through the parapet. And suddenly he spoke to Glaukos son of Hipplokhos; 'Glaukos, why in fact are we honoured'.

The portrait of the king is now complete. By turning suddenly to Glaukos and by asking: 'Why . . .' its human traits emerge and take prominence. Unlike the lion whose noble heart and need of meat constitute the unique sources of motivation, Sarpedon needs to know 'why . . .' and for eighteen lines he analyses his motivations. For unlike a God, the king is also mortal.

To introduce the lion features among the divine and human traits that the *Iliad* is outlining and ascribing to the *kleos* of Sarpedon is not critically otiose, or erratic. Readers so eager to appreciate the aesthetic values of the *Iliad* should not miss the extravagant complexity of this portrait which exhibits savage brushes, sublime tones, violent and untamed contrasts. Our Sarpedon is not a modern gentleman.

My critical reasons for insisting on this portrait, however, are more specific. Sarpedon ultimately considers it his duty to uphold his *kleos*, his glorious portrait, and to substantiate it in the eyes of his subjects, the Lycians, with an heroic gesture, by which he stakes his life. It will not be otiose therefore to ask which sort of portrait he wishes to live up to, and which (epic) portrait the *Iliad* wants him to uphold and to support. One of the most troubling critical questions the *Iliad* raises for its readers is in fact the consistency of the theological (mythological) premises and underpinnings of its narrative, and when once we ask such a concrete question, we begin to unravel it.

The banter

The ferocious banquet *(dais)* of the lion in which he feasts on meat is a sort of mirror image of the tamer banquets of the kings. Sarpedon mentions them, listing accurately all the features of this gala, the place of honour, the meat, the wine, the respectful attitude of the Lycians (12. 310–12). This list is conventional and traditional, and it occurs, complete or partial when the privileges of the kings are described. Food is a serious matter in Homer,[9] even if it also serves jocular purposes. The jocular purpose occurs in the type of mockery that the kings like to level at each other, when they compare their greed for these privileges (*timē*) with their poltroonery. Typical of this mockery is the insult Agamemnon hurls at Odysseus:

O son of King Peteus, fosterling of Zeus, and you master of evil tricks, greedy of gain,[10] why are you recoiling and standing apart and waiting for the others? It benefits you to stand among the foremost, (*meta proto-isin*) and to face the fiery battle,[11] for you are the first to be heard at my banquet for the Elders. There you love to eat roast meat and drink your cups of honey-sweet wine, as long as you like.

(*Il.* 4. 338–46)

This mockery intimates the kings' awareness that their exalted position (*timē*) and their glorious portrait (*kleos*) create expectations of heroic behaviour and that those expectations are not infrequently frustrated by their cowardice. At the gala of the banquets there are not always gallant kings.

The text therefore plots with its characters to attach suspicion to the truth of kings' *kleos*, and even if it does so only in these scenes of a bantering mood and even if generally it unveils this suspicion only in order to assert, with greater assurance, the truth of the kings' *kleos*, nevertheless, to attach doubt and suspicion to their heroic portrait is a sore business for epic poetry. Since this poetry is the source of the kings' *kleos*, the text exhibits itself and its own fabrications. Accordingly, as we will see more clearly, the text confirms the unstable meaning of *kleos* which names either the truthful, imperishable glory which Achilles gains by his death, or a mere 'rumour', even the 'gossip' of the town.[12]

By raising the intimation that the *kleos* of the king may be exaggerated or contain mere flatteries, the text of the *Iliad* is perverse, for it reverses, amusingly, its normal function which is that of edifying a real, well-deserved renown for the kings, what I call in this paper the 'glorious portrait' of the king.[13] Of course the *Iliad* would not allow a character like Thersites to twice repeat this undoing of the royal *kleos*; and even in the case we are considering, the *Iliad* allows Odysseus to reconfirm his renown with a noble response. Yet, perhaps because it is a question of Odysseus, the *Iliad* speaks tongue in cheek. For, indeed Odysseus has no great reputation as a *promakhos* (a fighter among the front ranks), but a splendid one for his shrewdness (*metis. Od.* 9. 19–20; 13. 287–95, etc).[14] Besides, it is certainly true that an Odyssean trait of Odysseus represents him as indulging in the pleasures of the belly (*gastēr*)[15] and the *Iliad* seems to recall this tendency here and in another passage.[16] Be it as it may, Odysseus' answer for all its apparent nobility, does not entirely refute Agamemnon's reproach.

Atreides, what word has escaped from the barrier of your teeth? How can you say that we are slack in battle? When we Achaeans excite sharp Ares against the horsetaming Trojans, you shall see, if you wish and if you care, the dear father of Telemachos mingling among the front ranks (*promakhoisi*) of the horsetaming Trojans. What you say is empty air. (*Il.* 4. 350–5)

Formally Odysseus' answer is noble and enhances his warrior's reputation. On the surface, at any rate, Agamemnon's reproach seems to have served only as a foil in order to spell out with greater energy the excellence of Odysseus. But in fact, even if Agamemnon now praises Odysseus (358–63), the reproach does not function simply as a foil. There is an interesting rest. I follow Risch in interpreting the line

You will see . . . the dear father of Telemachos mingling among the front ranks.

as a pun.[17] The name 'Telemachos' etymologically means 'fighting from afar' and therefore Odysseus is made to say: 'You will see the father of "fighting from afar" mingling among the front ranks.' Since by epic convention the children often are named from some characteristics, accidents or events in the life of the father,[18] the *Iliad* humorously forces Odysseus to say that though he is known as a man of the rear lines, (that is a man of the bow, or the ambush, and so on) he will be seen fighting as a *promakhos*.[19] When the *Iliad* is humorous it is splendidly so. Here the text takes its pleasure in tantalizingly suspending and keeping undecided the 'Iliadic' *kleos* of Odysseus, and, at the end the text gives it back to him, at least partially, in the form of his heroic determination to fight as *promakhos*. that is to become, against his tradition and *kleos*, an Iliadic hero. Just as Odysseus is made to respond with an heroic decision to the legitimate suspicion that his son's name Telemachos attaches to his *kleos* as *promakhos*, so Sarpedon will feel his duty to prove his force and thus to dispel the suspicion the Lycians attach to his *kleos*. In both cases the text initially presents a contested and dubious portrait; apparently the text uses this initial move as a foil in order to produce unquestionable evidence for the truth of the kings' *kleos*. Yet in the case of Odysseus the text seems unwilling to re-establish his heroic portrait without a humorous touch; in the case of Sarpedon the text unquestionably aims at substantiating the truth of Sarpedon's *kleos*, but it fails to do so fully. Sarpedon's speech is no joke: its sublime pathos makes more emotional for the reader the textual incapacity to demonstrate the truth of the portrait for which he is determined to die.[20]

What the Lycians think of the king's portrait

When Sarpedon, the lion, turns to address Glaukos, like him a king of Lycia, he questions his peer and himself as to why they are honoured as they are. He begins to speak, therefore, as a king, conscious of the prerogatives a king enjoys and aware of the questioning, admiring glances the subjects bestow on their king:

310 Glaukos, why in fact are we honoured (*tetimēmestha*) so greatly
311 by a distinctive seat (*edrē*) and meat and full cups
312 in Lycia and all people look at us as at gods?
313 And why are we granted a domain (*temenos*) by the bank of Xanthos
314 a fair domain with orchard and wheat bearing arable land?
315 Therefore now we must (*khrē*) stand among the front ranks
316 and face the fiery battle
317 so that some of the well-corseleted Lycians may say:
318 Truly our kings are not without glory (*ou . . . akleees*) as they rule over Lycia
319 and eat fat sheep and choice wine, sweet like honey,
320 but they have also excellent might (*is*)
321 since they fight in the front ranks of the Lycians

There is no doubt that the introductory question: 'Why are we honoured . . .' constitutes, so to speak, the framing of Sarpedon's speech as far as line 321, and therefore intimates that the duty (*khrē* 315) Sarpedon feels is somehow attached to his being a king and receiving the *timē* he so effectively evokes (*tetimēmestha* 310). And yet the precise logical connection between the *timē* and his awareness of duty is lacking: the text deviates from *timē* and evokes the glances the Lycians bestow on the king. It is in relation to those glances that Sarpedon conceives his duty to take a stand.

As a consequence, critics vary in their appreciation of the specific connection between the king's *timē* and his duty to stake valiantly his life. Some consider that Sarpedon embraces this duty idealistically as the commitment that alone justifes his royal prerogatives;[21] others, denying that in Homer moral decisions are even autonomous and self-grounded[22] reverse the order of priorities and read the passages as a statement of *noblesse oblige*. Thus for instance Jasper Griffin paraphrases it as follows: 'We are noble and wealthy, therefore we must fight in the front rank.'[23]

The difficulty in this matter is that the question, 'Why are we honoured so greatly . . .', is not answered in Sarpedon's words, by the *direct* suggestion that royal honours entail the duty to fight, but the question is transformed in the evocation of the Lycians' expectations; and the Lycians do not expect the king to behave valiantly on the ground of his *timē*, but on the ground of his *kleos*, that is of his royal portrait:

Therefore, now, we must stand among the front ranks . . . so that (*ophra*) some of the Lycians may say: 'Truly our kings are not without glory . . . but they have also excellent might'[24]

Sarpedon considers it his duty (*khrē* 315) to give his Lycians some evidence, a demonstration of the qualities that are written in his royal portrait. But the syntax and the style of 318–21 deserve more careful analysis, and the disruptive force of *kleos* must also be considered within that frame:

Truly our kings are not without glory (*a-kleees*) . . . but (*alla*) they have also (*kai*) excellent might.

This adversative *alla* and the adverb *kal* add a new idea to the previous one, either with opposition or without opposition.[25] I do not see any way to determine the exact extent of the adversative clause. Sarpedon may only wish that his Lycians witness something besides his *kleos*, its truth for instance, or something different from his *kleos*, something that his *kleos*, his royal portrait, does not say or says falsely.

In both cases Sarpedon's full identity with his royal portrait turns out to be fractured in the eyes of the Lycians, but the measure of their disbelief, or of their mistrust, varies in accordance with the reading we offer of his remarkable passage. For, on the one hand, we could read the Lycians' attitude as sarcastic and as cynical like that we encounter in the mockery by Agamemnon or Achilles. The instability of the meaning of *kleos*, the ironical mention of the banquets during which that *kleos* is fabricated, the adversative clause and the possibly sarcastic litotes ('not without glory' or 'not unglorious'), the concrete, almost physical meaning of *is* (force) would allow us to paraphrase the Lycians' thinking as follows:

Yes, during the rich banquets we prepare for the kings in Lycia, they of course are not without a glorious renown; indeed, they are extravagantly praised by all sort of divine epithets; they are vaingloriously described in incredible adventures,[26] but as we see them now in the front rank, we must say that they have, flatteries aside, also excellent force as well.[27] There is something true in all that old flattery.

Sarpedon would prove, by taking a valiant stand, that, really, the royal portrait is not all boasts, only part of it. Alternatively the Lycians' thinking may be represented less ironically and less sarcastically: 'Our kings do not only enjoy their due honours and their proper reputation, but as we see them now in the front rank, we must say that they also live up to that reputation'.[28]

Therefore Sarpedon feels that he must substantiate or validate the truth of his royal portrait by giving evidence through his action. He feels that fighting as a *promakhos* provides the Lycians with the ultimate test of his might.

Should we say that the former reading of the Lycians' sarcastic disbelief in the royal portrait is inappropriate to Epic poetry? The scenes of bantering are built on this very disbelief and prove that the answer is no. Nor is this interpretation at odds with our passage which begins with the mention of concrete privileges before turning to the ascetic views of 322–8.

It remains also undecidable what Sarpedon thinks of the Lycians' suspicion, whether he would agree with them that his *kleos* is exaggeratedly flattering, or a correct representation of what he is.

Accordingly it remains uncertain whether he means to substantiate some of the reasonable and still heroic features of his flattering portrait, or to live up to his full *kleos*. If he thinks that his portrait, however flattering, is nevertheless a correct representation of himself, he considers it a duty to show that he is as good a king as his portrait says he is. The *Iliad's* premises would encourage us to uphold this interpretation. Sarpedon considers it a duty to prove that he is as good a king as his *kleos* says he is because he is afraid of the criticism or of the mockery that the discrepancy between his portrait and his deeds would allow the Lycians to level at him. He would then respond to a sense of fear and reverence that the Homeric Greek calls *aidōs* and which induces kings to act valiantly on other occasions as well.[29] As a result, Sarpedon would consider it a duty to substantiate *a posteriori* the portrait which the Lycians have of him. He would grant the evidence of truth to his portrait by a gesture that logically and morally should lie at the origin of his *kleos*.[30] Therefore while his response to the Lycians' criticism or suspension of belief can be considered a moral decision, the specific goal of behaving *a posteriori* just as his portrait – which he did not compose – prescribes, is gratuitous. Or, even if we assume that Sarpedon agrees with the moral prescriptions that are contained in that portrait, that goal remains unmotivated, since he produces no argument to uphold those moral prescriptions. Consequently his acceptance of the prescriptive, authoritative force of his portrait is unconditional, gratuitous and it is fully accounted for only by the ideological premises of Epic poetry. Such lack of motivation characterizes some of the greatest Homeric heroes at the moments of their entry in the epic story. A sort of reckless and seigneurial gratuitousness must lie also at the source of Achilles' decision to come to Troy in order to win imperishable glory (*aphthiton kleos*). He, like Sarpedon in the passage I have commented upon, must put his life in jeopardy to serve, so to speak, the creative purposes of Epic poetry. Analogously Hector dies with poignant elegance looking at his immortal *kleos*.

Sarpedon has argued until now that he must live up to his splendid *kleos*. The question that Sarpedon leaves open to the reader is why does he – like the other great heroes – treasure this glory so much? The last words of Sarpedon try to give us the answer to this question:

322 'O friend! If we could escape from this war[31]
323 and if we could live for ever ageless and immortal
324 then myself I would not fight in the front rank
325 nor would I send you into the battle that gives glory to men (*makhēn es kudianeiran*)
326 but now – for all the same countless fates of death stand upon us
327 and it is not possible for a mortal to escape or to avoid them –
328 let us go: either we shall give the boast (*eukhos*) to others or others to us.' (*Il.* 12.322–8)

The passage contains one of the strongest statements in Homer. The huge portrait of the king with its epic paraphernalia and rhetorical embellishments, shrinks to the frail image of a mortal man, even more, to the portrait of a man who knows that he is besieged at each moment by the menace of death. Homer spells out the recognition that the awareness of death is the quintessence of man, and by defining man uniquely in all of nature, among beasts and gods, by this awareness, he founds, for us, a notion that will reappear insistently in the history of western metaphysics.[32]

The consoling aspects of this conception reside in the implication that what is 'proper' and 'essential' to man is stronger than or as strong as the insuperable force of death. For man is somehow made able to take up death and to administer, through his awareness, the economy that makes death simultaneously a menace and a resource, other and self.

Accordingly Sarpedon too lets himself be affected by this economy, when he describes the countless fates of death constantly standing over him as an inevitable menace, and yet also as a resource for an heroic decision that somehow anticipates and therefore masters those countless fates. One should not miss, in this powerful text, the astuteness of its formulation: Sarpedon impresses upon himself the inevitable presence of countless *Keres* 'destinies', 'fates of death', and with enormous energy he opposes to them the vitality of the imperative, 'let us go' (*iomen*), and the force of his will to take a gamble, a hopeful chance.

As a master and accomplice of his own death, Sarpedon would also free himself from the haphazardness, anonymity, facelessness of death. And here there is probably another strong consoling element implicit in his words. His willingness to go to face a hero and gamble his life acquires the specific implication of protesting against the necessity of death and its anonymity.[33] He capitalizes on the distinction of his gesture, on the public splendour of his attitude. For all these reasons his gesture names his desire to battle death.[34] And of course he is sure of outwitting death as he knows that the splendour of his gesture will survive. Accordingly the *eukhos* he speaks of in line 328 must also name – though improperly as we shall see – the 'glory' and the 'fame' that the epic song celebrates. If Sarpedon should die he would substantiate, or found, the truth of his royal portrait (*kleos*).

These views are powerful and deeply affect the reader. The Epic text produces motivations for gallantly accepting death that seem capable of reducing the power of death, and accordingly have the force of the greatest power of all. By gaining some mastery over death the hero shows how his acceptance of death also makes fuller sense of his life, how in fact, through glory he – on a different level – immortalizes himself.[35] And yet this comforting vision of man's mortality seems simultaneously to domesticate the issues which it faces with such force. First of all this comforting vision presupposes that the consciousness of death and its controlling economy parallel the economy of real death. But this is not the case. Consciousness of death implies life, but death extinguishes all consciousness.[36] Consciousness of death involves a discourse that in Sarpedon's experience survives, as epic song, the death of the kings, and develops – as indeed it does also in the case of Achilles for instance *Il.* 21.106–13 – the themes of the equality of all men before death, of the shortness of life, of the inevitability of death.

Furthermore to appropriate death as what is proper, close, essential to man looks like an unstable, paradoxical appropriation since death is other than he is.[37] Indeed, in our passage, it is paradoxical that Sarpedon's awareness that death menaces him at each moment should persuade him to actually stake his life, now, immediately (cf. *nun.* 315 and 326).

In fact, it is undecidable whether Sarpedon suspends his heroic decision totally on his existential awareness that death is inevitable or also on the edifying advantage that *kudos* and *eukhos* finally would bring to him. The answer to this question remains uncertain, for the text could be construed so as to satisfy both meanings. To begin with, we do not know exactly what *kudos* and *eukhos* meant for the epic poets; furthermore the last line (328): 'let us go: either we shall give *eukhos* to others or others to us' presents an odd gamble which could end with no *eukhos* for Sarpedon. Finally, the whole train of thought, as we shall see, is unclear.

Let us start from *eukhos*. I incline with Emile Benveniste to attribute to this word the meaning of 'voeu de victoire' and then 'victoire'[38] though it is possible to reach the same result by postulating 'scream or boast of triumph' and then 'triumph', 'victory'. This meaning appears in the only other example of the formula (*Il.* 12.328: *Il.* 13.327), where *eukhos* does not imply death of one hero, or his glory, but the victory of a wing of the army.[39] As concerns *kudos* in Sarpedon's *machen eis kudianeiran* of line 325, not even here would there be specific mention of glory.[40] On the ground of these elements we could sustain the pure existential inflection of the passage: defeat (death) in battle is only one of the countless fates that threaten men, and the hero gambles whether god will give power (*kudos*) and victory (*eukhos*) to him or to his adversary.[41]

There are passages, however, in which *eukhos* seems to mean the boast and glory of victory (see, for instance, *Il.* 7.203, and especially 7.81–91) and we cannot confidently exclude this sense from our passage.[42] Accordingly the gamble that Sarpedon raises in line 328 could still look at death in the battlefield as a privileged death, one that would be marked off from the countless fates of death. The *eukhos* in the battlefield might be prolonged in the *kleos* that immortalizes the hero.[43]

The decision between a pure existential interpretation and an edifying reading of Sarpedon's willingness to embrace death remains difficult to take. It is easier, on the contrary, to perceive and to appreciate the vocal connotation of *eukhos*. For this speech act certainly designates a 'marked utterance', and therefore its meaning is contained within the semantic field of *kleos*, *logos*, *mythos*.[44] It is with a view to this special utterance – whether or not connected with *kleos* – that Sarpedon raises his gamble with death, or his dalliance with epic glory: accordingly his speech – the one we are commenting upon – anticipates and rehearses that cry of boast (*eukhos*) he hopes to scream in the battlefield. Then the awareness that death is close and proper to man emerges as a voice and an utterance which are even closer than that consciousness, because they are prior to it. They affect the character while being produced by the character himself.[45]

Iliadic writing

With the last turn of argument I have begun a deconstructive reading that exposes the comforting and/or edifying force of the voice (*eukhos, kleos*) in Sarpedon's speech and accordingly in the Iliadic 'writing' in general.[46] This reading continues in the analysis of textual reflexivity. For it is clear that when Sarpedon speaks of his duty to perform the originary act that logically and morally starts the edification of his *kleos*, or when he urges himself to rush into the battle in order to obtain *eukhos*, he reflects the textual premises of the *Iliad*, its *raison d'être*, and even the effects that the poem, as an oral one, creates. For there is no reason to doubt that the poem knows the power of the voice, and that it develops in its 'writing' the situations and the structures in which the power of the voice obtains more powerful effects: dialogue, prayers, self-exhortations, invocations and so on.[47]

Now to start from the critical view that merely shows the reflexive consciousness a work has of itself is not yet a deconstructive move; the business of deconstruction is to unravel the process of signification, to expose the metaphysical premises that found all texts, the complicity of the readers with those premises, and to look, if possible, beyond them. Yet the critical concern of showing the reflexive consciousness of a text is a necessary premise of deconstructive discourse. It problematizes and suspends the reader's confidence – inspired by the text – that a responsible author is simply narrating a story about a referent. The text of course narrates a story, but it simultaneously reflects its textuality, reads itself as a text among other texts, glances at its compositional conventions, at the protocols, at the constitution of its self-making, at its readers' reading.[48]

In the text I have commented upon there can be no doubts that Sarpedon's glance at the Lycians' appreciation of his *kleos* is almost a glance at the Lycians' reading of the Epic text that is productive of his *kleos*. The *Iliad* gives us empirical evidence – if it were needed – that Sarpedon's *kleos* literally precedes him as a sort of *proklut'epea*.[49] He speaks of himself as if he were borrowing some of the traits of his portrait,[50] and finally he accepts it, somehow *a posteriori*, fulfilling an image of himself that, ideally, wants him dead in order to increase his posthumous glory. Consequently

Sarpedon as a character is a mere function of a structure which precedes him and of which he fulfils the needed role.

Curiously this function does not weaken the representation of his image, but, on the contrary, strengthens it. For the huge super-human power that his royal portrait outlines *lives* only as an image. It is as if the real person's immense force of heroic life were drained out and made image. That is why the representation of Sarpedon's power turns out simultaneously to illustrate the power of represen-tation.[51] By this I do not mean that Sarpedon's image is an image: I mean that Sarpedon's portrait represents him *already as* an image and therefore also already as a text, as other than himself and as dead. For what *kleos* tells of him is what can be said even before and after him. Hector's mother for instance, will celebrate Hector's death with words similar to those with which Sarpedon celebrates himself borrowing the terms from his portrait.[52] The portrait of the king, therefore, lives only as a dead and deathless image, even while the king is alive. And one portrait resembles the other.

Later in his speech when Sarpedon simply considers his human destiny, rather than his royal image (322–8), he confronts death as any other mortal would. Here the force lies in his capacity to impress on himself the will to confront and somehow master the power of death.

Here the text taps a different metaphysical resource, as I have shown, a stronger and more universal one. Yet, by embracing death as he does, he also fulfils the implicit programme of his portrait, a programme that inscribes his death both in his imperishable glory and in the text of that glory as well.[53]

The structure of supplementarity

To say that the real person, Sarpedon, is already an image, a text, suspends, within an indecidable logic, the question of his truth. Of course we recall here that *kleos*, the image he fulfils by rushing into the battle, is itself troubled by an unstable meaning. We remain closed within the prison of the text, unable to predicate anything about its referent.

Kleos intimates simultaneously and contradictorily the truthful and imperishable renown (*aphthiton kleos*) and the irresponsible, occasional rumour. As such, *kleos* contains in itself a contradiction in which one term is constitutive of the other while displacing it (supplementing the other), and vice versa. Therefore truth in *kleos* is constitutive of *kleos'* falsehood. The meaning of *kleos* can never rest, but must constantly oscillate in a movement through which at each moment one meaning delivers – and is deferred by – the other, anticipates the other and destabilizes itself. The oscillating supplementary meaning of *kleos* impinges on the very image the text presents of itself.

Sarpedon's decision to fulfil his *kleos*[54] and to validate it with the evidence of truth, at the price of his life, at once reveals the advantage the text looks after, and intimates the inevitable lack that marks the *Iliadic* writing. Even if Sarpedon fulfils *a posteriori* his (epic) image, still he becomes the guarantee of its *truth*; by performing the 'originary' act that validates his (epic) *kleos*, he demonstrates its truth. Yet, by this same gesture, Sarpedon also shows how badly epic poetry needs to validate itself as truth.

The supplementary structure of *kleos* does not rest and does not leave any rest to the Iliadic writing. Here we touch the critical move whereby the *Iliad* both intimates its truth and unveils its impossibility to give evidence of truth. For of course Sarpedon's statement merely enlarges his already existing *kleos*, which by itself, notwithstanding all its theological underpinning, was already insufficient to prove its own truth. The Lycians suspected it and Sarpedon agrees to add to it the force of truth. But it still remains *kleos*. *Kleos* therefore cannot provide that textual evidence that would stop its endless, restless movement. In fact the more the text plots and conjures up evidences for its own truth, the more it parades not only its need for truth, but also the impossibility to satisfy that need.

The consequences for our interpretation of the *Iliad* resulting from this supplementary force of *kleos* oscillating within the well-built structure of epic self-representation are easy to imagine.

The theological underpinnings, the divine inspiration are as much 'evidence' in favour of the truth of *kleos*, as Sarpedon's will to fulfil it with his own life. They all hide and expose the supplementarity of *kleos*. But even the psychological characterizations become impenetrable for our analysis.

We have already seen how difficult it remains for us to appreciate the way the Lycians read (sarcastically, unreasonably) Sarpedon's *kleos*. Nor is Sarpedon's own appreciation of his *kleos* made evident by his will to validate it. For this does not tell us either how much of his *kleos* he upholds, or what it means for him to validate a *kleos* which presents him as a god, as a lion, as a king, while recognizing that only the inevitability of death makes sense of his gesture.

The image of the king could appear to the king himself and/or the *Iliad* to be a noble fabrication: as the king comes to realize his human frailty he would be aware of that fabrication, or, alternatively the text would expose – without the character's awareness – that fabrication. Or again the portrait of the king could appear to himself and/or to the *Iliad* to be the true image of a superhuman person that only death separates from the gods.

In the former reading the text would exercise a sort of rationalistic criticism; in the latter it would uphold its superhuman heroes with all the theological and rhetorical underpinnings it masters. Both readings are inseparable and this explains not only why it is possible to speak of the text's awareness of its fiction, but also why the readers are constantly and simultaneously tempted by both views.

The text's reading of itself[55]

We have seen that the Lycians are the first who sometimes admiringly (313) and sometimes suspiciously (318–21) read the portrait of Sarpedon. As readers, they function as mirror figures of us, readers of the *Iliad*. We too, just like the Lycians, are not sure to which extent the *kleos* of the kings is a portrait the text fully upholds or allows us to feel critical about. We both know that the *kleos* is the main business of the epic song, and that there will be always portraits of kings until kings will exist. The Lycians of course know also some of the poets who sit at the table of the kings when singing their portraits.

The text of the *Iliad* with seigneurial assurance and ironic understatement represents the suspicion of those readers of the epic poetry, and gives them their due. It has the king recording their relative lack of trust, and stating that he must, at the cost of his life, prove the *truth* of that truthful *text*. The Lycians must therefore feel ashamed to be such suspicious readers. And accordingly the text induces us, mirror figures of the Lycians, to feel like them. We know the success the text has reaped with this strategy.

I have shown that the Lycians' suspicion about Sarpedon's *kleos* arises just because his portrait *precedes* the king's actions and *bios*. In the eyes of the Lycians, therefore, the precedence of the text with respect to its truth remains unchallenged. First is the word . . .

Yet if Sarpedon (even *a posteriori*) means to validate the implications of his portrait, he is presented by the text as a different reader, an exemplary one, on whom the text has a tremendously edifying effect. Indeed Sarpedon is exemplary of all those noble readers whom the *Iliad* has affected and has persuaded to accept, valiantly, their own death.

The text's awareness of its reflexivity is admirable. It is as though the text knew in advance the possible readings it was offering. On an empirical level it is true that the poets of epic poetry were able to appreciate the reaction of their listeners, immediately, as the reading scene of *Od.* 1 325–59 shows.[56] But the text's rehearsal of its own readings is not an empirical feat: it intimates the sense the text has of itself as a text, of its manipulation of language, of its awareness of itself as fiction.

And yet there is one effect that the text cannot presume and mirror, its unreadability.

At the end of Sarpedon's speech a crossing of possible significations makes uncertain the precise inflection of Sarpedon's thought. I have shown that *eukhos* may designate mere victory or glory (*eukhos* pointing to a *kleos*),[57] and that accordingly an existential and an edifying interpretation of Sarpedon's utterance are possible. For Sarpedon may imply that to die in the battlefield constitutes either one of the countless ways of death that constantly threaten men or a qualitatively different sort of fate. His train of thought from 322 on could follow two different directions. Either he would belittle the importance of *kleos* in the evaluation of the heroic death and would therefore stare at the stern comfort of considering death as that which is proper and close to all men, or he would finally suspend heroic death on the exclusive privilege of *kleos*, and repeat essentially the train of thought of the first part of his speech. Both inflections are present in the ideological premises of the *Iliad*, and, though they are slightly incongruous or inconsistent, they are oddly readable here in the same words.

Furthermore, even the specific identity of Sarpedon's subjectivity which should be the source of his words and decision is blurred. For the *Iliad* presents Sarpedon as being affected by his own voice which is actually also the voice of the *Iliad*, and, in each oral performance, the voice of its poet. Of course as Sarpedon speaks with the epic poetry's diction and ideas, and he affects himself, his subjectivity emerges as a function of that auto-affection. That diction, those ideas, the voice that insistently and solemnly repeats them – and attributes them to a divine source, the Muses – combine in *kleos*, which contradictorily is also what the poets, in their human blindness and ignorance, only hear, a rumour, a voice, which they repeat, insistently and solemnly:

Tell me, now, Muses living in the houses of Olympus – for you are goddesses, you are present and you know (see) everything, but we (poets) hear only *kleos* (rumour) and know nothing – tell me who . . . (*Il.* 2.484–6)

The knot of crossing contradictions becomes insoluble: the subjectivity of the hero emerges with the auto-affection that is exercised by a discourse/voice which is 'other' (*kleos*); glory (*kleos*) is the effect of a repeated voice that insistently declares this effect to be a valuable (divine) voice and a valueless rumour; *eukhos* is either a variant of that same voice, or 'victory', which is meaningless since it is a momentary result of the gamble . . .

The power of the negative that I have liberated with this reading, deeply shakes all the articulations that should hold the text tightly together. We are left, to some extent, in a predicament or *aporia* that would seem to force the reader into silence.

But this is not the case. The exposure of the power of the negative reveals how the text makes sense, how it holds itself together and how it manages, hides/exposes the negative itself, the difference, the supplementarity, the unreadability. This operation of simultaneous hiding/exposing is the mark of a great text, one that does not offer itself to an easy demystification of its metaphysics, nor allow the reader to know exactly where it stands – either on the side of hiding or on the side of exposing.

Furthermore the deconstructive analysis sharpens our knowledge of the forms (protocols), the power and the effects of all linguistic structures, each staging different strategies and supplementary constructions. The epic language of the *Iliad* as we have seen, builds its whole immense fabric on the ground of *kleos* and on its several functions and protocols (or 'etiquette') as 'glory', as 'portrait' of the king, as 'repeated voice' (rumour, renown); and therefore it exhibits the 'voice' as the main means of its production, and of its effects against death and in taming death.

The *Odyssey*, on the contrary, elaborates its strategies through *metis* and polytropy as protocols of a 'writing' that seeks to captivate and imprison the most powerful enemy, death, in its own movements and figures.

The power of the negative, of course, also marks the writing that liberates this power in deconstructing other texts. To this extent, the deconstructive discourse cannot assert any truth for itself, but implement a strategy that simultaneously points to truth and suspends it. It gains nevertheless power over the text it deconstructs. The question, then, is whether this strategy is a seductive literary manoeuvring or a troubling necessity . . . or both.

Acknowledgments

I have read this paper in the seminars of Nicole Loraux in Paris, of Jean Bollack in Lille, of Umberto Albini in Genova, in the Rhetorical Workshop at the University of Chicago, and at the University of Southern California in Los Angeles. On all these occasions I gathered useful criticism, agreement and disagreement that have sharpened my arguments. I thank all the participants of these meetings.

Notes

1 On the theme of the beautiful, glamorous death of the hero see the important papers of Jean-Pierre Vernant, '*Panta Kala*: d'Homere a Simonide', *Annali della Scuola Normale Superiore di Pisa*, se. 3 9–1979, pp. 1,367–74; 'La belle mort et le cadavre outragé' in G. Gnoli and J.-P. Vernant, *La Mort, les morts dans les sociétés anciennes*, Cambridge, Cambridge University Press, and Paris, Maison des Sciences de l'Homme, 1982, pp. 45–76; Nicole Loraux, 'Mourir devant troie' in the same collection, pp. 27–46; Pierre Vidal Naquet, Preface to Helene Monsacré's *Les Larmes d'Achille*, Paris, Albin Michel, 1984, p. 23; and Hélène Monsacré, ibid., pp. 51 ff.

2 Among these, one cannot omit Achilles' statement on the choice he faces between a long joyful life and an immediate but immortally glorious death (*Il*. 9. 410–16); Achilles' desperate knowledge that, godlike though he is, he is doomed to die like everybody else (*Il*. 21. 106–13); Odysseus' short but moving speech in *Il*. 11. 404–10 where he asserts his will to be an *aristos*, a hero and to take a stand alone against the Trojans, and so on.

3 Sarpedon is Lycian and not Trojan; he has no revenge to take; finally no divine compulsion induces him to run in the front rank of the battle.

4 I recall here Epictetus (*Diatribai* 1. 27–8), who quotes the final part of this passage as an argument which can calm the fear of death. An even more noble use of Sarpedon's words is illustrated by Lord Granville (Carteret) at the end of the Seven Years War (1763): he fixes his attention on the last part of Sarpedon's speech (322–8), as R. Wood relates: 'he insisted that I should stay, saying, it could not prolong his life, to neglect his duty; and, repeating the following passage out of Sarpedon's speech, he dwelt with particular emphasis on the third line (324)' (quoted by Walter Leaf, *The Iliad*, 2nd edn, Amsterdam, A. H. Hakkert, 1960, bol. 1, p. 548). William E. Gladstone, *Studies on Homer and Homeric Age*, Oxford, Oxford University Press, 1958, vol. III p. 58, calls Sarpedon's speech 'incomparable' and comments on it with admiration.

5 The most recent commentary is that of Jasper Griffin, *Homer on Life and Death*, Oxford, Clarendon Press, 1980, who touches upon this passage with short notes on pp. 14, 73 and 92–3.

6 I derive these interpretations from M. M. Willcock, *A Companion to the Iliad*, Chicago and London, 1976, p. 142; J. Hogan, *A Guide to the Iliad*, New York, Garden City, 1979, pp. 192–3, and from Griffin, *Homer on Life and Death*, 1980, p. 73:

Sarpedon utters the fullest and most explicit statement of *noblesse oblige*: 'We are noble and wealthy, therefore we must fight in the front rank' and then he goes on to say 'If by avoiding death today we could make ourselves immortal, then I should not fight; but we must die some way, so let us go, to win glory ourself or to serve the glory of others.'

7 The image of the lion to represent the fierce force of kings is conventional and could be described as a fixed piece of the 'portrait' of the king. There are about forty occurrences of lion similes in the *Iliad* alone. Of the extensive bibliography on the lion in Homer, I quote here only a few recent essays: Annie Schanpp Gourbeilloun, *Lions heros, masques. Les representations de l'animal chez Homere*, Paris, Maspéro, 1981; Christian Wolff, 'A note on lions and Sophocles' *Philoctetes*', in *Arktouros*, Berlin, New York, 1979; Rainer Frederick

'On the compositional use of similes in the *Odyssey*', *American Journal of Philology*, 102, 1982, pp. 120–37.

As the reader will see, I am identifying the 'portrait of the king' with the 'glorious renown' (*kleos*) that epic poetry celebrates for each king or prince. In this sense *kleos* is used for a living hero, as for instance in *Il.* 6.446 or even more clearly in *Od.* 9.20. On the question whether the 'Basileus' is a king, and whether all '*Basileis*' are kings and what sort of king they are, cf. R. Drews, *Basileus: The Evidence for Kingship in Geometric Greece*, New Haven, Conn., Yale University Press, 1983, who agrees that the word defines different types of monarchs and leaders; Pierre Carlier, *La Royauté en Grèce avant Alexandre*, Strasbourg, AECR, 1984, who argues that 'Basileus' always designates a king but 'Basileis' also names various types of counsellors. I call 'king' the great leader who is designated as 'Basileus' or who is mentioned among the *Basileis*, or among the *Boulephoroi*.

8 Gods, kings and even lions feast in *daites*, the princely banquets which, without the kings' presence are off limits to commoners. Occasionally the meal of a lion is also named *dais*, see *Il.* 24.43. The *dais* is a ceremonial meal: it has social and religious importance because the eating of meat implies the sacrifice, see Gregory Nagy *The Best of the Achaeans*, Baltimore, Md, Johns Hopkins University Press, 1977, pp. 277 ff.

9 See Jasper Griffin, *Homer on Life and Death*, Oxford, Clarendon Press, 1980, pp. 13 ff; Fausto Codino, *Introduzione a Omero*, Turin, Enaudi, 1965.

10 *Kakoisi doloisi kekasmene, kerdaleophron. Kerdaleophron* is also used by Achilles to insult Agamemnon in *Il.* 1. 149. This word is never used in the *Odyssey*. On *kekasmene* see M. Durante, *Sulla preistoria della tradizione poetica Greca*, Roma, 1976, 11, p. 41 who rightly considers *kekastai* a 'literary' expression of the *Epos*. Notice the heavy, expressive alliteration of *k* which of course emphasizes and repeats the consonant sound of *kakoisi* and *kerdos*.

11 These two lines occur in Sarpedon's passage *Il.* 12. 315–16. The antithesis between the rear and front line of battle is almost formulaic, and occurs many times, see *Il.* 11. 596, 12. 35, 13. 330, 668, 17. 253, etc.

12 I have analysed the unstable meaning of *kleos* in 'The Language of the Muses' in Wendell M. Aycock and Theodor M. Klein (eds) *Classical Mythology in 20th Century Thought and Literature*, Texas University, Lubbock, Texas, Texas Tech Press, 1980, pp. 166–86.

13 In all epochs, the king or queen of every monarchy is known through a specific 'portrait'. Such a portrait is inevitable because being a king means, basically, to respond to a set of representations and prescriptions. The sheer fact that the king has authority over others entails a series of images, that of the father, of the god, and so on; the king's

role to represent and defend his people confirms and enlarges that set of images and includes his being a lion, close to gods, and so on. It would be preposterous to try in a note to open up all the aspects and the articulations of the image or portrait of the king. I simply state here that this portrait is unavoidable, that all sorts of politicians and artists work at this portrait, and that the *Iliad* is for us a gallery of such portraits, a gallery of king's *klea*. See Louis Marin, *Le Portrait du Roi*, Paris, Editions de Minuit, 1981: he analyses the general features of the royal portrait in the specific one of Louis XIV.

14 As a hero of *metis*, Odysseus' military excellence appears mainly in the activity of the *lokhos* (ambush). It is by virtue of this skill that he is involved in the plans concerning the Trojan Horse. See Anthony T. Edwards, *Odysseus against Achilles: The Role of Allusion in the Homeric Epic*, Beiträge zur Klassichen Philologie vol. 171, Königstein/ Ts: Hain, 1985, and Pietro Pucci ΜΗΤΙΣ 1. 1986, pp. 7–28.

15 See *Od.* 7 215–221; 17.284–290, etc.

16 On this theme see my *Odysseus Polutropos*, Ithaca, NY, Cornell University Press, 1987, pp. 157 ff.

17 E. Risch, 'Namendeutungen und Worterklärungen bei den altesten Gr. Dichtern', *Eumusia*, Festgabe fur E. Howald, Zurich, 1947, pp. 72–91. Odysseus probably puns on his name in *Od.* 5. 423: this linguistic gusto could therefore be attributed to him in the *Iliad*.

18 Max Sulzberver, 'ONOMA E ONYMA', *Revue des études grecques*, 1926, pp. 383 ff. The classical example of this convention is the name Odysseus itself: as we learn from *Od.* 19. 406 ff., Odysseus is named in this way by his grandfather's immediate concerns.

19 On the opposition between Achilles, the *promakhos* and Odysseus, the man of the *lokhos*, see Anthony T. Edwards, *Odysseus against Achilles: The Role of Allusion in Homeric Epic*, Beiträge zur Klassichen Philologie, vol. 171, Königstein/Ts, Hain, 1985. See also Joachim Latacz, *Kampfparänese, Kampfdarstellung Kampfwirklichkeit in der Ilias, bei Kallinos und Tyrtaios*, Zetemata München, 1977, p. 159, where summarizing his long analysis of *promachoi* he writes that the substance of the notion *promakhos* does not lie either in the social aspect or in the ethics. The substance lies in the fact that the *promakhos* fights in the front ranks. The *Odyssey* picks up line *Il.* 4. 354 (characterized also by the unicity of *migenta*) in 18. 379: Odysseus boasts, just as in *Il.* 4. 354 that he will be seen 'mingling among the front ranks' but he does not – and in fact he cannot at this point – call himself 'the father of Telemachos'.

20 Perhaps the reader feels uneasy about the comparison I have established between the passage *Il.* 4. 338–55 and 12. 310–21. I recall however that two lines recur in both passages (4. 341–42; 12. 315–16), an evidence that the passages echo each other. It would also be instructive to analyse *Il.* 20. 178–86 where Achilles scoffs at

Aeneas' military prowess by asking him if he intends to gain royal prerogatives.

21 See William E. Gladstone, *Studies on Homer and the Heroic Age*, Oxford, Oxford University Press, 1958, vol. III, p. 58: 'So entirely is the idea of dignity and privilege in the Homeric King founded upon the sure ground of duty, of responsibility and of tail.'

22 Georg Finsler, *Homer*, Leipzig and Berlin, G. B. Tinbuer, 1914, vol. 1, p. 163.

23 Jasper Griffin, *Homer on Life and Death*, Oxford, Clarendon Press, 1980, p. 73.

Dans son exhortation à Glaukos, après avoid rappelé les privilèges materiels dont jouissent les rois lyciens, Sarpedon ajoute qu'en contre-partie, il est de leur devoir de se battre 'en premier rang des Lyciens'. (II.XII.315) Tous les rois homeriques n'ont pas de leur devoir une idée aussi exigeante. (Pierre Carlier, *La Royauté en Grèce avant Alexandre*, Strasbourg, AECR, 1984, p. 172)

This interpretation is canonical. Already Plato in *Rep.* 468 d–e when he thinks of which compensations, and prices will honour the valiant warriors, he does not find anything better than to quote our passage (livre 311) and suggest the compensation of song, seat or honour, meat and cups of wine . . .

24 *To* (*therefore*) of line 315 is proleptic of *ophra* (317) so that the previous question ('why are we honoured . . .?') merely introduces the frame of the royal honours (*timē*) among which there is also that of a splendid royal portrait (*kleos*).

25 LFGE 1, p. 531 Col 1, 1 ff. takes this *alla*-clause as introducing a stress on a new idea without opposition. Accordingly the previous clause 'they are not without glory' turns out to be incomplete and partially negative even if we take this *alla* as introducing no opposition. But how to determine that this adversative adverb here has no oppositional force? On the other hand the new idea is stressed also by *kai* (also), not only by *alla*.

26 As we learn from the *Odyssey*, the epic songs of praise were sung during the banquets at the royal palace. The Lycians are thinking (319–20) of these occasions. Among the extraordinary adventures that are sometimes attributed to the kings, see for instance Diomedes' fight with the Gods in book 5 of the *Iliad*. The Lycians would be sarcastic in using litotes and speaking of *kleos*, as 'mere rumours'.

27 *Is* names the physical force of men, or of natural phenomena like the wind or the sun.

28 In this case the mention of the banquets (319–20) would simply function as a textual reference to Sarpedon's first lines, when he evokes the royal privileges and would harmonize the two passages. The litotes, instead of being ironic, would stress the relative modesty of the king's

portrait, and *kleos* would name the proper, deserved, truthful representation of the kings.

29 cf. Hector in *Il.* 22. 99–110 when he decides to wait for Achilles
because he feels *aidos*, that is he fears the criticism of the Trojan men
and women: he had resisted Polydamas' proposal of withdrawing the
troops within the walls, and now after heavy losses, the Trojans would
reproach him for having presumed too much of his force. Another
interesting example is found in *Il.* 20. 83–5, where Apollo provokes
Aeneas by recalling his previous boasts and menaces against the
Achaeans.

I do not believe that Sarpedon feels the duty because the Lycians
expect him to act as a hero in response to the royal privileges they
grant him. First I suspect that the Lycians, in Sarpedon's view, would
under no circumstances imagine ceasing to grant honours to the king
and to listen to his splendid reputation; and moreover, the statement
of *noblesse oblige* must come from the king, not from his subjects.

Achilles' argument in the ninth book of the *Iliad* proves empirically
that royal prerogatives do not justify the loss of life, and even the
desire for imperishable glory (*aphthiton kleos*) is unaccountable and
can be dismissed in favour of a long life.

30 Sarpedon's decision would be marked by a modern sense of ethics if
he were considering it a duty to substantiate an ideal, noble reputation
(*kleos*) that he, himself, has built in the course of this life through a
consistent noble behaviour. But his royal reputation exists, in part at
least, independently from his behaviour – as the Lycians' suspicions
prove – since it is to some extent traditional and conventional.

31 The phrase would also be translated as a wish: 'Would that we could
escape ... and that we could live for ever ageless and immortal!
Then ...' Pierre Chantraine, *La Grammaire Homerique*, tome II,
Syntaxe, Paris, C. Kliencksieck, 1953, p. 219, considers the phrase
potential rather than a wish and I follow him.

32 See Jacques Derrida, *La Carte postale*, Paris, Flammarion, 1980.
p. 376 ff, where the author, analysing Freud's speculations on the
Death instinct in *Beyond the Pleasure Principle*, and Heidegger's
notion of authenticity writes pages that could be read as an inspiring
commentary on our Iliadic passage.

33 In analogous terms, W. Thomas McCarry explains this sort of death
wish that Sarpedon utters here by the Hegelian notion that life-and-
death struggle is essential to self-definition, *Childlike Achilles*, NY,
1982, p. 197.

34 In view of Sarpedon's desire for real immortality, we may also understand J. Griffin's comment: 'It is not unreflective or unconscious
heroism that drives these men on. Facing death they see both the
obligation and the terror and their speech reflects the totality of their

situation and response', *Homer on Life and Death*, Oxford, Clarendon Press, 1980, p. 73.

35 On the awareness of mortality as a source of morality for the Homeric hero, see J. Griffin, *Homer on Life and Death*, Oxford, Clarendon Press, 1980, p. 93.

36 One is reminded of the criticism which has been addressed for instance by Georges Bataille to Hegel's analysis of the encounter of consciousness that results with a master and a slave. Because Hegel visualizes an encounter of consciousness he cannot confront the actual death of one of the parties.

37 Jacques Derrida, *La Carte postale*, Paris, Flammarion, 1980, p. 379, develops this point.

38 Emile Benveniste, *Le Vocabulaire des institutions indo-européennes*, Paris, Les Editions de Minuit, 1969, vol. II, p. 242.

39 Here Idomeneus says: 'Let us see whether we will give *eukhos* to others or others to us'; the context and the governing verb 'let us see (know) *eidomen*' imply that Idomeneus speculates whether the Achaeans or the Trojans will have victory as the enemies are pressing on the left side of the battlefield.

40 Emile Benveniste, *Le Vocabulaire des institutions indo-européennes*, Paris, Les Editions de Minuit, 1969, vol. II, pp. 57–69, maintains that *kudos* names 'the magical power' the god grants to a victorious hero.

41 'A hero', Odysseus says, 'either is wounded or he wounds another one' (*Il.* 11, 410). But of course, *balein* may mean a fatal wound. It is noteworthy that the lion in the simile with Sarpedon (12. 299–308) is willing to undergo the same: *eblet'en protoisi* (306).

42 Often *eukhos* seems to be used as a full synonym of *kudos* and *kleos*; but in some passages differences appear. In *Il.* 7. 81–90 the difference between *eukhos* and *kleos* is evident: *kleos* is attached to a *sema* and accordingly becomes permanent and personalized glory, so much so that Hector can say 'my kleos will never die'. *Eukhos*, on the contrary, points to the actual (scream of) triumph the god will grant Hector at the moment of the fight. In fact most often *eukhos* indicates the victory the hero is hoping for (*Il.* 7. 203; 11. 290; 7. 81; 15. 462; 16. 725; 21. 297; 5. 654 = 11. 445 = 16. 625). In *Il.* 7 200–5, the difference between *eukhos* and *kudos* lies in the fact that *eukhos* goes along with the verb *eukhonto* (200) while *kudos* repeats *kudiste*, epithet of Zeus. In *Il.* 11. 290–300 *kudos* appears to be a solid, post-factum reality in relation to *eukhos*.

43 Hector, sensing his defeat, boasts of his future glory: 'May I die', he says, 'not without struggle and glory (*a-kleios*) but with the accomplishment of a great deed to be known to future generations' (*Il.* 22. 304–5). The last line not only explains what *kleos* is, and why a *kleos* is to some extent always permanent, but also calls the attention shamelessly on the textual selfreferentiality. The negative form *a-kleios*

occurs, though not adverbially, in Sarpedon's passage (12. 318) and elsewhere, in *Il.* 7 100; *Od.* 1. 241 = 14.371.

44 *Eukhos*, in fact, is corrected to *eukhomai* whose usages, as Pierre Chantraine writes, refer to 'une déclaration insistante et solennelle', *Dictionnaire etymologique de la langue grecque*, Paris, Editions Klincksieck, 1970, vol. II, p. 389. See also L. Ch. Mullner, *The Meaning of Homeric* EYXOMAI, Innsbruck, 1976, pp. 108 ff.

45 I allude here to the phenomenon of 'autoaffection' and its interference in the production of 'consciousness', see Jacques Derrida, *La Voix et le phenomene*, Paris, PUF, 1967.

46 It is not necessary today to explain what 'writing' means in this context. It has of course little to do with the technique which we call 'writing' but with the specific notion that deconstructive criticism has elaborated to speak of the texts. For 'writing' names the lags and gaps in the process of signification, the repetition, the dissemination of meanings, supplementarity; the arbitrarity or better the unmotivatedness of the sign and its discontinuous signification. I refer here essentially to the notions that are illustrated in the writings of Jacques Derrida, and I apologize here for reducing to mere labels such an original and masterful thought.

47 On this 'dramatic' oral part that the poem stages and which is as large at least as its descriptive part, see the formal analyses that Carlo Ferdinando Russo has been unravelling in these last fifteen years, in *Belfagor*.

48 Paul De Man has written eloquently on this question, in his *Allegories of Reading: Figural Language in Rousseau, Nietzsche, Rilke and Proust*, New Haven, Conn., Yale University Press, 1979.

49 Part of the royal portrait is conventional and traditional. For instance in Sarpedon's portrait the divine genealogy — he is the son of Zeus — the lion simile, the special epithets, are traditional marks of royalty. Together with individual traits and features, the traditional marks compose a royal portrait by which the king is known. When Aeneas answers in *Il.* 20. 204ff. to Achilles' mockeries, he says that both of them know well each other through the *proklut'epea*, that is through 'the previously heard tales' or 'verses' that celebrate them. *Prokluta* is composed by *pro-* and *kluta* which is connected, through *kluo*, to *kleos*.

50 Sarpedon picks up the godlike (*antitheon*) feature of this portrait when he says (312) that 'all people look at *him* as at a god'. This is a rare compliment in Homer. Besides this passage, we have *Od.* 8. 173, for an almost mythical king and 7.71 for Alcinoos! There are several variations on this theme. 'To honour as a god': *Il.* 9. 155, 297, 302 (of Achilles); *Il.* 5. 78 (Eurypylos); *Il.* 10. 33 (Agamemnon); *Il.* 11 58 (Aeneas); *Il.* 13. 218 (Thoas); *Il.* 14. 205 (Castor); *Il.* 16. 605 (Laogonos); *Od.* 5. 36; 19. 280; 23. 339 (Odysseus). 'To receive a

hero as a god': *Il*. 16. 434 (Hector) 'To be a god among men': *Il*. 14. 258–59 (of Hector, who, a rumour says, boasts of being son of Zeus 13. 54, but the genealogy is denied in *Il*. 10. 49–50). 'To pray to someone as to a god': *Il*. 22. 394 etc., Hes. *Theog*. 91.

51 I borrow here the formula which Louis Marin illustrated in his Seminar at the Ecole des Hautes Etudes in the spring of 1981 on the 'Portrait of the king'. I read there a first version of this paper.

52 See *Il*. 22. 433–5.

53 See Nicole Loraux, 'Mourir devant troie, tomber pour Athènes: de la gloire du heros à l'idée de la cité', in G. Gnoli and J. P. Vernant (eds) *La Mort, les Morts dans les sociétés anciennes*, Cambridge, Cambridge University Press; Paris, Maison des sciences de l'homme, 1982, p. 32: 'la mort du guerrier appelle irrésistiblement le chant du poète, la prose de l'orateus, alors il s'avère que *la belle mort est toujours en elle-même déjà un discours*'.

54 I pursue here only one of the alternative readings of the passage. The other one, that *kleos* is mere flattery, invalidates already the truth of *kleos*.

55 I follow here some of the critical concerns that Paul De Man has illustrated in his work.

56 Here Penelope intervenes and stops (*apopaue* 340) Phemius' song about 'the wretched return of the Achaeans': see my analysis in *Odysseus Polutropos*, Ithaca, NY, Cornell University Press, 1987, pp. 195 ff.

57 See J. Griffin's paraphrasis of the passage in *Homer on Life and Death*, p. 73: 'if by avoiding death today we could make ourselves immortal, then I should not fight, but we must die some day, so let us go, to win *glory* ourselves or to serve the glory of others' and his translation on p. 92: 'so let us go either to yield victory to another or to win it ourselves' (italics mine).

'Knowledge is remembrance': Diotima's instruction at Symposium 207c 8–208b 6

DAVID FARRELL KRELL

The phrase 'knowledge is remembrance' sounds familiar. It is reminiscent of Socrates' formulation in *Phaedo*, 'learning is recollection (*hē mathēsis anamnēsis*)'. And, as we know from *Theaetetus*, if learning is recollection, the goal of learning, knowledge, must be the actual having in hand (*ekhein*)[1] of what is recollected. Knowledge is remembrance. Socrates says (*Phaedo*, 75d 8–11), 'For to know [*eidenai*] means to possess the knowledge attained [*labonta tou epistēmēn*] and not to have lost it; or does not forgottenness [*lēthē*] mean the loss of knowledge [*epistēmēs apobolē*]?' 'Knowledge is remembrance'. What could be clearer than that? Is there any other Platonic notion we can feel so sure of? Is there any other Platonic formulation that moves us so quickly and effortlessly to the very heart of what is called the Platonic philosophy?

At the beginning of Book VI of the *Republic* Socrates and Glaucon again conduct us to that core. The philosopher-guardians, the lovers of wisdom, 'are those who are capable of possessing what is always the same and unchanging [484b 4–5: *aei kata tauta hōsautōs ekhantos . . .*]'. Philosophic souls 'always love knowledge that discloses to them something of that being which is forever in being [485b 1–3: *ekeinēs tēs ousias tēs aei ousēs*] and which is not made to wander through coming-to-be and passing away [*kai mē planōmenēs hypo geneseōs kai phthoras*]'. *Love* of such knowledge spawns all the other virtues that the guardians must exhibit –

truthfulness, temperance, liberality, courage, justice, sociability and gentleness – when it mates with native *intelligence*, which from Plato to Piaget has always been associated with a good memory, that is to say, a good *active*, recollective, 'anamnetic' memory. Socrates and Glaucon continue (486c–d):

Nor will you overlook this, I fancy.
What?
Whether he is quick or slow to learn. Or do you suppose that anyone could properly love a task which he performed painfully and with little result from much toil?
That could not be.
And if he could not preserve [*sōizein*] what he learned, being steeped in oblivion [*lēthē*], could he fail to be void of knowledge [*epistēmē*]?
How could he?
And so, having all his labor for nought, will he not finally be constrained to loath himself and that occupation?
Of course.
The forgetful soul, then, we must not list in the roll of competent lovers of wisdom, but we require a good memory [*mnēmonikē*].
By all means.[2]

A mighty memory and a love of knowledge together constitute the philosophic nature. But what about this ever-present, constant love (cf. 485b 1: *aei erōsin* . . .)? How is such love related to recollection and to remembrance? How is *erōs* related to actual possession or having in hand, *hexis prokheiron*?

Plato writes about *erōs* in many places, but with special concentration, as we remember, in *Phaedrus* and *Symposium*. There is a passage in the latter dialogue that defines the relationship of love, possession, knowledge, and remembrance in a way that leaves little to be desired when it comes to vivid depiction. Yet commentators for the most part have neglected the passage, so much so that I believe we can call it one of the 'forgotten' passages in Plato. It appears in the midst of Socrates' recollection of Diotima's instruction in *ta erōtika* (at 207c 8–208b 6 in the Stephanus pagination).[3]

We have perhaps forgotten the passage because Diotima's instruction here – if I understand it well – threatens the entire edifice of doxographic Platonism, that is the structure of Platonic 'doctrine', and with it no small part of the western intellectual tradition. Tradition always preserves selectively: it always remembers to forget the troublesome and recalcitrant pieces among its building blocks. In his well-known book, *The Greeks and the Irrational*, E. R. Dodds says that Plato himself failed to integrate fully the erotic teaching of *Phaedrus* and *Symposium* into the remainder of his philosophy.[4] I am not convinced that Dodds's way of posing the problem of such integration is very helpful. Yet it does serve to remind us that *erōs* is not for Plato a bloodless, sentimental metaphor of philosophic education, of easy ascent to the ethereal realm of ideas, but an issue and a task. Diotima's words at 207c – 208b offer a kind of rugged access to that issue.

We remember the immediate context. Remember it more vividly than anything else in philosophy. Diotima identifies *erōs* as a *daimōn* (202d 13) who serves as an interpreter and envoy between gods and mortals. Ambiguous offspring of Need and Resource, servant to Aphrodite, *erōs* is 'neither mortal nor immortal', 'neither poor nor rich', and he hovers undecidably 'always in the middle between wisdom [*sophia*] and ignorance [*amathia*]'. Hence *erōs* is a *lover* of wisdom, beauty, and the good, *not* one who *has* them: he is the *philosophos* (204b 4) par excellence, forever *in between* (5: *metaxy*) those who are wise and those who do not know, forever *desirous* of possessing the good (206a 11–12). Now comes Diotima's famous definition of love's *praxis* (cf. 206a–e): *erōs* is every sort of producing, begetting, and giving birth in beauty, both of body and of soul, for the sake of immortality. 'Producing', 'begetting', and 'giving birth' all try to translate *tokos*. This noun derives from *tiktō*, an action attributed to both a father and a mother, and meaning the entire process whereby men and women come together (*synousia*) in order to conceive and generate offspring (*hē kyēsis kai hē gennēsis*).

I interrupt the exposition at this point to say aloud what all have surely observed by now. The philosopher-guardian of the *Republic* forever loves and is capable of having in hand knowledge that discloses to him something of being that is always in being (*tēs ousias tēs aei ousēs*); he spurns the advances of all derivative beings that wander the necessitous path of generation and corruption (*hypo geneseōs kai phthoras*). Yet Diotima now defines the practice of love itself in terms of *genesis*. it is here that we enter the 'forgotten passage'.

What is the *telos* of erotic *praxis*? Diotima replies (297d 1–2) that 'it belongs to the mortal nature [*hē thnētēte physis*] to strive, in accordance with its powers, to be forever and immortal [*zētei kata to dynaton aei te einai kai athanatos*]'. Yet the only way it can do that is 'through generation [2–3: *tēi genesei*]'. The outcome of generation is that another individual who is young remains back behind to assume the place of the one grown old. Diotima continues:

We say of every single living creature that it lives and is as the selfsame [5: *to auto*], just as we call someone by the same name from the time of his infancy until he has grown old. He is always called by the same name, even though he never remains the selfsame but is forever becoming something new [7: *necs aei gignomenos*], losing what is old in hair, flesh, bone, and blood, and in his entire body.

In other words, mortal nature generates not only in the *synousia* of man and woman but also in the all but anonymous life of one's own body. Reproduction is but an image of the ongoing living, dying and renovating in the human body. Of course, none of this need concern the philosopher-guardian, if his love and possession of knowledge have brought him to the point where he can dispense with his body. However, Diotima does not stop with hair, flesh, bone and blood. She goes on.

However, not only in the body, but also in the soul, there are changes [e 2: *hoi tropoi*]: character traits [*ta ēthē*], opinions [*doxai*], desires [*epithymiai*], pleasures [e 3: *hēdonai*], aversions (*lupai*), fears [*phoboi*] – none of these remain the same, but come to be and pass away.

Indeed, we might interject, what sense would philosophic education have if these things did not change? What good would Diotima's instruction do the youthful Socrates if his soul were incapable of growth and change? 'But still more astonishing', Diotima proceeds,

is the fact, not only that elements-of-knowledge [e 5: *hai epistēmai*] in part come to be and in part pass away, and not only that we are never the same in relation to them, but also that each element of our knowledge undergoes the same process [208a 2–3: *alla kai mia ekastē tōn epistēmōn tauton paskhei*].

Diotima is not stating the obvious about knowledge – that it is learned, that it therefore changes, and that it alters us in the process. She is saying that every single 'particle' of knowledge (to speak for a moment the language of the Titans!), every single insight, suffers ongoing alteration within itself. She is talking, not about *mathēsis*, the learning process, but about *epistēmē*, knowledge *itself*, as we say.

Diotima tries to demonstrate the alteration of *epistēmē* by describing what goes on when we pursue something in thought. The word she uses (a 4–5) for such thoughtful pursuit is *hē meletē*. It derives from the verb *meletainō (meletaō)*, meaning (1) to take thought or care for (cf. *melō*, to care for, take an interest in); (2) to attend to, study, pursue, or exercise oneself in; (3) to rehearse in one's mind. It is the word Plato uses in *Phaedo* when he describes the philosopher's life as the practice or pursuit of dying and being dead (cf. 67e 5; 81a 1).[5] Diotima appears to be using the word in the somewhat restricted sense of rehearsing in one's mind, studying, pursuing in thought. Schleiermacher translates *hē meletē* here with *Nachsinnen*, to ponder, mull over, think back to, dwell and meditate on a thing. Diotima says – and here we reach the central point of the passage –

For what we call *meletē* pursues knowledge that is on its way out [208a 4: *exiousēs . . . tēs epistēmēs*]. For forgetting is the departure [5: *exodos*] of knowledge. But *meletē* induces a freshly minted memory to take the place of what is departing [5–6: *palin kainēn empoiousa anti tēs apiousēs mnēmēn*], and so preserves knowledge [*sōizei tēn epistēmēn*] in such a way that it seems to be the same [6–7: *hōste tēn autēn dokein einai*].

Thinking-back-to (*hē meletē*) is pursuit of a knowledge-in-departure. *Exiousēs* is a present participle in the feminine genitive, a form of *exeimi*, to go out, leave, quit, abandon; in relation to time, to come to an end, cease, expire.[6] Michael Joyce translates the phrase beautifully as follows: 'When we say we are studying, we really mean that our knowledge is ebbing away'. Schleiermacher translates: *Denn was man Nachsinnen heisst, geht auf eine ausgegangene Erkenntnis.* 'For what we call thinking-back-to goes toward knowledge that has departed'. *Eimi* (with the stress on the first syllable), 'to go', is of course enticingly similar (judged by the contemporary reader's eye, if not by the Greek ear) to *eimi* (stress on the second syllable), the verb 'to be', nowhere more so than in the participial form *ousia*. I wonder whether Plato was altogether blind to the significance of such a similarity: *exiousēs . . . tēs epis-tēmēs* at least *suggests* the departure of knowledge *from being*. The *exodus* of knowledge, forgetting (*lēthē*), is a retreat into conceal-ment and obscurity, a withdrawal into nonbeing or absence. Think-ing-back-to bears witness to that withdrawal, however, and, following the traces of fugitive knowledge, institutes a kind of retrieval. Care brings back (*palin*) a souvenir of the departing knowledge. it produces a fresh memento (*kainēn empoiousa mnēmēn*) to take the place of the knowledge that will have vanished irrevocably from being (*anti tēs apiousēs*). As a result of such mnemonic minting or production, knowledge is preserved (*sōizei tēn epistēmēn*). Now, *sōlzein* is a word of complex origins, but it means to rescue from death, to keep alive, spare; to preserve or to help recover. It also has the sense of 'keeping in mind', remem-bering, as in the above passage from the *Republic* (486c 7; cf. 455b 8) where Socrates and Glaucon agree that a guardian must be capable of preserving or keeping in mind what he learns. However, the 'preservation' Diotima speaks of here is actually the coining of a new mnemonic image to take the place of the dying one; it is generation, not mummification. knowledge is preserved in such a way that it *seems* (*dokein*) to be always the same (*hōste tēn autēn . . . einai*). Diotima concludes:

And in this way all that is mortal is preserved (208a 8: *sōlzetai*), not as though it were forever entirely the selfsame, like divinity, but in such a way that what grows old and deteriorates leaves behind a youthful other [b 1: *heteron neon*] who is somewhat the same as it was [b 2: *hoion auto ēn*].[7]

Let us make no mistake about Diotima's instruction concerning *epistēmē*. The kind of knowledge we have always identified as the bulwark of what is called the Platonic philosophy — eternal and immutable knowledge — suffers alteration in itself. Diotima uses the word *paskhein*, subjecting active thought to passivity. Yet subsequent tradition distinguishes epistemic knowledge from all sorts of inferior representation and intuition precisely by means of the absence of passivity: knowledge *per se* is spared the passion of existence in time, the inglory of departure. Diotima defines mortal thought, on the contrary, as pursuit of that which is in withdrawal — but which is amenable to leaving behind an image of itself.

Mortal thought, thinking-back-to, retrieves and recovers a memento. It preserves, not by clinging forever to the selfsame, but by harbouring seeds of identity within an inexpungeable difference. It accepts the new in place of the old, the generous fruits of remembrance. Yet these seeds of identity themselves disseminate and disperse. Mortal thought recovers a knowledge it *believes* to be the same: *epistēmē* is grounded in *dokein*. Is that to say that knowledge is mere opinion, *doxa*, and that verisimilitude is sheer deception, so that all knowledge is a ruse?

Who *is* this Diotima? Is she to be trusted?

At the end of his encomium to Erōs Socrates professes himself a 'believer' who is 'persuaded' by Diotima's instruction (cf. 212b 2–3; *pepeismai, pepeismenos, peithein*). Yet *pistis*, belief or trust, is hardly secure grounds for knowledge. And young Socrates himself is from time to time dubious. 'O Diotima, most wise [208b 8: *sophōtatē*], I wonder whether all this is really true?' She reassures him. Her manner in reassuring him is that of one who is utterly knowledgeable – Michael Joyce translates, 'with an air of authority that was almost professorial' – literally, 'after the manner of perfect sophists [208c 1: *hōsper hoi teloi sophistai*]'. Plato invites us to ponder the juxtaposition of *sophōtatē* and *sophistai*, to wonder whether Diotima is most wise, that is whether she remembers her own origins, function, and limitations, or whether she is indeed a perfect sophist.[8]

How can we find out who Diotima is? Perhaps by expanding our reading of the passage to include its situation among the other Platonic dialogues and its context within the *Symposium* itself.

The first is of course an impossible task. It would require a careful reading of the *Republic, Meno, Theaetetus, Sophist*, and *Parmenides*, among others, where *epistēmē* is a central theme. Let me therefore attempt a 'shorter way'. I will try to provide something of a primer for Diotima's instruction, 'knowledge is remembrance', by referring to Plato's magnificent opera buffa, *Cratylus*, and then to that more earnest dialogue, *Sophist*.

In the *Cratylus* Socrates tries twice to define *epistēmē*. The first time he speaks as a kind of inspired oracle for the silent Cratylus, proclaiming in neo-Heraclitean style the adequacy of names to express the nature of things, while taking the nature of things to be perpetual flux. Socrates elaborates etymologies for all of philosophy's pet terms, and the zany result is as follows:

Phronēsis [deliberation or thoughtfulness] . . . may signify *phoras kai rhou noēsis* [perception of motion and flux], or perhaps *phoras onēsis* [the blessing of motion], but is at any rate connected with *pheresthai* [motion]; *gnōmē* [judgment], again, certainly implies the pondering and considering [*nomēsis*] of generation [*gonē*]. . . . Or, if you prefer, here is *noēsis*, the very word just now mentioned, which is *neou hesis* [the desire of the new]; the word *neos* implies that being is always in process of becoming. The giver of the name wanted to express his longing in the soul, for the original name was *neoesis* [i.e. desire of the new or young]. . . . *Epistēmē* [knowledge] is akin to this, and indicates that the soul which is good for anything follows [*hepetai*] the motion of things, neither anticipating them nor falling behind them; wherefore the word should rather be read as *epeistēmē*, inserting an epsilon.[9]

Here we recognize in caricature several elements of Diotima's instruction: judgment is related to the seed of generation, thought is desire for what is new and young, this implying that beings are forever in process of generation; and knowledge chases after the whirligig of beings, in pursuit, anxious not to fall too far behind. But that implies the identity of knowledge and mere opinion, since *doxa* (cf. 420b 7) comes from *dioxis* (pursuit), 'and expresses the march of the soul in the pursuit of insight'.

When Socrates' galloping enthusiasm succeeds in getting Cratylus to re-enter the dialogue, Socrates himself begins to doubt his inspiration. In fact, he now swings to the opposite pole, defining all in terms of stasis. He says:

Let us revert to *epistēmē* [knowledge], and observe how ambiguous this word is, seeming to signify stopping [437a 4: *histēsin*] the soul at things rather than going round with them, and therefore we should let the initial epsilon alone, merely inserting an iota and reading *epiistēmē* [stopping upon].

Socrates adds, for good measure, 'And again, *mnēmē* [memory], as anyone may see, expresses rest [b 3: *monē*] in the soul, and not motion'. At the end of the dialogue he expresses his belief in the stability of knowledge, encouraging Cratylus to put off his acceptance of the Heraclitean view of things until he has studied the matter further. Cratylus reasserts his Heraclitean predilections and closes the dialogue with an injunction to Socrates: 'Very good

Socrates. But I hope that you yourself will continue to ponder these matters'.

We do not know about Socrates, but Plato surely does continue to think about names, knowledge, permanence and change. He also continues with the effort to distinguish the philosopher from the sophist. And yet even the more persistent of those efforts, the dialogue entitled *Sophist*, is, to say the least, not unequivocally successful: in the final attempt to distinguish *eikastikē* (production of likenesses) from *phantastikē* (production of semblance), one division of *mimēsis* – which is itself a division of *phantastikē* – requires judgment (*gnōsis*). Yet judgment ought to be reserved exclusively for philosophy and the production of likenesses. A 'serious shortage of names', as the Stranger says (267d 8), prevents a perfect distinction and identification, one that would allow us to insert Diotima into one category or the other. If both Homer and Parmenides, both *mimēsis* and *antimimēsis*, are banished from the city, if not murdered by their children; if no binary system, whether in literature or philosophy, can survive dissimulation; then how are we to decide?[10]

If the dialogue *Sophist* fails to resolve the problem of Diotima's identity, it does help us to penetrate more deeply into the dilemma posed by the interpretations of being (and knowledge) as total flux and as absolute stasis. On the one hand, we hear the philosopher-guardians declare their love for and possession of knowledge of being that does not come to be and pass away; on the other hand, Diotima tells us that knowledge is itself an image of generation and dying. The positions these two parties adopt are not identical to those assumed by the Friends of the Forms and the Titans, respectively, but they are similar enough to aid our labours to provide a primer for Diotima's instruction. If the *gigantomakhia* between the materialistic Titans and the idealistic Friends of the Forms has an outcome, it is a kind of 'draw' which the Stranger describes at 249c–d:

It seems that only one course is open to the philosopher who values knowledge [*epistēmē*] and the rest [i.e. *phronēsis* and *nous*: cf. 249c 8] above all else: he must refuse to accept from the champions either of the one or of the many forms the doctrine that everything [d 1: *to pan*] is changeless, and he must turn a deaf ear to the other party who represent being [2: *to on*] as everywhere changing. Like a child begging for 'both', he must declare that being, everything that is, is both at once – all that is unchanged and all that is in change.[11]

Bafflement over being surely does not end there – some have thought that Plato's *Sophist* is precisely where it *begins* – but at least we may now try to rehabilitate Diotima's reputation. If the authentic man or woman of knowledge is like a child begging for both rest and motion, permanence and change, then Diotima may be the very woman who succeeds in reconciling these contrary traits. She does not say, as the sophist does, 'Error cannot be, hence I am always right', or 'All is flux, hence my opinion is as good as yours'. Rather, she tries to instruct Socrates in the way mortals forever are, namely, subject to change, birth, departure, death. Change is their permanent abode. Nor does she say, 'There is no knowledge, hence I am the measure of being'. Rather, she speaks of a recovery of knowledge, *sōizein tēs epistēmēs*, albeit a recovery at the cost of absolute identity. She invokes rebirth from the womb of difference.

Is knowledge therefore a ruse? Yes and no. Yes, if we insist on occupying the standpoint of the gods, if we forget our mortality and lose faith in the erotic venture. No, if the *dokein* that founds *epistēmē* is not 'mere opinion' (*doxa*), fleeting and fickle, but a sowing and cultivating that combine in some mysteriously fertile way motion and rest, dissemination and gathering.

So much for a rather hasty effort to situate Diotima's instruction within the whole of what is called Plato's philosophy, or at least amid some of the other dialogues. Discussion of the essential neighbouring dialogue, *Phaedrus*, I must reserve for another time. Earlier I promised to say something about the setting of Diotima's instruction within *Symposium* itself. Let me conclude therefore with a few equally hasty remarks on Diotima's theme, 'knowledge is remembrance', in the context of the great drinking party.

Diotima is of course not present at the party. Her knowledge is *remembered* and *reproduced* by Socrates, who went out in pursuit of her when he was a young man. Moreover, Socrates himself is absent from the narrative situation that frames the dialogue, since the tale is being recounted some fifteen years after its occasion – Agathon's victory in the tragedy competition. The story is told by Apollodorus, 'the gift of Apollo', who is 'crazy' about philosophy (cf. 173d 8: *to malakos*; and e 2–3: *mainomai kai parapaiō*). Now,

Apollodorus was not at the party either, but he remembers the account of Aristodemus, who, they say, was there. Apollodorus is telling the story told him by Aristodemus – partially corroborated by talks with Socrates himself (cf. 173b 5) – to a 'friend', or perhaps several friends, two days after he has recounted it to Glaucon. In fact, Diotima's instruction is a retelling of a retelling of a retelling of a retelling. What does such retelling presuppose?

The dialogue begins with Apollodorus saying, 'Oh, if that's what you want to know, it isn't long since I had occasion *to refresh my memory*'.[12] Translated more literally, the first lines of *Symposium* read: 'I believe [*Dokō*] that I am not altogether unable to think back to [*ameletētos*] the matter you are asking about'. The entire *logos* of *Symposium* rests on Apollodorus' *dokein*, his seeming to remember. Thus his tale can be only somewhat the same. Yet we may have some confidence in his memory, since crazy Apollodorus has dwelled on the matter, studied it, thought back in pursuit of it, *cared* for it: *hē meletē*. Certainly for Apollodorus and for all the unnamed friends who hear his story, knowledge is remembrance. Precisely because the tale has an extraordinarily intricate *genealogy*, having gone through *generations* of retelling, of mintings and coinages, it is like one of those little *sileni* (cf. 215a 7) that you open at the belly to find images of the gods inside. Yet only images!

After Diotima instructs Socrates in the matter of knowledge as remembrance, she tries to teach him how to climb the ladder of *erōs*, advancing from rung to rung from love of body to love of the soul, to love of laws and institutions, to love of every kind of *epistēmē* (210c 6), and finally, at the top of the ladder, to the vision of beauty-in-itself, which is beyond all *epistēmē* (211a 7). What is the nature of this 'beyond'? What are we to say, now that Diotima has enticed us to the upper ionosphere of love and beauty? Shall we intone hymns, don the robes of immortality?

Not to worry: whatever we might have sung will be silenced by the approaching flutes. and yet somehow, perhaps because of Diotima's instruction on the *erōs of epistēmē*, we are not totally unrehearsed in the kind of plunge initiated by Alcibiades and his Bacchantes, who come to remind us where we are. We who pursue. We who love to know.

Notes

1 cf. *hexis*, in contrast to *ktēsis*, in the *Theaetetus*, at 197b 1–2. For 'having in hand', cf. *prokheiron*, 198d 10.

2 Plato, *Republic*, trans. Paul Shorey, in Edith Hamilton and Huntingdon Cairns (eds) *The Collected Dialogues of Plato*, New York, Bollinen, 1961. All English translations, unless otherwise specified, are based on this collection, with minor alterations.

3 I cannot claim to have surveyed the vast secondary literature on Plato's *Symposium* sufficiently to make my assertion perfectly convincing. Yet apart from Gerhard Krüger's wonderful *Einsicht und Leidenschaft: Das Wesen des platonischen Denkens*, Frankfurt am Main, V. Klostermann, 1939, I have not seen a commentator treat this passage with the puzzlement it deserves. Paul Friedländer, *Plato*, 3 vols, London, Routledge & Kegan Paul, 1969, trans. Hans Meyerhoff, vol. 3, pp. 267, simply skips over it. Stanley Rosen, *Plato's Symposium*, New Haven, Conn., Yale University Press, 1968, pp. 250–5, recapitulates the entire speech in a lapidary manner. Rosen never really poses a question, never allows the surface of his own or Plato's texts to be ruffled. In contrast, Krüger (see especially pp. 165–72) affirms the 'astonishing' radicality of Diotima's doctrine of knowledge. Indeed, he takes her notion of the 'perpetual renovation' of knowledge as the fitting site for a discussion of the 'problem of time' as such in Plato. We will therefore have to come back to Krüger's *Insight and Passion*, inasmuch as Diotima's instruction is about the passion of all mortal insight.

4 E. R. Dodds, *The Greeks and the Irrational*, Berkeley, Calif., University of California Press, 1951, pp. 216–19 and 231 n. 60–2.

5 *Meletē* itself means 'care'. In his first lecture course on Nietzsche (winter semester 1936–7) Martin Heidegger employs the word as a contrast to *tekhnē*. *Meletē*, *epimeleia*, means 'an ability [*Können*] in the sense of an acquired capacity to carry something out'. He takes the word in its most general sense to mean 'the mastery of a composed and resolute openness to beings [*Entschlossenheit zum Seienden*]', which in *Being and Time* he designates as 'care', *Sorge*. For Heidegger, *hē meletē* constitutes the being of that being called *Dasein* – human existence as such. (For the quotation from Heidegger's lecture course, see M. Heidegger, *Nietzsche, vol. I: Will to Power as Art*, New York, Harper & Row, 1979, para. 21.)

6 cf. the form *exiousēs* employed by Lysias Orator in Liddell-Scott, p. 589b, lines 24–5. A classicist friend assures me that *exiousēs is* a *present* participle. To me, initially, and (as we shall see) to Schleiermacher, it seemed to be *perfect*.

7 cf. the Aristotelian definition of 'essence' as *to ti ēn einai*, *Posterior Analytics*, 82b 38.

8 Rosen (see note 3 above) acknowledges the 'Aristotelian' traits in Diotima's doctrine (perhaps having learned this from Krüger); yet he never takes the threat of sophistry seriously. He takes Socrates' ironic reference to the 'perfect sophists' as one 'which points to the theoretical aspects of her next speech' (p. 256); yet he never penetrates to those 'theoretical aspects' that ought to cause genuine astonishment. Gerhard Krüger (see also note 3) takes Diotima's insistence that *epistēmē* itself is subject to the vicissitudes of coming-to-be and passing-away as evidence of Plato's resistance to what Krüger anachronistically calls 'the illusion of the Enlightenment'. While acknowledging those famous passages from *Phaedo* with which my chapter began, passages that appear to contradict Diotima's instruction and to reassert the reign of immutable *eidē* in Platonic philosophy, Krüger none the less takes the *erotic* Plato to be the fully integrated Plato, and Diotima to be Plato's own priestess. For Diotima 'puts her finger on the simple yet enigmatic fact of the humanity of knowledge' (p. 171). Krüger, true to his phenomenological heritage, takes Diotima's instruction as evidence from the *temporal acts* of 'discursive' cognition. There are no *pure* contents that could be preserved in an autarchic logic and no *mere* acts that can be relegated to a lowly psychology. 'This forced separation, which turns the unity of our actual thinking into a subsequently insoluble puzzle, becomes superfluous if we do not set out to achieve "scientific consciousness" as something divinely sovereign – at the cost of leaving a spiritless humanity as its dross' (p. 171). Diotima as phenomenologist? That may seem less strange now that we have come to see her as a theorist of *dissemination*. Unless of course diotimic dissemination threatens the project of phenomenology 'as such'.

9 I cite the Jowett translation, with changes. The Schleiermacher rendition is ingenious, but (atypically) is farther removed from the original.

10 See J. Derrida, 'La double séance', in *La Dissémination*, Paris, Seuil, 1972, pp. 211–23, n. 8; and Jean-Luc Nancy, 'Le ventriloque', in *Mimésis des articulations*, Paris, Aubier Flammarion, 1975, pp. 304–7.

11 Translation by F. M. Cornford, with changes.

12 Translation by Michael Joyce, my emphasis.

· 8 ·

On the saying that philosophy begins in thaumazein

JOHN LLEWELYN

He was a good genealogist who made Iris the daughter of Thaumas. (Socrates).

I

'Wonder is the only beginning of philosophy,' Plato has Socrates say at 155d of the *Theaetetus*. And at 982b of the *Metaphysics* Aristotle says, 'it is owing to their wonder that men both now begin and at first began to philosophize'.

'Wonder', *thaumazein*, is one of those wonderful words that face in opposite directions at one and the same time, like Janus and the androgynous creature of whom Aristophanes tells in the *Symposium*. It seems possible to use it in opposite senses at once; *thaumazein* both opens our eyes wide and plunges us into the dark. It is both startled start and flinching in bewilderment. Reflection on it might well have made Theaetetus' head swim as much as do the aporias Socrates leads him into in the pages culminating at 155 in Theaetetus's exclamation: 'By the gods, Socrates, I am lost in wonder *(thaumazo)* when I think of all these things. It sometimes makes me quite dizzy'. His condition would be well described by analogy with the stunning effect of the sting ray to which Meno – and, according to the response he makes to Meno's comparison, Socrates himself – are perplexed by aporias. Theaetetus, for example, is puzzled at the suggestion that six dice can be both fewer than twelve and more than four. And Meno is paralysed by the less readily solved problem of how to define virtue. Despite the greater depth of Meno's problem, he too suspects Socrates of performing conjuring tricks, *thaumatopoios* being puppetry, juggling and suchlike acts of prestidigitation that dumbfound. As at the beginning of the *Meditations* Descartes is so stupefied at not being able to identify any sure mark by which to distinguish waking from dreaming that he can almost persuade himself that he may be then and there asleep. *Obstupescam*, he says. His Latin also speaks of *stupor*, for which the French gives *étonnement*, astonishment.

Thaumazein, astonishment, Aristotle says, is provoked by aporias. According to him the difficulties that arose for the early philosophers were first to do with matters close at hand but later concerned remoter questions, questions about the solstices, for example, and the genesis of the universe, *peri tēs tou pantos gene-seōs* (982b 17). As with Plato, the aporias often have the form of apparent contradictions, such as the prospect of dolls at a puppet show behaving as though they were alive, and the idea that the diagonal of a square is incommensurable with the side. When the cause of the puppet's movements has been revealed and when we have learned a little geometry our astonishment disappears. What would astonish us then is the suggestion that what we now believe to be possible is not. These are two cases that Aristotle regards as ones that might give rise to astonishment with anyone at some stage. He mentions them immediately after stating that 'all men begin, as we said, by wondering that all things are as they are', *archontai men gar, hōsper eipomen, apo tou thaumazein pantes ei outōs echei* (983a 12). The 'as we said' refers back to a passage that attributes wonder to any beginning philosopher. It appears to follow that any puzzled person is a philosopher provided he seeks to remove that puzzlement and that his desire to achieve the knowledge that will remove it as a desire for knowledge for its own sake, not just for the sake of removing the puzzlement and not as a means to some further end. As support for his analysis Aristotle appeals to what he sees as the historical fact that it is only when man's economic needs are secured that he begins to seek knowledge for its own sake.

Given the triviality of some of the aporias Aristotle has in mind, it might seem that a further condition would be required to distinguish knowledge from the specific kind of knowledge called *sophia* for which philosophy is the *philia*. Such a further condition is stipulated. It is that the knowledge sought should be of the universal, knowledge ultimately of the first cause. This condition is compatible with philosophy's beginning with perplexity over 'obvious difficulties', that is to say, over aporias which can be explained away by the discovery of causes that are not far to seek. For these difficulties and their removal may be on the way to knowledge of first causes, divine science, the science of being. So we have the picture of a teleological progress of inquiry from proximal causes to the ultimate cause, a cause being for Aristotle one of the four kinds distinguished in the *Physics*. This suggests an Aristotelian parallel to Heidegger's assertion that existing as *Dasein* is to be already concerned with being. If there is a parallel here it implies that already in our concern with the problem of earning our daily bread we are taking our first steps in philosophy. This would be an awkward implication for Aristotle at least, because it would endanger his thesis that philosophy is not concerned with production, that it is *ou poiētikē*. How could this danger be met?

It could be said that in his absorption in solving the problem of his biological survival man is only potentially a philosopher. However, this still clashes with Aristotle's thesis if the potentiality just mentioned means that man has already begun to philosophize, though only in an undeveloped way. On the other hand, if the potentiality is no more than a possibility, all we shall be saying is that concern with the immediate problems of survival and comfortable living is consistent with going on to become concerned with seeking wisdom for its own sake. Heidegger is not himself faced with the particular difficulty that confronts Aristotle, because he says that *Dasein*'s world is everyday only *zumeist*, that is not always, but only as a rule (SZ 370).[1] Although Heidegger is not himself giving a genetic account, what he says leaves room for anyone wishing to give one to say that there is philosophy as soon as there is Dasein. It is not only because his account is not historical (*historisch*) that Heidegger would refrain from saying that where there is Dasein there is philosophy. If philosophy is an articulated theory of being, an ontology, Dasein's pre-theoretical concern with being does not make him a philosopher (SZ 12). Of course there is an Aristotelian parallel to this distinction, and it is this that provides him with the best defence against the above-mentioned danger.

We shall come back to the German Greeks and to what they say about the saying that philosophy begins in wonder. Meanwhile, what else can we learn from what the Greek Greeks say relative to this, for instance on the idea that philosophy seeks knowledge for its own sake?

This idea sets philosophy apart from sophistry. But does it not let into philosophy the solving of crossword puzzles, provided the solutions are not sought for the prize or self-conceit that may follow? Not if solving crossword puzzles and suchlike activities are indulged in to pass the time or to relax so that, as Aquinas puts it in the *Summa contra Gentiles*, 'we may afterwards become more fit for studious occupations' (III, XXVI).

As for the collection of facts, even facts about natural causes, just for the sake of having them in one's collection, we shall post-pone mention of one of the reasons why this is not philosophy. A reason that may be mentioned forthwith is that in so far as philos-ophy is what Aristotle means by metaphysics it comes after physics conceptually, whether or not it is called metaphysics on that account or on grounds of bibliographical history. Philosophy is not only a search after *epistēmē* and where possible *nous* concerning causes, but also that pursuit given direction by the hope of wisdom, *sophia*, knowledge of the most honourable kind. This ultimate aim is what impresses the stamp of philosophy on the humbler questions with which it begins. It is important that this be remembered as we pursue the question what Aristotle means when he says that philosophy begins in *thaumazein*. Does it go without saying that a hierarchical structure analogous to this must be kept in mind when we ask what Plato means when he says this?

On Aristotle's conception of philosophy, but not on Plato's, philosophy keeps its roots in 'the things we see'. But is it true to say that the *thaumazein* from which philosophy springs according to the *Theaetetus* has, at the beginning, its roots in the Forms? The following passage of the *Parmenides* could be taken to suggest that the answers to both of these questions must be No:

if anyone sets out to show about things of this kind – sticks and stones, and so on – that the same thing is many and one, we shall say that what he is proving is that *something* is many and one, not that Unity is many

176

or that Plurality is one; he is not telling us anything wonderful, but only what we should all admit. But, as I said just now, if he begins by distinguishing the Forms apart by themselves – Likeness, for instance, and Unlikeness, Plurality and Unity, Rest and Motion, and all the rest – and then shows that these Forms among themselves can be combined with, or separated from, one another, then, Zeno, I should be filled with wonder. I am sure you have dealt with this subject very forcibly; but, as I say, my astonishment would be much greater if anyone could show that these same perplexities are everywhere involved in the Forms themselves – among the objects we apprehend in reflection, just as you and Parmenides have shown them to be involved in the things we see. (129c–e)

From this it would appear, perhaps to our astonishment, that Platonic *thaumazein* is of less noble birth than the Aristotelian kind. The down-to-earth Artistotle would seem to allow for *thaumazein* over the ultimate causes of things, whereas the otherworldly Plato would seem to limit *thaumazein* to our questioning about 'the things we see'. Is Plato not saying through Socrates that we can be astonished at the idea that a stone can be both many and one, but not astonished at the idea that Unity is many? On closer inspection we find that this is not what Plato is saying. Since he goes on to tell Zeno that he would be astonished if it could be shown that the Form Unity taken separately from the counted things was also many, he cannot be contending that the Forms are not appropriate objects of wonder. Someone who had not made the distinction he has just made between the Forms considered in themselves and the particular things in which they are unsubstantiated might well be astonished at the propositions Zeno advances. What Plato is denying is that such *propositions about* the Forms considered in themselves can be proper objects for *aporetic* wonder when we understand their logical and ontological status. Aporetic wonder about such propositions would suffice to show that we had not understood this status.

Once we do understand the status of the Forms and the ultimate causes, is wonder at an end? Is *thaumazein* only the beginning of philosophy? Is its *telos* its own end, the end of philosophy? All we have shown so far is that neither Aristotle nor Plato denies that there may be a place for *thaumazein* when aporetic, interrogative, *thaumazein* is superseded. But do they argue positively that a kind of *thaumazein* may persist? Or do they show any signs of recognizing that aporetic *thaumazein* has a positive side that may be capable of surviving the solution of a problem, surviving into *sophia*? Interpretable as such a sign perhaps is the suspicion Aristotle evinces that it may be blasphemous to entertain the thought that one might attain *sophia*, or at least that others might think so, this 'might' becoming articulated a few sentences later into the disjunction that only god can possess *sophia* or, at any rate, god will possess it in a degree above others. Knowledge of the highest kind of the final cause may be beyond human capacity. This is something Aristotle admits, speaking for himself. But it is only speaking as a mouthpiece for the poets that he brings in the idea that divine wrath might descend on him who supposed *sophia* to be within his reach. And there is no explicit statement by Aristotle that the separate and permanent objects of the divine science, if not of mathematics and physics, may be objects of such *bewunderung* as Kant confesses to experiencing when he contemplates the starry sky above. Plato too avoids the word *thaumazein* when he speaks of the separate and unchanging Forms. Also when he refers to the gods, as at *Republic* 379, though there, as in Aristotle, the language of the traditional myths is used self-consciously. Perhaps this is a clue. The myths have lost their hold. Invocation of a god has become a mere stylistic device, and the god a *deus ex machina* before which the only sort of wonder possible is of the lowly sort caused by the puppeteer. That this is so for Aristotle is borne out by his remark that 'even the lover of myth is in a sense a lover of wisdom, for the myth is composed of wonders'. Here still the wonder is provoked by something one cannot explain, an aporia before which one has the feeling of being trapped, of there being no way out, no way out of the flybottle.

Interrogative or aporetic wonderment is based then on a sense of one's ignorance, where the ignorance is not any absence of knowledge, but an ignorance that challenges us to dispel it because it is presented dramatically in the form of an apparent contradiction or dilemma and is therefore difficult to live with. The object of the wonder is incredible. The stupidity we feel before it is not the stupor of dull indifference that Hegel speaks of when in connection with Aristotle's dictum that philosophy begins in *thaumazein* – for which Hegel's word here is *Verwunderung* – he writes in the *Philosophy of History*: 'the Greek spirit was excited to wonder at the natural in nature. It does not maintain the position of stupid (*stumpf*) indifference to it as something existing (*als zu einem Gegebenen*)' (PH 234). This *Stumpfheit* is not that of being stumped for an answer. It is not just failure to hear an answer. It is failure to hear a question. Ignorance of ignorance, alogicality, it is below the threshold of mental laziness, since laziness does rise to the level of perceiving that there is something that calls to be done, for instance a question that demands to be answered. But the stupidity of *Stumpfheit* is unquestioning. However, it is neither of this, the blank look, nor of the stupidity of interrogative *thaumazein*, the puzzled look, that Aquinas can be speaking when in his comments on Aristotle's dictum he writes in the *Summa Theologiae*:

What laziness is to outward behaviour, amazement and stupor are to mental effort.
  One who is amazed refrains for the moment to pass judgement on the object of his amazement, fearing failure. But he does look towards the future. When stupor envelops a man he is afraid either to form a judgement here and now or to look towards the future. Hence amazement is a source of philosophizing, whereas stupor is an obstacle to philosophical thinking. (1a2ae, 41, 4)

The stupor of which Aquinas speaks here is not the stupor of dull unquestioning indifference. The latter is consciousness of a state of affairs, and it has an intentional object, therefore it is not so thick a stupidity regarding something that nothing regarding that thing enters our ken. The thing is not something of which we are unconscious. But our consciousness of it does not include consciousness of any question it poses. The stupor of which Aquinas speaks has an intentional object, but the person's attitude to it is not one of indifference. He sees that a question is raised, but he is afraid to even seek an answer. He buries his head in the sand. He wants nothing to do with the question, hoping that if he diverts his eyes from it, the question will go away. Aquinas therefore rightly distinguishes this *stupor* from what he calls *admiratio*, concluding that wonder or amazement motivates philosophy whereas stupidity is an impediment to it. It will be recalled that our proposal in the present essay is that there is a kind of *stupor* that is intrinsic to *thaumazein*. We are pursuing the idea that 'wonder' is a wonderful word in something like the sense of the 'speculative' word '*Aufhebung*' that delights Hegel because it incorporates opposite meanings, and like the sense of the antithetical words Karl Abel claims he comes upon in Ancient Egyptian, words that he finds as astonishing (*erstaunlich*, he says) as one would find it if 'in Berlin the word "light" was used to mean both "light' and "darkness" '.[2] We are wondering whether this may be how it is with at least one of the varieties of *thaumazein*. So far we have been addressing ourselves mainly to its dark side. Now we must turn towards the light, return to the question whether astonishment can be sustained in wisdom.

II

Can astonishment be sustained when we issue from the cave into the light? As we emerge the light blinds us. This confusion by bedazzlement of which Plato speaks at *Republic* 515 f is the counterpart of the confusion by dizziness that comes over us as we make the passage from seeming understanding (*Schein*) into the darkness of aporetic wonder. As we move into the light of real understanding the object of our vision is, in the words of the hymn, hidden by the splendour of light. Our eyes cannot accommodate themselves to its brilliance any more than our darkness can comprehend aporia. Aporetic astonishment persists as long as there is aporia, lack of passage; as long as the puppeteer or geometer has not administered the aperient. Paradoxically the laxative that is a *pharmakon*-remedy is at the same time a *pharmakon*-poison in so far as aporetic astonishment is a healthy state compared with blank indifference.[3] It is the very source from which philosophical inquiry springs, the springboard of its *Satz vom Grund*, the point from which its spirit spirits. Astonishment is the *pathos* of philosophy, as Plato says: as Heidegger says, its *Stimmung* (WP 79), the very timbre of philosophy's voice.

This being so, how can we contemplate with equanimity the prospect that contemplative wisdom promises or threatens? How can we face its apparent lack of dis-ease? We shall perhaps be happy with the satisfaction of *sophia* if we ever reach it. Who knows? One thing we do know here and now is that we do not value highly the satisfaction of pre-aporetic indifference. How then can we with consistency value highly here and now post-aporetic bliss conceived as satisfaction of all our needs, including the need for philosophy? Can Paradise be paradise unless it continues to have something like the shortcomings of existence in Purgatory? It is not simply that heaven threatens or promises to be uneventful and *ennuyeux*. Presumably the gods are not bored up there on Olympus. Nor are we bored at the peaks of, say, aesthetic ecstasy. But would we not here and now prize their and our experience less if it lacked a sense of wonder? Theologians at least since Heraclitus have recognized this. It is recognized in what one reads about the experience of mystical union being at the same time an experience of feeling apart: feeling oneself apart and feeling oneself a part. It is manifest in the apartness that is a part of love, in what is wanting in love, as this is recognized by Levinas when he writes:

Intersubjectivity is not simply the application of the category of multiplicity to the domain of the mind. It is brought about by Eros, where in the proximity of the other the distance is wholly maintained, a distance whose pathos is made up of this proximity and this duality of beings. What is presented as the failure of communication in love in fact constitutes the positive character of the relationship; this absence of the other is precisely his presence qua other. The other is the neighbour – but proximity is not a degradation of, or a stage on the way to, fusion. (EE 95 [163])

As well as this Judaic tradition there is a fusionist tradition. To this latter Hegel belongs. This is the tradition of belonging and of longing that ends in belonging, the tradition announced in Hegel's remarks on the way wonder is the origin of philosophy among the Greeks. The Greeks, as Hegel reads them, are a home-loving lot. Home-builders and cultivators of *Heimatlichkeit*, their gods are really all gods of the hearth.

It is this veritable homeliness, or, more accurately, in the spirit of homeliness, in this spirit of ideally being-at-home-with-themselves in their physical, corporate, legal, moral and political existence; it is in the beauty and the freedom of their character in history, making what they are to be also a sort of Mnemosyne with them, that the kernel of thinking liberty rests; and hence it was requisite that philosophy should arise among them. Philosophy is being at home with self, just like the homeliness of the Greek; it is man's being at home in his mind, at home with himself. If we are at home with the Greeks, we must be at home more particularly in their philosophy. (LHP 151–2)

And in a passage of the *Philosophy of History* from which we have already had occasion to cite, Hegel says:

According to Aristotle's dictum, that philosophy proceeds from wonder, the Greek view of nature also proceeds from wonder of this kind. Not that in their experience spirit meets something extraordinary which it compares with the common order of things; for the intelligent view of a regular course of nature, and the references of phenomena to that standard, do not yet present themselves; but the Greek spirit was excited to wonder at the *natural* in nature. It does not maintain the position of stupid indifference to it as something existing (*als zu einem Gegebenen*), but regards it as something in the first instance foreign, in which, however, it has a presentiment of confidence, and the belief that it bears something within it which is friendly to the human spirit, and to which it may be permitted to sustain a positive relation. This *wonder* and this *presentiment* are here the fundamental categories. (PH 234)

Here we are at the beginning of a history in which the foreign gradually becomes the friend, the *Fremd* the *Freund*, to the point that in the end the distance between philosophy and the *sophia* it loves vanishes away completely in an infinite consciousness of its loved self, Hegel's version of Aristotle's *noēseōs noēsis*.

Philosophy proper commences in the West. It is in the West that this freedom of self-consciousness first comes forth; the natural consciousness, and likewise mind disappear into themselves. In the brightness of the East the individual disappears; the light first becomes in the West the flash of thought which strikes within itself, and from thence creates its world out of itself. The blessedness of the West is thus so determined that in it the subject as such endures and continues in the substantial; the individual mind grasps its being as universal, but universality is just this relation to itself. This being at home with self . . . . (LHP 99)

Compare this view of the history of philosophy with the history as Heidegger sees it issuing from the same source, the *thaumazein* experienced by Heraclitus and Parmenides. We quoted earlier Aristotle's statement that 'all men begin by wondering that things are as they are'. That is also how Hegel sees the beginning. He sees both the end and the beginning in an Aristotelian light. And that, in Heidegger's view, is how philosophy tends to see itself. But this is only one aspect of philosophy as Heidegger describes it in his lecture 'What is Philosophy?'. To bring to thought philosophy's hidden side, wonder that things are as they are must be supplemented by wonder that things are. That is what astonished Heraclitus and Parmenides in their astonishment that things are as they are; The seven or seven million wonders of the world of which the poets sing are set within the context of the wonder of all wonders, *das Wunder aller Wunder, that* that which is *is* (EB 386 [W 307]). What Heidegger might at one time have called fundamental ontological wonder, the *thaumazein* of the thinking of being, prepares the way for another beginning in which man is not only the preserver of the unconcealment of beings but also the guardian of the openness of being (GP 190). No attempt will be made in the confines of this essay to interpret what Heidegger says at different stages of his work on the question how the tasks of the *Wahrer, Wächter* and *Wegbereiter* are related to those of the scientist and the poet understood in the wider and the narrower senses of *Dichter*,[4] to ask how far one is helpmeet of the other and how the wonder of the thinker bears upon ontic wonder, whether that of the *Dichter* who names the holy or that of the scientist whose wonder, although it is the wonder of the *se demander*, the demand for an explanation, may coexist with a wonder of a different kind: the wonder expressed by the zoologist who named the *sabella magnifica*, the *aranea mirabilis* and (with less Greek) the *thaumetopoea processionea*.[5] This last-named is the caterpillar to be seen trailing across the Mediterranean countryside head-to-tail in processions up to eight metres long. The accounts that Fabre and more recent naturalists have given of the behaviour of these creatures are studded with words like 'remarkable', 'singular', 'puzzling', 'extraordinary'. However, in the final section of this chapter it will be relevant to remember that it is not only the puzzling and extraordinary that the natural scientist explains.

III

In this final section we apply to questions raised in the first and second some of the distinctions Heidegger makes in the *Grundfragen der Philosophie*, his most detailed treatment yet published of the saying that philosophy begins in *thaumazein*. So far we have rung the changes on the various ways this Greek word may be translated into Latin, German, French and English. Within limits that I shall not attempt to make precise the terms are often inter-changeable. There is therefore some arbitrariness in the choice of terms Heidegger uses to indicate the outlines of a thaumatology, and this *Spielraum* is allowed for in translating those terms into English.

Heidegger distinguishes *Verwunderung*, *Bewunderung*, *Bestaunen* and *Er-staunen* with a hyphen, the unhyphenated *Erstaunen* being employed usually to range over all four of the notions he distinguishes. The first three he regards as the ordinary terms for the unordinary. He examines what they mean with a view to eliciting clues to the meaning of *Er-staunen*, ontological *thaumazein*.

Verwunderung (and *Sichwundern*) is marvel at what one finds surprising, remarkable, what one cannot explain and does not want to have explained. It is a manifestation of a craving for novelty, a cult of the unusual and unique that turns its back on the ordinary.

Bewunderung is admiration. What is admired, like the object of marvel, is the singular as contrasted with the ordinary, but, in contrast to the marvellous, what is admired is *recognized as* unusual. Instead of being swept off his feet by it, the admirer stands back and appraises it. To the extent that he gives it marks he achieves a kind of mastery, however lacking he may be in the competence being judged.

Bestaunen, amazement, like marvelling, recoils before its object. But it does not evaluate or patronize. Admiration, however wanting in the skill or talent it assesses, assumes it has critical gifts of its own that confer authority to evaluate. Amazement does not grade. Furthermore, what amazes me does not stand out only as unordi-nary. By comparison with the ordinary it is extraordinary, so surpassingly extraordinary that the very idea of putting a value upon it would never enter my head.

In all three cases so far considered there is some particular thing that causes surprise. And all three involve comparison of the ordinary with what is out of the ordinary to a lesser or greater degree. *Er-staunen*, ontological astonishment or wonder, on the other hand, is wonder at the most ordinary itself. The utterly ordinary in everything strikes us as utterly unordinary. The most commonplace overwhelms us. Like the commonplace where and of which, in the anecdote told by Aristotle and more than once retold by Heidegger, Heraclitus says to his slightly disappointed visitors 'The gods are also even here (*kai entautha*)', here being the humble kitchen where the daily bread is baked. The gods are everywhere. There is no place that they do not haunt. As Aristotle in his way puts it, as he is about to tell this story in *De Partibus Animalium, en pasi gar tois phusikois enesti ti thaumaston*, 'every realm of nature is wonderful' (645a 17). As Heidegger in his way puts it, wonder knows no exit from the unordinariness of the most ordinary. There is no escaping it, because the attempt to escape by explaining the unfamiliar presents us with something familiar in its stead which however is again utterly strange. Nor does ontological wonder know any way in. Whichever way it turns, it is always already faced by the superlative unordinariness of the ordinary. There is no transition to or from wisdom here, since the wisdom of ontological wonder is an ontological between, a *Zwischen*. It is a passage, and it is only in this moment of passage, *poros*, from the most ordinary to the most unordinary that ordinariness and unordinariness as such are highlighted. In that moment dawns the wonder that and what the totality of being is, the wonder of what elsewhere Heidegger calls the ontological difference and here the *Spielräum* of the between of the being of beings. Here too in the *Grundfragen der Philosophie* we come upon the stunning statement that our wonder before the totality of what is is wonder '*dass es ist* und das ist, *was es ist*', that it is, *and that is to say*, what it is (GP 174). This points up strikingly the betweenness of the ontological difference and the near-farness of the *Denker* and the *Dichter* who, in one of the images Heidegger borrows from Hölderlin, 'dwell near to one another on mountains farthest apart' (EB- 392 [W 312]). There is a complicity between them, but also an abyss. How that can be is the mystery of this *und das ist*.

Returning to the Greeks, Heidegger quotes from the first chorus of Sophocles' *Antigone*:

> *There is much that is strange, but nothing*
> *that surpasses man in strangeness.*
> *He sets sail on the frothing waters*
> *amid the south winds of winter*
> *tacking through the mountains*
> *and furious chasms of the waves.*

'Here', Heidegger says, ' "sea" is said as though for the first time'

(IM 129 [EM 117]). The dialogue between thinking and poetry is the dialogue of the between. The between 'is' man's transitivity before the totality of what is, his displacement, *dépaysement*, before the question of the ground, the wonder at there not being nothing. Hegel too speaks of the totality:

The position of hearkening surmise, of attentive eagerness to catch the meaning of nature, is indicated to us in the comprehensive idea of *Pan*. To the Greeks Pan did not represent the *objective* Whole, but the indefinite that is at the same time connected with the moment of *subjectivity*; he is the inexplicable frisson (*der allgemeine Schauer*) that comes over us in the silence of the forests; he was, therefore, especially worshipped in sylvan Arcadia (a 'panic terror' is the common expression for a groundless terror). (PH 235)

It would be precipitate to identify this *grundlose Schreck* with the objectless *Angst im Sinne des Schreckens* of the Postscript to 'What is Metaphysics?' (EB 392 [W 312]), notwithstanding that Heidegger there and Hegel here are describing a stance with regard to totality. For the meaning of nature of which the Greeks have a presentiment will turn out to be the overcoming of terror and outlandishness when the Greek spirit finally comes home. When at last it is fully *bei sich* in its *Wohnung* everything about it is *gewöhnlich*. The ordinary has no trace of the extraordinary.

   Heidegger's *Heimatlichkeit* is otherwise, as is his reading of the Greeks. Provoked by his reading of *Antigone*, a work that gropes in vain for a way out from the tragic aporia of the between of the *heimlich* and *unheimlich*, he writes, referring to the violence (*deinon, Gewalt*) with which man is enabled to break open new paths, as when the *Dichter* for the first time discloses the sea *as* sea, the earth *as* earth, the animal *as* animal (IM 132 [EM 120]):

Immediately and irremediably, all violence comes to nothing in the face of *one* thing alone (*Nur an* einem *scheitert alle Gewalt-tätigkeit unmittelbar*). That is death. It is a term beyond all termination, a limit beyond all limits. Here there is no breaking out or breaking up, no capture or subjugation. But this strange thing (*Un-heimliche*) that banishes us once and for all from everything in which we are at home is no particular event that must be named among others because it too ultimately happens. It is not only when he comes to die, but always and essentially that man is without exit in the face of death. In so far as man *is*, he stands in the exitlessness of death. Thus being-there (*Da-sein*) is the very happening of strangeness. (IM 133 [EM 121])

Strangeness, *das Unheimliche*, on Hegel's interpretation, is alien to man's final home. On Heidegger's interpretation it is the very finality of man's being at home. No wonder that Freud, in his paper 'Das Unheimliche', like Karl Abel before him, exclaims that '*heimlich* is a word the meaning of which develops towards an ambivalence, until it finally coincides with its opposite, *unheimlich*'.[6] And no wonder, therefore, that we should find that 'wonder' is a word that points in opposite directions. Ontological wonder is wonder over the between of the *heimlich-unheimlich*, over the *entre* of the exit, death's entrance.

Ontological wonder is a *Grundbestimmung*. There are at least two ways in which we can get wrong what Heidegger means by this. In *Vom Wesen des Grundes* he warns that *Begründung*, founding, 'should be understood, not in the narrow and derivative sense of proving ontical or theoretical propositions, but in a basically primordial sense. Founding is *that which makes the question "Why?" possible in the first place*' (ER 113 [W 168]). The *Bestimmung* is a ground base attunement of temper and disposition that is a dis-position in that it is a displacement of man from the condition in which he sees things in an everyday light to the condition in which he sees this seeing as blindness, now that it is disclosed to his astonishment that everything as thing is *phusis*, and that *phusis* is *a-lētheia*, unconcealment, as Heraclitus saw at the very same time that he saw that *phusis* loves to conceal itself, at the first beginning of philosophy and when history first began. The first beginning of philosophy and history (*Geschichte*) is the happening (*Geschechen*) of word, work and deed. It is incalculably rare, *das Seltenste* (GP 170). *Geschichte ist selten* (EHD 76). The astonishing passage between the ordinariness of beings and the unordinariness of the being of beings is utterly and unutterably unordinary. It is therefore inexplicable, whether in terms of the causality of beings outside man or of the agency of man himself. The *Grundbestimmung* is not a psychological *Erlebnis*, a passion undergone, nor is it an act of will. It is a way in which one deports oneself. It is an *Erfahrung*, a displacement. Not a mental state in which he luxuriates, but a luxation beset with risks: a *gefährliche Erfahrung*.

In posing the *Grundfrage der Philosophie*, 'Why are there beings, not rather nothing?' (GP 2; EB 380 [W 122]) man finds himself disposed toward another beginning of philosophy. This disposition is a being possessed by a *question-savoir*[7] which recognizes that first philosophy is more and more fundamental than it is conceived to be by Plato and Aristotle, who begin to bring the first beginning to its end when the latter conceives philosophy as the quest for the most universal causes underlying the secondary causes of physical phenomena, and the former, through his doctrine of ideas, prepares the way for a conception of truth as adequacy and correctness and conceives *logos* as assertion that can be repeated and passed on, no longer as gathering, *legein, sammeln*.

Before Plato and Aristotle, Parmenides, with whom, as Hegel says, philosophy proper begins (LHP 254), is wonder-struck at the belonging together of gathering thinking with being that at once makes possible inquiries that demand answers and runs the risk of being forgotten on account of such inquiries. Following Aristotle, Alexander of Aphrodisias speaks more truly than he knows when, in his commentary on Aristotle's dictum that philosophy begins in *thaumazein*, he says that wonder precedes inquiry.[8] But meanwhile *technē*, which at the first beginning is neither passive suffering nor active exercise of will, but receptivity toward *phusis*, a disposition of disponibility, *Bereitschaft* (GP 170), is on the way to becoming technical control, and the 'for its own sake' which Aristotle identifies as a mark of philosophy comes to be interpreted as theory opposed to practice, instead of what that distinction presupposes. Paradoxically, the conception of philosophy as quest for wisdom understood as knowledge of the first cause or Ideas imposes upon philosophy the means-end structure of *praxis*, so that Plato sometimes gets perilously close to regarding philosophy as a machine for producing statesmen. Paradoxically too, this peril is what keeps open the possibility of philosophy. If philosophy is the desire for the possession of knowledge, if its *philia* is represented as the *Symposium* represents erotic desire, then the attainment of *sophia* will be the attainment of a *petite mort*, the substitution of indifference for wonder. If, however, *philia* is not a variety of *epithumia*, if it is being possessed by love that does not seek to possess, but to let being be, wonder will belong to *sophia* as to the beginning of philosophy. The *archē* of philosophy which is *thaumazein* is not just a beginning that is left behind. It remains its ground and guide.

Das Erstaunen trägt und durchherrscht die Philosophie (WP 80). The lecture in which Heidegger says this was delivered in 1955. In it, as in the lectures entitled *Grundfragen der Philosophie* given in 1937–8, the word 'philosophy' covers metaphysics and what will be called essential thinking in the 'Letter on Humanism' of 1946 and 'The End of Philosophy and the Task of Thinking', a lecture given in 1964. However, what he earlier calls coming philosophy, *die künftige Philosophie* (GP 2), and what he later calls the thinking of another beginning is a thinking of and a thinking on the first beginning, a remembrance of it:

The preparatory thinking in question does not wish and is not able to predict the future. It only attempts to say something to the present which was already said a long time ago precisely at the beginning of philosophy and for that beginning, but has not been explicitly thought. (BW 379 [SD 67])

What was said at the first beginning but not explicitly thought (*nicht eigens gedacht*) is what Parmenides and Heraclitus named *alētheia*, unconcealment. They also experienced *lēthe*, oblivion, as a dispensation of concealment (EGT 108 [VA 264]). But they did not think this explicitly as such, and so did not think explicitly what Heidegger calls *Lichtung*, opening or clearing, as of a forest: the complicity of concealing and unconcealing, which makes possible the opposition and play of darkness and light in which things appear and disappear; which makes possible the language of Platonic and indeed all metaphysics (BW 386 [SD 74]). To stress the irresolubility of this complicity Heidegger says, not without poignancy, that self-concealing belongs to light. It is not a simple supplement, not *eine blosse Zugabe* (BW 390 [SD 78]). It is because concealment, *lēthe*, is a syncope at the very heart of unconcealing, *a-lētheia*, that Heidegger says that philosophy understood as love toward wisdom cannot be superseded by *sophia* understood as absolute knowing (BW 242 [W 3364]). If indeed there is necessary concealment, then philosophy, *zukünftige* philosophy and essential ·thinking will never cease being underway. This means that in principle wonder will never cease, even though its aspect as awe before the stupendous may from time to time give way to its aspect as stupor so dark that it forgets its own oblivion. The very interplay of concealment and unconcealment will be 'what is ever and again worthy of wonder and is preserved in its worth by wonder' (EGT 121 [VA 279–280]).

But if what this *denkende Er-staunen* wonders at is the ground of the distinction between darkness and light, must not our own characterization of wonder be itself replaced by one that is no longer framed in the language of chiaroscuro, the language of Platonism, the language of metaphysics? Can this be done? Can Heidegger himself describe the *Zwischen* of concealing and unconcealing except by the light, and the shadow, cast by the idea of the interplay of darkness and light? That we do not yet see how this can be done is perhaps what Heidegger is wishing to bring out by employing the ambiguous word *Lichtung*. But whether or not thinking at the beginning of another beginning can accomplish the task of thinking beyond the language of the end of the first beginning, it will be, as we have seen, a thinking on that first beginning. It will therefore inherit the *thaumazein* which is the only beginning of philosophy.

Notes

1 The following abbreviations are used in the text:

BW *Martin Heidegger: Basic Writings*, ed. D. F. Krell, New York, Harper & Row, 1977; London, Routledge & Kegan Paul, 1978.

EB Martin Heidegger, *Existence and Being*, trans. R. F. C. Hull and A. Crick, London, Vision, 1949.

EE Emmanuel Levinas, *Existence and Existents*, trans. Alphonso Lingis, The Hague, Nijhoff, 1978 [*De l'existence à l'existant*, Paris, Vrin, 1981].

EGT Martin Heidegger, *Early Greek Thinking*, trans. D. F. Krell and F. A. Capuzzi, New York, Harper & Row, 1975.

EHD Martin Heidegger, *Erläuterungen zu Hölderlins Dichtung*, Frankfurt am Main, Klosterman 1981.

EM Martin Heidegger, *Einführung in die Metaphysik*, Tübingen, Niemeyer, 1953.

ER Martin Heidegger, *The Essence of Reasons*, trans. T. Malick, Evanston, Northwestern University Press, 1969.

GP Martin Heidegger, *Grundfragen der Philosophie*, Frankfurt am Main, Klostermann, 1984.

IM Martin Heidegger, *Introduction to Metaphysics*, trans. R. Manheim, New York, Doubleday, 1961.

LHP G. W. F. Hegel, *Lectures on the History of Philosophy*, vol. I, trans. E. S. Haldane, London, Kegan Paul, Trench, Trübner & Co., 1892.

PH   G. W. F. Hegel, *The Philosophy of History*, trans. J. Sibree, New York, Dover, 1956.

SD   Martin Heidegger, *Zur Sache des Denkens*, Tübingen, Niemeyer, 1969.

SZ   Martin Heidegger, *Sein und Zeit*, Tübingen, Niemeyer, 1967; *Being and Time*, trans. J. Macquarrie and J. Robinson, Oxford, Blackwell, 1962.

VA   Martin Heidegger, *Vorträge und Aufsätze*, Pfullingen, Neske, 1954.

W   Martin Heidegger, *Wegmarken*, Frankfurt am Main, Klostermann, 1976.

WP   Martin Heidegger, *What is Philosophy?*, trans. E. Kluback and Jean T. Wilde, London, Vision, 1958.

2 Sigmund Freud, *Standard Edition of the Complete Psychological Works*, London, Hogarth Press and the Institute for Psycho-analysis, vol. XI, 1957, pp. 154 ff.

3 See Jacques Derrida, 'Plato's pharmacy', in *Dissemination*, trans. Barbara Johnson, Chicago, University of Chicago Press (London, Athlone Press), 1981.

4 See especially Robert Bernasconi, *The Question of Language in Heidegger's History of Being*, New Jersey, Humanities Press (London, Macmillan), 1984.

5 For a discerning treatment of the question whether scientific explanation reduces the scope for wonder, as well as of other topics related to the ones raised in the present essay, see R. W. Hepburn, 'Wonder', *The Aristotelian Society Supplementary Volume* LIV, 1980, pp. 1–23.

6 Freud, *Standard Edition*, vol. XVII, 1955, pp. 218 ff. See also John Llewelyn, *Derrida on the Threshold of Sense*, London, Macmillan, 1986, pp. 94 ff.

7 Maurice Merleau-Ponty, *Le Visible et l'invisible*, Paris, Gallimard, 1964, p. 171.

8 Alexander of Aphrodisias, *In Aristotelis Metaphysica Commentaria*, ed. M. Hayduck, Berlin, Reimer, 1891, pp. 15–16.

· 9 ·

Entertaining arguments: Terence Adelphoe*

JOHN HENDERSON

It is easy to see that we are living in a time of rapid and radical social change. (Terence)*

1 'Postquam "since"; causal' (Martin on Ad. 1)*

Pas d'au-delà! One more step back, I think, to consider what we may learn to learn of what obstructs our moving ahead, contests a future beyond the aporiai we have learned to recognize. I shall suggest here some of the ways in which Terence's last play, the *Adelphoe*, has collaborated with certain histories of reading – which are themselves folded into the play's text – to shrug off or cancel its productivity as a text. A sketch, then, the outline of which is indicated in my title: serio-comic problems in the valorization of and refusal to valorize textual pedagogy.

2 Ludus*

In school,* a characteristic performance from Roman boys learning to be Romans, *by* learning, need I say, to be Roman boys: 'older boys' (*adulescentes*), learning to learn. Sent off to acquire pronunciation, delivery, personation with the professional (the actor, *comoedus*); to act out emotions, perform roles, regulate entry into social discourse. . . . via the correct material, namely bits of

Menander and the Roman Menander, Terence (Bonner 215 f, 261). And back in school, to learn narration, characterization and in a word *ars* from instruction and exercise in replay and re-reading of chosen scenes. Class learns 'polite letters' – bons mots and *sententiae*, purity of style and style as purity, *Latinitas*. 'Terence was important in education. Boys were made to read him for his Latinity and his moral sentiments' (Sandbach (1977) 150). An imperial system of instruction, run by the rhetor *in loco parentis*. Cutting up, ingestion of culture as a course in 'reading'. It's important to our Roman literature that Terence was conserved in this educational scene (the comedies of Plautus and Terence are the only texts to survive from before Cicero's maturity across what is now a century of lacuna). Was it important to the production of Romans that Terence's texts be utilized in teaching in ways that precluded learning from them what they teach about teaching? Perhaps their design already predestined them for this role – the naturalization of a society's tacit covenant about what it has determined not to know. In the mythic scene of Roman education – 'primal' education – Father stands in as teacher of his son and the son will (come to) acknowledge Father as Teacher; they must both learn the *praecepta paterna*, the son-now-Father, the Father-to-be who is now son (Bonner 10 f, 16 f). The school texts which stood-in-for this mythological pater commonly staged just such scenes (e.g. Plautus *Most.* 120 f, *Trin.* 275 f . . .). And the *Adelphoe* may be their *locus classicus*: discussion of 'What kind of father . . .' would lead axiomatically to this play (e.g. Cic. *Pro Cael.* 37 f with *Ad.* 120 f, a speech/script in court which also poses 'What sort of brother (and sister)' and 'Can defending counsel adopt prosecutor and defendant', cf. Geffcken 23; and Horace's father is fashioned from Terence, *Serm.* 1 4 105 f with *Ad.* 412 f, cf. Leach; Duret; Cic. *De Sen.* 65 for Cato on the peripeteia of *Ad.*, Quintilian 11 1 39 on the *Terentianus pater* . . .).

The playscript, though, must remain highly duplicitous material for instruction in the positions of instructor and instructed; the comedy, perhaps, doubly so, '*Adelphoe*' itself as title, a pointer to the shifting positionality which is constitutive of the paternal scene; for in this play Fathers are Brothers and Sons are Brothers, the double re-doubled. Back in school do sons learn that their fathers aren't sure of their position, must learn to be fathers? It's not on the syllabus. . . . But the valorization of the drama is a precarious mytho-logical business, anyway, which calls for the firmest management. As the text is tooled into existence and then parcelled up in an envelope of assurances that it is already read, there arises a phenomenon of self-pronounced poetic art, a classic of national culture, a masterpiece of literature, 'the most read and studied Latin poet after Virgil' (Hunter 8). Thus Terence as prey to those routines of mastery – his text treated as pure linguistic object, *the* instance of linguistic range as the decisive constituent of cultural purity; his subtly inflected verse a halo sanctifying doxa; a paradigmatic endorsement of expressivity working on the maxim as the gentleman's 'wisdom'. . . . The lessons of Terence as teaching-text concern the projection of a 'modesty' on to 'culture', an extremely controlled model of restraint, the classic classics. (A useful outline in Duckworth's Index s.v. Terence 497 f, e.g. 'avoids . . . eliminates . . . few . . . seldom . . . lacks . . . not interested in . . . omits . . . lacking in . . . rare in . . .').

3 *In comoediis elegantia et quidam uelut 'αττιχισμός; inueniri potest* (QUINT. 1 8 8)*

It is to be emphasized that the modern emergence of western critical theory through the gaps in standard close-reading techniques, the palimpsestic recovery of critical practice from practical criticism, presents schemata for writing about texts which are without significant parallel in the institutions of Graeco-Roman Antiquity. We may nevertheless catch a containment of textuality within the classroom at work within the canonization of Terence in the interests of that familiar construct, the standard language. The hegemonic post-Hannibalic Rome became a world-state and called into existence a political entity, Italy, and its linguistic register Latinity; the chief site for this fabrication became education.

Terence's texts, and the *Adelphoe* in particular, have for various reasons been caught up in a traditional dispute over their alleged participation in a putative 'philhellenism'* surrounding their original production, usually labelled 'Scipionic' and conceived of as an attempt to introduce enculturation* to the public arena in Rome, an effort to found a Roman 'Atticism'. The terms of such a hypothesis are all contested, but in any case it is more important to recognize the continuing participation of these plays in the communal construction of *Romans*, the provision of a language which could speak 'civilization' as bearer of a new 'ruling' culture: Terence's characters all talk 'the same elegant, undifferentiated* conversational Latin' (Duckworth 331); the plays fashion the easy Latin of aristocratic Rome (1. Roman aristocrats) with 'a certain nobility' (Beare 112); 'the tongue of the future' (Salmon 122). While we should resist acceptance of linguistic unification* in Italy as an imperial 'solvent' of differences in any (other) field, we may just notice the structure of cultural imperialism at work here according to which the unbridgeable, unshaken incommensurabilities of local cultures *were* threatened by the centripetalism of the refusal of the Other as 'foreign' (Salmon 121 f). Common cause in the untranslatability of Greek culture could function as the axiom of the national language.

4 *Translativity*

It is the task of such prestige languages to appropriate for their nationalism an adequacy to conceptual mastery of the universe, a paradoxical task made (to seem?) feasible by a businesslike approach to sense: the Roman-centred universalism of Latin dealt with what was 'sound' in Greek culture, marking out a translatability* based on double criteria of 'success' in incorporating Greek systems of thought, value, expression and of 'practical' conformity with realities. . . . A language regulated through and through by translation, a constantly reformulating check on its performance: an educated Roman's Latin was in an important sense a 'good translation', 'a double interpretation, faithful both to the language/ message of the original' (Greek) 'and to the message-orienting cast of its own language' (Lewis in Graham 37).

To take first the 'in-put' side, Terence's creative authorship, the interpretant 'fidelity' has commonly figured in accounts which see his formalist purity as a cul de sac of transparency:

It is likely that this [his presentation of a constant, if unobvious, Hellenic milieu] is to be connected with an increasing demand in educated Roman circles for 'pure' reproductions of the classics of Greek culture. In this attempt to fossilize a genre whose life came from its contact with the changing demands of a popular audience we may perhaps see the seeds of the genre's decline. (Hunter 23)

Teleological 'shape' to the development of theatre at Rome – as from Plautus to Terence – would chime with other forms of transcendence and displacement of plebeian Roman culture in this period and would constitute a plausible enough scenario of supervenience by exemplary Art (cf. Bristol 118 f, 122). Here, 'translation' comes progressively to the fore as the force regulating production, the measure of that 'double interpretation' of faithfulness; translation invents Latinity in its measured difference (Lewis in Graham 33 f).

On the side of the 'event', Terentian impact, effect, the programme of moral platitudes – measured measure – which seems to survive the cultivation of translation as purism is customarily whittled away by interpreters to isolate at core a virtually mindless creator and creation, as moralism, didactic purpose, philosophical insight is shuffled into comic technique, theatrical genre, popular entertainment (cf. McBride 3 f). Though his plays did not, as we've seen, 'entertain' their audiences, they were finally but 'entertainment':

Terence has preferred to play the scene [the end of *Ad.*] strictly for its farcical possibilities. In doing so he has managed to offend the sensibilities of generations of critics, but in fact he is merely following a traditional preference,* which flourishes at all periods of ancient comedy, for humour over dramatic coherence. It would be attractive to interpret the remarks at the end of the *Adelphoe* as a victory for stern Roman morality over Greek laxness, but the very ambiguity of the ending should warn against any attempt to associate this play with a very specific social and historical context. (Hunter 108 f)

The operator 'That's Entertainment' 'reduces all cultural achievements indiscriminately to the same level of innocuousness' (Wood in Altman 63).

5 The cruelty of theatre

The play-text won't ever quite settle down to burying its self as performance, though, it won't profile as our 'classic', for example, without re-awakening its *mise-en-scène* within the *mos maiorum*. *Adelphoe* always stages again the burial of the Roman republican theatre; the same late Republican culture in which the long-ossified classic drama collapsed consecrated the era of Ennius and Cato, Plautus and Terence as its heyday, mythologized the age of the Scipios and post-Mannibalic conquest as its zenith and nostalgia; and built the imperial schooling system (Rawson (1985) 267 f). The prestige of the Ciceronian corpus as the memorial to Republican eloquence was a prime agent in this canonization, particularly in the form of the 'Scipionic circle' (Zetzel 173 f; Earl (1962) 480 f). *Adelphoe*'s display of its dimension of performance in and before its text makes it bearer of this legend, faithful or otherwise.

This, Terence's last play, comes like the rest framed by a firmly 'extra-dramatic prologue',* an 'outside' to the play's 'inside' which orients the play through its didąscalia, the production details of its 'first performance' which precede the text in editions of Terence; 'period piece', perhaps, but the classic script keeps ajar the question of its traditionality, its place within its theatre, within, precisely, a 'very specific socio-historical context'. The question of closure.

6 *Prologomena*

Postquam poeta sensit scripturam suam is the first verse of the play. A 'poet' 'wrote' *Adelphoe* – and this prologue. Author, authority, back of the script is that thrust, the intelligence of a design, of mind. Animating and motivating throughout: the prologue ends with *poetae ad scribendum . . .* in its last line, for a start. This move marks an originality which gives an account of itself in a characteristic shift from a popular to a re-vamped quasi-literary pedagogic theatre (cf. Bristol 118 f on Jonson's Prologues). The threat is to annul performance, the difference of actorial mediation, the material significance of the rendition. The problem of the dissembling actor, despised mimic as bearer of 'authority', is tamed as the play is commandeered by its 'poet': in Plautus 'the poet' and 'his writing' were not used of Plautus – but were used, in his prologues, of the Greek playwright whose play was being 'abused' by its incorporation in Latin farce.* In this respect, too, the relative homogenization* of the text's Latin co-operates with a battery of formal decisions – abandonment of lyrical effusion, selection of a narrow band of plays from a strongly compacted 'Menandrian school', restriction of numbers on stage and contact between the dramatis personae, concentration on purposive interchanges, intent soliloquy, a steadiness of progress and pace through the body of a play – to produce a background 'rule' of a directed 'point of view'. Our package of the 'comoedia' in its clutter of didascalia (classical scribes/scholars), Periocha (late antiquity précis), dramatis personae (modern restoration in the case of *Adelphoe*), and indeed the conventionality of the prologue to a classical drama itself should help us see this construction of the author and his work as scripted performance; for all that 'The *prologus* never acknowledges his own role as actor', he cannot stand 'totally outside the play that follows' (Slater 56). Indeed the *Adelphoe* makes use of this prologue frame to claim the play for its writer as the enabling device for a re-framing of the writing as the work of *his* masters, as we'll see, and so rhetoricizes the pre-framed script as bearer of a message, working on the audience toward an orientation of their reading in a controlled explosion. The pursuit of this guided reaction, in the form of a reconstructive articulation of an originary performance, can pressure us toward asking if the prologue seeks to 'teach' us, to teach us the teaching of its play, to teach us that both teach, what they teach and what teaching is – always again the lability of the preface, invocation of polysemic drift, surprise, circulation.

7 Contamination

The first half of the prologue concerns play-writing as a craft (1–14): under attack, Terence/*poeta* pleads in our court that he informs against himself that he has for better or worse rescued a scene passed over by Plautus and stuck it into *Adelphoe*; theft, this, or rescue from neglect? A document,* one of a series through Terence's prologues? Literary polemical apologetics?* Distancing device or directive? Could it be a joke? It does in due course initiate a scholarship which observes keenly the 'imperfectly integrated'* graft (Gratwick in CHCL II 120). In obedience to the order that we don't pass negligently by the scene which has been rescued from negligent by-passing (*pernoscite . . . praeteritus neglegentiast*, 12–4). Red herring? We could prefer to learn of the theatrical positioning of the play's discussions at the level of our reception and re-enactment of it. We shall be the best judges of *that*? It will be inserted into our reading that we side with or against the play, willy-nilly. We stand pre-condemned as the villains of the piece, since the poet began by claiming that he will be trying to clear himself· from the invidious denigration he re-cites as *ab iniquis* (2) in a play which circles round insistently claims by the characters to represent *aequum* (MacKendrick 24 n 2). Are we learning that learning is caught up in the invidious watch of the spectator? The 'point' is made again at the close of the prologue where the poet requests our *aequanimitas* to increase his industrious, non-negligent, zeal to write (24–5). The formulaic blandishment projects on to the level of our reception the *argumentum* which the prologue has just ostentatiously deferred from its formulaic prefatory position as chief function of the dramatic prologue (22–4). As the 'plot' summary-in-evidence is evacuated from the prologue, the empty space has been filled with thematic imbrication of the audience into the plot that awaits us. The play begins as it promises us that the play is still to begin – as it points to the characters who will 'open up some of the play/plot and show some of it in the doing/acting of it' (23–4, note *ostendent* here, for later), the prologue is already at this work.

8 Ghosts

The presence of the writer is contested by the prologue which invokes it, in the 'second' of the self-arraignments of rehearsed malevolence (15–21): the proudest boast* there could be, the infidelity of his claim to authorship. Some unnamed 'nobles' help and constantly co-write Terence's plays; they like him, the audience and people like them, they have been of service to the state in war, peace – and business. The 'Scipionic circle' was already supplied in ancient scholarship as the obvious bunch of candidates – Scipio and Laelius. . . . – and contested, by one Santra,* on the grounds that Scipio would be too young to do Terence's handiwork . . . (Suet. Vit. Ter. 4, Rawson (1985) 276 f).

The specific socio-historical context for *Adelphoe* proposed by the didascalia* fixes the play to the celebration in 160 b.c.e. of the *ludi funebres* of L Aemilius Paullus, a massively mythic spectacular of the representation to Rome of Rome. So much is always said. Next to disinter the strong thesis, pushed hardest by

Trencsényi-Waldapfel (esp. 136 f), that on that memorable day Paullus' surviving sons, adopted out into Rome's two most prestigious 'Mannibalic' families, buried their natural father: Q Fabius Maximus Aemilianus (b. c. 186 b.c.e.) and P Cornelius Scipio Aemilianus (b. c. 185/4 b.c.e.). They show through their poet in the guise of purist re-presentation of Menander's *Adelphoe* a representation of the question of their own fathering, their education and the problem of their learning to be Roman-(son)s. It is worth remarking, perhaps, that the second showing of Terence's *Hecyra*,* the Mother-in-law, that hated figure that none could stand – nor her play – was also part of the same funeral games; the gladiators* which are supposed by its grumpy prologue to have interrupted this performance were Fabius' idea, but Scipio paid up* half the cost, according to the slimy Polybius 31 28 5 f (Millar 10). And it is an often-voiced speculation that Pacuvius'* play *Paulus* may have been written for the same occasion (Trencsényi-Waldapfel 136). And I'd better observe that Scipio's adoptive father had died before this date (before 162 b.c.e., Astin (1967) 13, Dixon 151).

9 *Argumentum fabulae*

All points to Scipio (and his brother Fabius):

His wife was Sempronia; she is said to have been unattractive, unloved and unloving; and she was childless: there was no heir to the line of Africanus (App. B.C. 1 20 – ' cf. SMA 10 Sever. 21 1; his nephews Fabius Maximus and Aelius Tubero held *his* funeral' –). From such a situation the Roman aristocrat had two well-established avenues of escape: divorce followed by another marriage, or the adoption of a son. Scipio . . . took no action. Plainly he felt debarred from both courses.

'As for the failure to adopt, it may be relevant that his own experience as an adopted son seems not to have been wholly satisfactory' (Astin (1967) 235, 236). We can read snippets of his censorial speech on the subject of adopted sons (Gell. 5 19 15 f, Astin (1967) 322 f), find him modelling himself *exemplo patris sui* (Liv. Per. 51, cf. D.S. 31 27 2, Rawson (1973) 165; (re-)building the *pons Aemilius* and the *aedes Aemiliana Merculis*, Coarelli 7).

He looked up to his big brother (Cic. De Am. 69) – who became by adoption brother of the also adopted Q Fabius Maximus Servilianus (two of whose natural brothers succeeded him in the consulship in successive years) and whose son became Q Fabius Maximus Allobrogicus; who lived to help bury fathers and uncle. Scipio spent much of his youth, according to the embarrassingly corny excursuses* of Polybius (18 35 5 f, 31 22 26 f; cf. Plut. Vit. Aem. 39 5, Dixon 150 f), settling the financial affairs of the widows of his two intertwined families – he and Fabius had to return the dowry to Paullus' widow in favour of whom Paullus has divorced their mother Papiria, Scipio had to pay over the balance of the dowries owing for the two Corneliae his aunts/cousins, he turned Paullus' estate over to Fabius entirely, he handed over the wealth of Aemilia, Paullus' sister and the mother of his adoptive father, to Papiria and later passed all Papiria's property on to his two natural sisters, the Aemiliae... 'Marriage and even adoption tended to extend the ties of kinship rather than to divert them' (Dixon 169).

When Scipio was toddling, *his* father had divorced *his* mother, re-married and soon had produced a duplicate family of two sons (b. 181 and 179 b.c.e.). Sometime, several daughters were born, but as usual the details are lost; and the two elder sons were given to adoption between 179 and 168 b.c.e., aged between 5 and 18 as outer limits (Plut. Vit. Aem. 5 3, Astin (1967) 13)...

10 Fun-eral and games*

The theatrical rites for Paullus, who had come to Rome against doctor's orders to perform a religious function and pegged out there (Rawson 1973, 165), marked out a moment which acted, enacted and re-enacted his significance: everyone flocked from all over Rome and Italy in a long list, the community of living and dead; past glories, present commemoration, evocation of the future – reproduction of the power of the *gens*, the *gens as* power, smeared on to the dead man's memory as the balm of charisma –; the 'Janiform' procession of the *pompa funebris** – *imagines* of the ancestors, their magisterial regalia, the cortège and the surviving members of the *gens*, all hinged round the actor wearing the mask, triumphal insignia and robes of Paullus and imitating his gestures and gait (Plut. Vit. Aem. 39, D.S. 31 25 1 f, Polyb. 31 28 5 f, Trencsényi-Waldapfel 134, 163). This was a Roman.

11 Flashback . . .

27–29 Nov. 167 b.c.e. Rome. A huge procession* of prisoners-of-war and hostages from Greece, identified by placards and culminating in the family and person of the last King of Macedon, successor to Alexander the Great. Perhaps the largest single parade of enslaved there ever? Behind, the Roman legions singing their dirty chants of praise, headed by their general's lieutenants and natural sons: Fabius and Scipio. At centre in his chariot, plastered with Jovian vermilion and attended by the slave repeating 'Remember you're a man', Paullus. One of the very greatest of Republican celebrations (Livy 45 40, D.S. 31 8 10 f, Plut. Vit. Aem. 32 f) – *Ludi triumphales**.

12 . . . To the Scene

The mythological* battle of Pydna on 22 6 168 b.c.e. marked Paullus as Republican hero, legend in his lifetime. Defeat of Macedon made Rome the 'World State'. This was a 'turning-point', a 'telos', a 'zenith'. (For Polybius the hostage who turned live-in intellectual/Greekling and historian interpreter of Rome to Greek-speaking readers already the marker of a culmination and an impulse toward implosive decline, 1 1 5, 25 2f, Earl (1961) 41 f.) Fabius and Scipio both won their spurs and were given the pick of the royal library*, the bulk of which became the first library* at Rome (Plut. Vit. Aem. 28 6). The tuition* in Graeco-Roman excellence which became Scipio's legendary significance* prefigured the 'philhellenism' of imperatorial conquest.

Paullus' second brace of sons; the elder died aged 14 five days before the triumph in 167; the younger died aged 12 three days after it.

13 *Ab seriis rebus ludicrum*

. . . fecit. nam et artificum omnis generis qui ludicram artem faciebant ex toto orbe terrarum multitudo et . . . et . . . et . . . et quidquid aliud deorum hominumque causa fieri magnis ludis in Graecia solet, ita factum est ut non magnificentiam tantum sed prudentiam in dandis spectaculis, ad quae rudes tum Romani erant, admirarentur. epulae quoque . . .

What Paullus was supposed to have said, they say, is that putting on a party and laying on games calls for the same man that knows how to win in war (Livy 45 32 8 f, from Polyb. 30 14). His son Scipio spent a lifetime reincarnating his fathers, most simply doubling his adoptive grandfather as conqueror of Carthage and second Scipio Africanus and thus practising the fantasy of playing father to his father, switching the roles, becoming in any event the incarnation of *mos maiorum*.

These classic tales of patriarchy and patrimony and patriotism and paternity I retell to amplify the *Adelphoe* in its funeral function. If the prologue can frame this performance for Paullus, then the play can force its audience toward interpretation of its brothers and fathers in the light of the view it takes of the Scipionic family– nexus – and its value within the mythology* of the *mos maiorum*. Such a reading would open in pre-judgment and close in discussion, perhaps. At any rate *Adelphoe* repeats that relay of re-presentations across the chain of Republican moments which seek to renew and incapsulate each other and in the process of pointing to itself as the monument to the Father, the wake of Tradition, the lesson of the Republic, scouts formalist registration as a literary 'entertainment' 'faithful' to a language at the despite of a disdained theatre.

14 'I do not think for all these reasons that "deconstruction" is a good word' (un bon mot) (Derrida in Wood and Bernasconi 7)

The 'social theatre' dimension to *Adelphoe* is an available gloss, then, a ready frame to refer a reading. A lesson that we can learn – that Fabius is (not) Aeschinus, Scipio is (not) Ctesipho, Demea is (not) Paullus, Micio is (not) one of the adoptive fathers . . . – we can repeat that this is a paradoxical invitation to rehearse the play as a mythological lesson in the learning of *praecepta paterna*, caught up in the shimmer of the script's array of Fathers dealing with Sons with never a hint of a hint of a school, or university; paradoxical because of those strongly prejudician pigeon-holes for Terence in his 'purity' *etc.* foregrounded by the first half of the prologue in its 'technical' angle on the translation of the *Adelphoe*. It's important that the 'poet' and his 'writing' can't delete their theatre entirely – the dramatist's control over his voices, the characters, their producibility is always shot through with the ironies of a necessary failure to construct a meta-level of authoritative authorial insistence – because of the paradox of the prefatory voice which must stake a claim to remain this side of the text and yet thus perform a rhetorical 'act', as an actor in the script. Nevertheless these original creations which are hollowed out by silent suppression of their former contents and substitution of faceless *'prologus'* and *'poeta'* for any of the regular masks in the repertoire of roles do make a turn within the theatre tradition from which they have mutated: 'With Terence there opens a permanent rift between higher and lower literary tastes' (Gratwick in CHCL II 127). From this point of view the formation of the 'classic' – its artistic literariness, placing as entertainment, reception as a crafted piece of Culture-as-formalist-blank – begins in the play's first lines and beckons the pedagogues forward to devise their exercises in and on the text as linguistic exemplar. More or less any reading of *Adelphoe* which allows it to propose discussion of whether it offers lessons* – including the sort which finds it offering the lesson that in certain terms it can offer no lessons – will allow its dramatic radical of presentation considerable importance in deciding on a view. Paper-author/characters/plot/(auto-) anagnorisis or peripeteia/dénouement jostle as factors involved in our getting 'into' a play*, for instance, and we can wonder whether a play can be other than a play, what that means. The comedy could be a way of showing that plays are always plays (always, then, comedies?). I think that Terence's bons mots always did evoke a reaction to the ideas they entertain, though this reaction was as we know it on the lines of Ciceronian creation of Terence the Wise, but it is worth proposing here that modern readings and re-readings of these *fabulae/comoediae* arise out of – and so vindicate, deny, question – a 'humanism' articulated in this century at least on the grid of 'literary close-reading' strategies. It is necessarily an ironic practice to challenge the relevance of this. Indeed it is always already the question, I suppose, pre-judged by the *Adelphoe* prologue's instructions that we 'judge' and be 'fair' to the play.

15 A knock-down argument

Enter Micio,* *senex*, beginning by (avoiding) thinking what Aeschinus, missing all night, has been up to by repeating proverbial folklore (*profecto hoc uere dicunt*, 28). Comic low-life connotations. Ironic expository tease,* too, since the saying concerns *uxor . . . irata, parentes propitii* (30–1), yet M's *filius* (35) is not his by birth but an adopted nephew (40) and *uxorem numquam habui* (44). A rift is opened, the finale will close with, precisely, the overdue wife for M. Meantime he can repeat the sayings, but is he qualified to pronounce them true, is experience vital to the authoritativeness of a father's views on fatherhood, is he being subtly characterized already as the genial verbalizer never stuck for a telling bon mot . . .? Just a comic cut that he should, in his 'deep' re-citation of the saying, be made to refuse to suspect the missing *adulescens* of amatory absence overnight on the grounds that he is a fond parent (36 f: the scold plumps correctly first for *amari*, 33, as does M at the end of this scene when he returns to the subject of Aeschinus, *amauit*, 149), a joke on the stereotypicality of comic adolescence. Subtlety in showing this 'different' sort of father to be empathizing with his child's paradoxical role in his father's thoughts to see, so to say, that anxiety is thinly disguised hostility and revenge for counting so much takes the form of lurid imaginings (32–9). When M continues, patting himself on the back for being so different* from his brother, the natural father of Aeschinus and of the younger son Ctesipho whom he has kept for his own, we may already be reading the clichés of *comoedia*: the two lives led by our two 'fathers' are the arbitrary whim of the script, working with the *rus/urbs* antithesis which corresponds with the theatrical convention that the stage-house be in town and 'others' arrive from the country. Whether these brothers chose themselves these lives – were they results or consequences* of their characters, their experiences, chance, reason, positional duty within the family . . .? – is irrelevant to the 'plot' and its entertainment value. Maybe the *fabula* will go on or set out to suggest that 'educational philosophy' is no matter of choice – that *it* chooses parents, if anything, as a rider to and rationalization of what suits them. Or to contest that view: the very idea of an 'educational philosophy' is unconvincing ('cerebral') blarney in the face of the totalizing challenge of parenthood, always likely to prove to be above the realm of any 'idea'; a trick, therefore, of the rhetorically minded, the urbane. No matter, I can teach you the play, at least partly, as a comic plot – the other part is just fun, colouring, art as the serious business of adapting the *argumentum* from Menander's prologue into Terence's 'first act' – although I recognize that the play will never say what its *argumentum* is now that the play itself is now, at least partly, its own *argumentum*: no précis (22–4). 'It is always too soon or too late to teach children about sexuality' (Johnson in B. Johnson 169). The comedy which focuses on its standard scenario of puberty (sc. male adolescence) as the site of a structural ambiguity at the level of the familial and civic orders feeds on the confused imperatives of paternal authority and filial obedience and on the insistence on a preference and autonomous desire in selecting a mate, to produce a socially threatening prospect of a failure to fit courting to marriage at the cost of family honour, a hiccup in the disposition of wealth, and so on, and worst of all a cloud of unhappiness over the community (Johnson in B. Johnson 175, Bristol 163 f). You can see why such plays are 'born' school texts (Johnson in B. Johnson 171) – and *Adelphoe* is 'just' the one which *thematizes* this nexus of adult authority and adolescent sexuality in its constitutive relations . . .

Just a comedy. The play promises the usual *senex/pater* to come: brother Demea, the outsider who will be closed to the audience as to the cast, but rigidity and age last to be teased and twitted. As father is doubled, he is split and the other masks will adjust to a novel re-disposition: M will be the *adulescens*' 'friend', more 'peer' cum 'inverse parasite' (a parasite with Dad's cheque-book), and the plot's talker and teaser, adaptive and conversant with the audience and cast, stealing much of the comedian slave's limelight (Syrus can twit D, but is allowed only to perform a 'faithful slave' role as vulgar facsimile of his master, M). M is the cancelled *paterfamilias*, the wild card. The females are all but extruded by all this. The *adulescens/amator* role is notionally doubled into Aeschinus, who will end the play, married, and Ctesipho who is to abduct a 'beloved', but it is the adopted son who has the ambiguity of two fathers who, of course, dominates the play, is the question of the play – if plays had questions. The marriage of Ctesipho is cancelled, so to say, as the *senex* M by generic logic joins A for the double-wedding comic finale.

We already know the plot, then. Four acts of experiment in the art of stereotype-confounding, pursued in the urbane seriousness adopted by faithful Terence from Menander, snapping back into shape for the fifth as the roles reverse, invert, follow the law of mirror-symmetry: D becomes *seruos callidus* and maverick ~~pater~~, acts out the new role of M in comic caricature, M is trounced and bundled out of his urban *otium*; and all this the joke on the audience that in so far as the play got you to take its serious mask at face-value, you were set up for the comic finale where all that occurred was the requisite generic procession at Chaplinesque* pace through multiple solution to exit for nuptials. After all, always already.

16 *A stand-up fight*

And if necessary, I suppose, *Adelphoe* – in concerning just the problems of post-pubertal boy-management (if it must concern, at all) – falls well short of such grandiosities as 'educational philosophy'. The play is a traditional and, to exaggerate, 'ritualistic' exercise in the ephebic narrative* which was so tightly wound into the Attic theatre: we have discovered that A is differentiated from C as the elder son (47), as the 'problem' of the play. Before we judge C 'a poor figure* who is entirely dependent upon A's assistance and whose utterances hardly rise above the level of a sigh or a melodramatic exaggeration' (Hunter 107), we'll have to take into account – besides the fact that C hardly receives *any* 'utterances' because of the pivotal expansionism of A's part – that comic plotting revolves around arbitrary but conventional binary/bipolar* symmetries woven out of just such archetypes as initiation into adulthood. C seems to have arrived at puberty 'today', crossing the teenager threshold into adolescence. (His father treats him like a child, a non-male, yes, the *uirgo* who must be locked away from sexuality, under surveillance, on the farm; over-rating of purity, over-discipline threatens to halt his life-cycle and destroy the father's objective, self-replication . . .) A seems to have arrived at adulthood prematurely, crossing into paternity before his father has married him off. (His father treated him as an adult in under-rating the importance of control, behaved himself, that is to say, as an adolescent in aiding and abetting teenage self-assertion with misplaced camaraderie; A's life-cycle is threatened with irretriev-able disorder, over the threshold before he's reached it.) The play overcomes the obstacle to C's development and successfully concludes A's restoration to the 'natural' order: C's first escapade of adolescence, a simple paradigm; A's last escapade of adolescence parachuting him into adult life as 'husband' and 'father' before he is married *and* – in strict parallel – before his father is married. (The 'end' of the play retrieves familial legitimacy, we could say, at the cost of an over-valuation of natural relation within family relations, since the new matron's position will be that of A's mother-in-law and 'mother', in an excess of quasi-incest.)

This structuralist (as it happens?) account shows again the lesson of plot's mastery of character. No chance of assessing the father's fathering? No way to regard the boys as products of an 'educational philosophy' or of an educational 'non-philosophy'? The limits of re-presentational adequacy. 'Come back in three years time and see how C makes *out*', the folly of teleological reading! 'That's entertainment', again, let's subside to the bottom line: a comedy is a comedy is a . . .

For instance,

In the live performance the audience could not reinterpret earlier scenes retrospectively in the light of the final verdict. On the other hand, caught up in a fast-moving dénouement, they would not have time to recall previous scenes which seemed to be contradicted by the outcome of the play. (Fantham (1971) 985)

'The position of the teacher is itself the position of the one who learns, of the one who teaches nothing other than the way he learns' (Felman in B. Johnson 37).

Istuc recte, the last words of *Adelphoe* (from the cast, that is; Micio in fact, who began the first act for us, significantly enough, by yelling back into the invisible and indeed non-existent interior of his lopsided parody of a house(hold) 'Storax!' (26, 'Gum-Arab!') to fail to fetch a slave who 'wasn't back' and was never to have a role . . .). We still have the all-important *plaudite* from the anonymous voice, appropriately the Greek omega in our texts, waiting to rein back the whole proceedings for Entertainment).

Does M simply add his approval because he has no alternative, or is there something in Don.'s suggestion that *istuc recte* implies *non ut cetera . . .*? Either interpretation is possible. When acted it can easily be spoken in such a way as to show whether M tamely acquiesces with D's last remark, or whether he makes a forceful and independent comment. (Martin on 997)

In the play, D has just used the words *finem faciat*, so M's reply may be to D *as* M to D. And in the comedy, M may *be* Comedy, picking up at random as a chance the cue for curtain-call, repositioning the script as an abusive mock-intentionality retrospectively denied any status but the inexorable ritualism of comic machinery . . .

17 'Even when we are trying to be open minded, we are likely to say, "Let's look at both sides of the question", or "Let's hear the other side of the story" ' (Postman and Weingartner 115)

M presents us with his summary of the difference between his brother D's views, and other fathers' too (proper fathers? Real ones? Real comic ones) with a verbal re-presentation of D in histrionic action (60–3). Pontificates, gilds his own lily: his views are urbane – 'nice' but no longer prefatory anonymity – and so loaded, of course. M's D is made to yell sarcastically at M, and this is M's sarcastic caricature of D; M's ideas of his difference from D's excessively excessive accusations of excess (63–4) are to convey his own equable adequacy, his sweet mildness (*aequom*, 64). When M predicts* that D will at once, on sight, 'quarrel as usual' (79 f), and in aside points out, 'Didn't I say this was going to happen?' (83) after the opening salvo, we are to savour the ironies of the situation, I imagine: M did 'break off' his claim to know best how to handle children with another unquestioning question, the comic formula stage-direction announcing an entrance *Sed estne his ipsus de quo agebam?* and the inevitable reflex *et certe is est* (78). And in the process, gave us the first half of the comic script's invitation to prohaeresis, completed at once by D's *te ipsum quaerito* (81); characters in plays are 'forever' looking to find each other, or else, I could say open-mindedly, failing to look for each other and so failing to find by default, in a quest for the truth of relationships, for 'where they're at',* as 'who they are' – 'their selves included' . . . M already told us he didn't know where A was . . . and that his guesses were no doubt paradoxically bound to the oppressive – and now we find the two brothers M and D both supposing they know each other, again, as of old. M is 'knowing', but what can his knowledge mean for his ignorance? What might seem to happen in the confrontation that ensues is that *we* learn more of the plot from D and M has some pieces of information on his son's whereabouts. And then, we witness in the exchange between M and D a first sample *in agendo* of what M has just 'revealed' about their differences so far as child-minding are concerned. . . . Some material for us to 'judge' as the case is argued, entertainingly enough, by both the 'sides' (100, *tu, Demea, haec male iudicas*, for instance). But we shall learn after D leaves that the exchange is caught up in an 'act': M, at least, tells us he finds more in what D said than he agreed to find in his saying it (*sed ostendere/me aegre pati illi nolui*, 142–3; cf. *ostendent*, 24).

The exchanges about A's putative 'injustice' (for D, his latest outrage; for M, that this extends a career of scrapes and japes which A had, good lad, indicated was over now, 98 106 vs. 148) makes the participants verge on 'insanity' (111, 147). The crunch 'argumen' that each produces in favour of his own authority to speak for Father **either** stands out, for us if not for them, as the point of the *argumentum, pater esse disce ab illis qui uere sciunt:: natura tu illi pater es, consiliis ego* (125 :: 126), **or else** folds away into the abusive exchange which produces the two lines, *te plura in hac re peccare ostendam :: ei mihi* (124, M :: D, of course, note *ostendam!*) and then *tun consulis quicquam? :: ah, si pergis, abiero* (127, D :: M). The play is at stake, here, no doubt, as the voice of the *prologus*, the summary of the *argumentum*, has yielded to M's voice as presumptive voice of the *argumentum*, within the poles of the *argumentum*, as one of its terms; has yielded to the contestation of any meta-level force to his representations in the displacement of *arguments* by (brute/human/comic) *argument*. A movement confirmed and ironized when M's voice retrospectively seeks to authorize this view *as* his view that whenever the brothers interact they speak their relationship – a known quantity, constitutional and in-grown . . . – which issues in M's manipulation of D. A view which will be reinforced as it is undermined in reversal by the new D, the ape of M, of the finale, who will use M-like tactics on M to act out the manipulative rhetoric* of M's 'position' as a comic argument: *ut id ostenderem, quod te isti faculem et festiuom putant, / id non fieri ex uera uita neque adeo ex aequo et bono* (986–7). One reading of the first confrontation between M and D will emphasize that M's reactions to D's 'rebukes', or should we call it 'teaching'?, consist of arguments with his brother, not arguments of the case – one of tricksy maxims (98–9), amplified by way of explanation to his simple brother in a presumptuous *argumentum* strictly *ad hominem* because *ad crumenam*, guaranteed to drive D wild (100–10) followed by another reaction, that it's not D's business, either. A is M's or he's not (114–24). M makes it 'sound' as if D only cares about the financial cost of A's escapades and makes a provocative boast to be able to prove to anyone that D is all wrong (123–4). As he does so, we notice he gives his game away by claiming that so far the troubles haven't been too much of a pain (122, *adhuc non molesta*), as he'll tell us once D is gone (141 f, *tamen/non nil molesta haec sunt mihi*). We should want to know when and so in what terms he *would* feel obliged to 'draw the line' and will be looking for this until the comic finale rubs our noses in the question with the concluding *istuc recte*, after M has yielded to all other sundry requests from the new D. In any case, M does not, 'so far', in Act 1 know how far A has gone, that's the question which D has underlined for M, that's the reason he must get rid of D so he can set about finding out more from A. That's the reason he *acts* as if he has the situation buttoned up, has nothing to think on, is toying with D, as always one jump ahead and behaving as though D could teach him nothing under the sun. He proposed 'fair' shares in the boys (130, *aequam . . . partem*), like a reasonable man, but this is to tell D to stop the *argument*, to turn his affected boredom with D's predictable hectoring (112 f, *ah / ausculta, ne me optundas de hac re saepius*) into emotional blackmail in stopping the discussion with an ultimatum, one son each (132, *ah Micio*, from D, caught in the trap). The controller of the verbal ring has used his control to void the argument of argument, to tease D and treat him as already read, to dispose of him . . . Has all this amounted to more than that drama must always show us in its script the insides of the 'verbal' characters, the remoteness and so woodenness, dullness, thingness of the Laconic, all we can get from the urbanity of drama we read, the comic festivity of wit – always vulnerable to theatre-production . . . We shall hardly be surprised to find that when the tide has turned and D wants to know why M hasn't kept to the 50/50 deal *he* proposed (130 f) – is this 'fair'?* (801, *aequom*) – M at once attacks with an accusation – 'That's not fair' (803, *non aequom dicis*) – and another old proverb (804), a lecture on money again (806–19), and some bland sophistries (820–35) . . . M, we could well agree, invented the 'fair deal' to avoid argument, and now he invents arguments to avoid discussing the deal . . . D tries sarcasm but is trumped again and when he presses on against M, he's treated with another yawn (853, *ah pergisne*, cf. 127 *pergis*) and once again M aborts the scene, not interested in hearing what D thinks.

18 'Teaching is a compulsion to repeat what one has not yet understood' (Johnson in B Johnson vii)

None of what I have written* has profited from any lessons we may draw from the insertion of the alien 'abduction' scene in Act 2 advertised in the prologue's first lines. Perhaps rightly: *that* reminder that Terentian theatre is but an adaptation of Plautine festivity, falsely concealing its origins, fit to adopt a prodigal scene which celebrates the threat to social order posed by the hostility of men as a group to the exclusions enforced on sexuality by male ownership of women (Bristol 166), the comic genre, perhaps, *in nuce*. Terence is just teasing us with his stereotype-busting and so comical 'no-fun' thinking-man's *fabula* which will snap back into shape in due course. Act 2 presents the closing moments of the kidnap of a pimp's property by A, announced as his latest outrage by D in Act 1. Normal behaviour for *adulescens/amator*. A 'livener-upper'. Should be a touch of venial violence playing in the margins where adolescent sexuality gets a chance to play with the tolerance of society, the doubleness of double standards, where the familial arguments are supplemented by social considerations. Machismo rules, OK. The scene should knit into its plot by providing a bride,

after recognition – as hinted at, but only as a momentary 'jest'*
by A (193 f). Whatever view we take of these proceedings – do
we agree with D (Outrage! So the pimp Sannio . . .) or with M
(Prank! So the slave Syrus)? – we shall find that we *have* taken a
view. We've 'seen' it, seen 'it' and given 'it' a description and an
evaluation. We've been framed into judging the thing. We've been
denied vital information until after 'it' is over, but that hasn't
stopped us from reacting. *If* we're allowing our selves to react to
this entertainment. A formulaic stage-direction is used to bring on
the fourth brother, to complete our set, and in it we learn oh-so-
casually that the skirt is for C, not for A. And what does that
change? A flowers, C's a runt? C's 'a schoolboy' looking up to the
'undergraduate' A? (Fantham (1971) 977). We feel less like liking
D's views on (this) abduction? Touché? We learn to defer, to see
that the *comoedia* is providing fun at our expense. . . . We think
differently about the two pairs of brothers, caught in their own
special(ly-contrived) ménage, exposed as a comic routine. . . . Yes,
we can avoid that silly 'fallacy' of our teleological reader who
wants to come back 'later' to give C a chance. We can see that
this play has devised a fail-safe problematic of undecidability* – a
funny crisis in which we are always too soon and too late,
obstructed from crossing our lives' aporiai and attempting to
correct with hindsight what we have been at, 'out of order' – in
that A will *never* have an elder brother, nor C a younger. The
point of '*Adelphoe*' is that we have no twins, precisely, 'just'
Brothers. The play's mythological axis is the provision of a double
father for A but we find that the 'dialectical' ironies of binarist
exploration of the father's role are then caught up in the questions
of positionality within the family. Questions which are well bigger
than any of us, which fold us in as fresh evidence in its verdict.

19 '*What can the impossibility of teaching teach us?*' (Felman in B. Johnson 22)

What is most unfunny in our 'close-reading' cultivation of
Adelphoe seems to me to be the refusal to read the tantalizing
lessons offered us as ourselves* 'characters' at work in and on the
script; that 'character' does not consist in what we may observe,
the quiddity of a description; that 'character' shows us how we

observe, what we (don't) know about how to observe; that
'character' insists that we plot how people get plotted (Docherty
ch. 1). The play works itself round the positions in the family, the
exchange and circulation* of its relay of mutually constitutive
relations. The dynamics of the doubles and their interrelations,
culminating in the sameness/difference of D-as-M in charade,
present us with the tease of familial positioning of its 'characters'.

20 The error of comedies

But the question of reading is on the edge of private/public,*
familial/social, individual/group definitions. The play makes itself
look at this. If 'our' primal 'Father–Son' dramatics have shifted
us toward the household, away from the community,* then the
replacement in the third act of the Brothers by the 'Neighbours',
the substitution of the outcast pimp parody of a citizen ('Sannio'
the prick*) by the pivotal concerned human being and pillar of
society Hegio (Our Leader), and the invention of a civic equivalent
to the fictional Fatherhood of M and the 'natural' Fatherhood of
D within the family in the patronal* position of Megio as 'family-
friend' to the Neighbour Widow are all emphatically powerful
pressures confronting us with the claims of the community on the
behaviour of its households, its determination to fix standards,
protocols, taboos.

Act 2, with its grafted scene of Abduction, matched younger
with the older brothers (seen in Act 1). Fathers discuss, Boy(s)
perform. What were the terms, the ties? Back in the *Adelphoe*,
faithful entertainment in Act 3: suddenly – of course – the second
door in the comic stage-front becomes a door in this play and
disgorges out of the blue an entire household and unsignalled Spilt
Milk. Parent, child and household slave inside, just as in M's
home. But quite its opposite, a Northern cold barbarian slave-name
(Thracian 'Geta'), not the Eastern hot luxuriance of 'Syrus'; a
natural parent/child, all-female, where M and A are adoptive.
Between them, the absent norm of D's unit – Father, Wife, natural
Son. D. if he forgets A, has just the task of safe delivery of his Son to
adulthood. M threatens to bypass women and 'procreate' without
exogamous social ties. Scandal.

21 *'Literary visions are a constant reminder of "society's" failings'* (Kampf in Roszak 60)

We learn that A has raped the freeborn citizen virgin daughter of Widow next door. The slave Geta has heard of the Abduction and supposes as had D that the girl was for A, who has therefore betrayed the family. We know better but see that their jumping to the same wrong conclusion as D is a far more vital issue for them – they stare at ruin. Is *this* adolescent fun? This time M must find arguments for himself to use on society, not his brother; in the form of Hegio the family friend of the rape-victim. (Thus he is social in Terence, where Menander made 'Hegio' the widow's brother. *Brother*!*) The reactions of Hegio, who responds to the news of A's criminal assault and apparent desertion of the family to D in the same terms as D had used in Act 1 and in apparent demonstration that M's values as set out in Act 1 have collapsed in their own terms* (*illiberale facinus . . . aequom . . . neque liberalis . . . uiri . . .* 449–64), is more complex than this suggests: he actually agrees to take M's view of the Abduction as his view of the Rape, so long as A does the decent thing, on the Spilt Milk principle (469 f, esp. *humanumst*). Otherwise, and as it seems that A is reneging, he agrees* with D to be outraged: he defines for D what is 'fair' (503, *aequo animo aequa*).

It seems clear that Hegio stands as the cast's own yardstick of behaviour so far as it affects the community. To impeach him is to impeach ourselves as not caring for our reputations (504). Here the play begins to rein back any apparent familial room for success for M's Unorthodoxy, begins to remove the isolation of the butt, D, as his ignorance continues but becomes a far less significant criterion for 'judging' him. Hegio does not know the 'truth', either, but he accepts the burden of straightening out the situation no-matter-what. We'll see, for instance, that the next time that Syrus tries to twit D as if he's the butt (548, *is solus nescit omnia*), he thinks wrongly that D is still after C and not M because he doesn't know about the new crisis. And, later, when M has dealt with A, fixed up a wedding better late than never, and confronts D once more, we'll be less inclined to be impressed by his teasing: M is calm now he knows of Abduction and Rape and is in control of things; D thinks that M thinks that D is still outraged over the Abduction (724–5) and when M puts him right about that, what he doesn't do is explain to D what the Abduction was really about, thus leaving D with the picture of a groom with a bride *and* the pimp's girl settling down inside M's. . . . The central presence of Hegio's arbitration insists that the 'person-centred' family threatens the social stereotype of the 'positional' family by substituting a creative, accommodating, autonomous bricolage for the strongly bounded age, sex and authority relations of the norm (Bernstein in Giglioli 174 f). And this opens up the household to public scrutiny, and to us. The context for 'our' reading of this play is also open to such scrutiny: only in the male schooling scene can we now find a reading which can read past the 'literary vision' of *Ad.* 486–7 at all: *miseram me, differor doloribus! / Iuno Lucina, der opem/ serua me, obsecro!*

The Rape has repercussions.*

22 Qui a peur de la philosophie?*

In the *Adelphoe*, the saying goes, 'philosophy is the servant, not the dictator,* of Comedy' (Arnott 16). Roman 'civilization' was built on a series of related refusals of Greek cultural practice, its institutions, specializations, valorizations. The Republic refused theatre – the permanent stone theatre half-erected was pulled down in 151 b.c.e.* in case it spoiled Roman fighting manhood (Livy Per. 48) – and staged its own spectacles of adaptation, translation, subsumption. Philosophers and rhetoricians were formally expelled from Rome by senatorial decree, for instance in 161 b.c.e., the year before the *Adelphoe* was staged. Round Latinity there organized resistance to Greek cóncepts, values, Otherness. Theatre became a different institution, one in which a classic repertoire was created to be a national treasure, one which traced a path in *comedy* 'up' from the vulgar carnival farcicalities of Plautus to the purged refinement of Terentian literariness (cf. Bristol 125). The blanking of schools of philosophy from Roman culture enabled a re-positioning of 'philosophy' within the public domain, ready for insertion within the aristocratic system of Roman patronage and, as a rhetorical faculty, within Roman education (André 49). The question of 'philosophy' at Rome is the study of translation, the re-distribution of conceptual knowledge across and through cultural difference. And in the service of *Latinitas*, *Adelphoe* taught that philosophical refusal of Greek culture – theatre, 'philosophy' – which consisted in the resistance to the play's teachings, 'our' textuality.

23 'We are all mediators, translators' (Derrida in Wood and Bernasconi 108)

Bons mots have an unphilosophical stance; they figure the refusal of philosophy, the 'philosophical' problem of creating a 'general public' and training it with vulgarized, non-specialist, conceptualizations (Ulmer 160 f on Greph): and language. Cato's famous refusal of Greece and its philosophers also creates the *mos maiorum* and its *Latinitas*: *rem tene, uerba sequentur* (Self-enacting rhetorical structures, cf. Astin 1978, 169 f).* Translation, the relaying of ideas in language, created a philosophy at Rome held in the pedagogy of rhetorical performance, though, despite and beyond its texts.

24 'No adult teacher is in loco parentis' (Owen in Rogers 10).*

... istuc recte ...*

Commentary

Asterisks in the body of text refer to a discussion of the word or idea in the commentary. The numbers of the paragraphs are followed in the numbering of the commentary.

Title cf. Shershow 32, 34, 'It is no laughing matter', 'that laughing matters'. '*Entertainment*' is discussed in (4) pp. 195–6 and in n. 14 p. 219. '*Arguments*' in the senses of 'plots', 'argumentation', 'argy-bargy' figure in (15) pp. 205–7 and (17) pp. 209–12 especially.

Epigraph This is, of course, the first line in each and every 'New Accent' published by Methuen since 1977, the introduction by the editor Terence Hawkes.

1 The main influences on this essay are (i) some of the essays in B. Johnson, (ii) around 200 separate supervisions on the *Adelphoe*.

2 '*Ludus*' in Latin spells 'school' as well as 'play' (and 'fun', and 'games'). '*In school*': cf. Kenney in CHCL II 7 'Literary criticism as it is now understood – concern with larger social and aesthetic values – was virtually unknown at any level of scholarly activity and certainly formed no part of the school curriculum. . . . The role of poetry in education was always ancillary to the overriding rhetorical purpose of the system'. Such 'current-traditional rhetoric' provided a dominant model for Latin models of 'textuality' just as, *mut.mut.*, today (cf. Crowley, in Atkins and Johnson 94).

3 This section looks, I think, toward White in *Gloversmith* 123 f, e.g. 143, 'Grammar, poetics and unitary language theory are modes whereby the prestige language simultaneously canonizes itself, regularizes and endorses its system and boundaries, makes itself teachable and assimilable in educational practice and above all "naturalizes" itself over against all competing sociolects, dialects and registers'.

'*philhellenism*': The important objections to this notion are assembled in Astin (1978) App. 9: 'additional note to Chapter 8: Cato and Education', esp. 342.

'*enculturation*': see Clavel-Lévêque 13 and *passim*.

'*undifferentiated*': i.e. *parsimoniously* differentiated, particularly relative to Plautine theatre and to the current living sociolects of C2nd b.c.e. Central Italy (e.g. Maltby shows that the masks are linguistically systematized in their mutual relations: but parsimoniously).

'*linguistic unification*': The telos of Beard and Crawford reads through 'the uniformity of Latin' as against other Italic languages to 'the homogeneous society of Italy from the age of Augustus onwards' (82–4): for objections cf. Foulkes 38 f, and Pêcheux 8 f on the process from 'uniformization' to 'an inegalitarian division inside the egalitarian uniformization', the putting in place of barriers 'within' the national language to bind subjects into hierarchic positions: the role of pedagogy?

4 '*Translativity*' is 'the conditions that make possible and govern the work of translation' (Lewis in Graham 33).

'*translatability*': For this Derridean point about 'national language' cf. Morris in Drakakis 48 f. Bassnett-Maguire has some good remarks on Rome as translation, esp. 43 f. '*a traditional preference*': The position that '*Adelphoe* doesn't teach – It entertains' is a traditional salient (e.g. Beare 110 f, Lloyd-Jones 283). Often, however, this is incorporated with other views, as in Hunter, by the technique of 'disavowal', 'I know all that is true, but nevertheless'?

5 For standard treatment of the '*extra-dramatic prologue*' see now Hunter 7, 26 ff, esp. 32 f.

6 cf. Knapp 38 for *poeta* and *scribo* usage in Plautus and Terence. '*homogenization*': for some good observations see Hunter 51 ff.

7 '*document*', as in RE Suppl. 7 419 f 'Luscius' (19) Lanuvinus, Donatus' and the Scholia's persecutor of Terence.

'*apologetics*': cf. Hunter 32. For exaggeration cf. Ehrman.

'*imperfectly integrated*': One of the chief focuses for interest in *Ad*. (e.g. Arnott 52 f; Ludwig 171 f; Grant (1973).

8 '*proudest boast*', cf. Williams in Gold 6, seeing this as a useful charge, 'invented or real'.

'*Santra*': cf. Earl (1962) 477 n. 29, Astin (1967) 15, Beare 93 for this topic. Most modern scholia accept the '*Scipionic circle*' connection to Terence a bit (e.g. Gratwick in CHCL II 123) – not so much as Trencsényi-Waldapfel 141 f! (For 'Scipionic' *Megio* cf. Callier).

'*didascalia*': Arnott 47 mentions worries over the status of these as would-be documents.

'*Hecyra*': See Konstan 130 ff for this play as an attack on the audience.

'*gladiators*': See Clavel-Levêque 29.

'*Scipio paid up*': See Dixon 147 f.

'*Pacuvius*': For speculation on the *praetexta* '*Paulus*' cf. Abbott, Clavel-Lévêque 51, Beare 43, Williams in Gold 5.

9 An '*embarrassingly corny excursus*'. For an 'Aemilian' *Ad*. (cf. Grimal, Orlandini, Lord 195 n. 24).

10 From this point of view, such lines as *Ad*. 109, *ubi te exspectatum eiecisset foras* become nicely sick jokes.

'*pompa funebris*': See Marshall 121, Scullard 218 f (Paullus' funeral on 219 f). On Roman *ludi funebres*, see Clavel-Lévêque 10, 29 f (cf. Bristol 179 ff, 'Treating death as a laughing matter').

11 '*huge procession*': Nearly half as many enslaved as adult male Romans? (Salmon 120). For the triumph cf. Scullard 214 ff (Paullus' on 216 f).

'*ludi triumphales*': see Clavel-Lévêque 31 for these.

12 '*mythological*', in the sense e.g. of Walbank 212, 'After 167 Rome was mistress of the world'.

'*library*': André 31 f treats *this* as inaugurating a new era.

'*tuition*': on the subject cf. Astin (1967) 15, 17; Earl (1967) 39.

'*legendary significance*': e.g. Astin (1967) ch. 1, Bonner 22 f.

13 '*value within the mythology*': Bloch and Parry Introduction 35 usefully assess the problem of the burial of the Great Man, whose individualism may threaten to offer death as End, as Blight to the Collectivity: identification of Him with the *gens* re-absorbs Him into the corporate body.

14 '*to propose discussion of whether it offers lessons*': Almost all criticism of *Ad*. has *decided*, e.g. Both Dads have faults (Grant (1975) 59), Both M and D are wrongly convinced they're right (Tränkle 248), or These 2 Self-Satisfied Men collide so that we can see the Universality of Self-Satisfaction and its inevitable Frustrations (W. R. Johnson 172).

Greenberg seems virtually alone in even suggesting a *question*: What *are* the goals and standards of social behaviour? (223).

'getting "into" a play': Altman in Altman 175 neatly observes 'By its very etymology, then, the term "entertainment" suggests a discursive phenomenon rather than an impersonal narrative form. "Let me entertain you" = "Let me hold your interest; let me create a bond between you and me".' Me contrasts this sense with that caught in the term 'diversion'. There is some overlap with the slippage 'paidia'/'paideia' of Derrida (cf. Ulmer in Atkins and Johnson 55)?

15 *'Micio'* means Titch. (So does Paullus!)

'tease': W. R. Johnson 173 'exposes' Micio as a teeny bit self-centred and self-approving in these lines (28–40).

'so different': Greenberg observes that Micio encroaches on Syrus' role as comic trickster (233), thus transforming his mask – he is *and* he is not a father – into a question-mask (236).

'results or consequences': Good decisions in Lord 192, 194; good questions in Greenberg 222.

'Chaplinesque': For the joke-structure of the end of *Ad.*, see Greenberg 233 f.

16 *'ephebic narrative'*: This is, true, generalizable beyond Attica (e.g. Suleiman 238 'The play of writing is perhaps none other than the coming of age of the reader').

'a poor figure': Fantham (1971) 976 for the kiss of death 'neither good nor bad enough to be interesting'.

'binary/bi-polar': The Brothers as Self and Other, as The Antithesis are an 'elementary scheme' (e.g. Suleiman 84 f, Irwin 33, citing Rank). *Adelphoe*, however, is neither elementary nor a scheme.

17 *'When M. predicts . . .'*: in mirror-image to this stands D's 'cue' for M. at 792 f, eccum adest / communis corruptela nostrum liberum (Painting him as 'pimp', cf. Sannio on Sannio – under pressure – at 188, Carrubba 17).

'where they're at': the formula recurs, always blank as stage-direction machinery, always re-opening and re-doubling the epistemological edge of character / plot, to form the beloved irony of the Terentian reprise which is heavily signposted on the level of point-of-view conception by the explicit quotations in the last act from earlier in the play and amplified exponentially on the level of phraseology, the telos of lexical homogenization. For some 'telling' collections and explorations of the echoing textuality of *Ad.* cf. W. R. Johnson, Grant (1971), Fantham (1971), 974 f and esp. Revesz, who brilliantly urges the speech at 821–4 on us as key to the irony. (It is, perhaps, 'keyhole' to the play, as it threatens to follow Micio's 'person-centred' creativity away from the bounds of social norms, cf. (*21*), pp. 215–16)

'manipulative rhetoric': Johnson in B. Johnson esp. 177 f explores the clash of didactic and mimetic pedagogy 'Do-as-I-say' and 'Do-as-I-do'

in their contestation of language theory in a critically different validation of the learning power of ambiguity. So does *Adelphoe*.

'*is this "fair"* ': Sandbach (1978) 139 conducts a fine plea in behalf of M's assistance of C. (Or, maybe, it's a 'protest'?)

18 '*None of what I have written*': This seems to include the Commentary *above*.

'*a momentary "jest"* ': On this see Fantham (1968) 200, 202, and, for the Answer, Lloyd-Jones 280 f.

'*undecidability*': The '*undecidability*' of the *Ad.* – its undecidedness on whether to be a 'free play' – deconstructively interrogates *all* critical positions, including of course deconstructive positions (were there such things), soon showing that they are *all* 'too soon and too late' (cf. Kanfer and Waller in Atkins and Johnson 69).

19 '*as ourselves*': B. Johnson in Atkins and Johnson 147 'Faced with the text, the reader's search for meaning is an examination of his own credentials'. Yes.

'*circulation*': Not merely on the level of a reading of the play, where so much spins round the Son who becomes in its course a Father, by criminal birth, but not yet Father (*paterfamilias*, for instance), but also at the level of the shifting terms of the criticism. This essay is thus constituted by a 'fiat' from Sandbach (1978) 139: 'These are all arguments which occur to any spectator who has in mind the realities of the situation'?

20 '*private/public*': It is possible pedagogically to sit on this edge, by refusing to entertain argument, e.g. Hunter 151, 'It may be helpful for an individual reader or spectator to analyse the play in Aristotelian terms, but this cannot be said to be necessary'. But the refusal here is, of course, also *decisive*.

'*the community*': 'Demea' means just this (try e.g. 93, where D says in orest omni *populo*).

'*the prick*': For *sannion* cf. Hunter 164 n. 24. Before we pooh-pooh the pimp's claims in the interests of A (e.g. Hunter 72), we should ponder the logic of his mask, e.g. Shershow 46 'Money stands for the power of society's regulations (the father), even as it sums up (!) the sources and resources of life.' The pimp's role is precisely the question of 'standing for', of 'substitution' and disseminative challenge to the Father. Sannio's cries are inevitably implicated in the ironic self-reprises of Ad. and by its share in the script's voicing of *libertatem* . . . *aequam* (182), however exclamatory, however discredited (see Fantham (1968) 203).

'*patronal*': Hegio is 'in loco parentis to the girl' (Sandbach (1978) 138, quoting Donatus on 351, pro patre huic est).

21 '*Brother*': cf. Sandbach (1978) 138.

'*in their own terms*': The play's textuality works meagrely through its Latinity to a comic / philosophical run of signifiers, e.g. 57–8 liberalitate liberos / retinere (with Donatus, cf. Lord 187) . . . 182–3 liber . . . libertatem, 194–6 libera . . . liberali . . . delibera (with Hunter 164 n. 26), 684 liberals – 828 liberum (with Martin on 828) . . .

'*agrees*': Greenberg 227 collapses here into *deciding* that Hegio condones A's 'crime'.

'*repercussions*': the rape institutes a linguistic scandal which overtakes all who (try to) understand it, e.g. Greenberg 227 'not quite' (nb) 'proper even in Roman Comedy, but there is a sense in which it is acceptable' is caught up in the double standard of Antiquity which *Adelphoe* always already questions (so too Anderson 130, at one remove, 'The happy Menandrian resolution turns sour'). Still, the Boys' Own pedagogy paints *itself* in its tar and feathers: Sandbach (1978) 140 (M gives A) 'a richly deserved awkward quarter of an hour (639–78)', for instance?

22 The title belongs to the Greph project (see Ulmer 160 f).

'*servant, not the dictator*': the non-match in this antithesis leaves the requisite space between 'philosophy-play but thoroughly integrated into comic conception' analysis (e.g. Lord, esp. 202) and 'traditional comedy but thoroughly imbued with contemporary ethics' analysis (e.g. Hunter 147 f, esp. 151).

'*151 b.c.e.*': cf. Earl (1962) 484. Pompey's theatre went up in 55 b.c.e., too late for the Republic.

23 From the lips of his heart Cato said, 'He thought in general that the words of the Greeks were born on their lips but those of the Romans in their hearts' (Plut. Vit. Cat. Mai. 12 5: in Greek the prepositions are *apo* and *apo*; in Latin they would be *in* and *in*).

24 cf. W. R. Johnson 186 'The play is about . . . the arrogance of adults'. The terms of teaching are always already unequal (Moger in B. Johnson 135): for some decisive ageism cf. Ludwig 170 'His *senes* are all quite' (nb) 'respectable, well-intentioned and serious fathers, who are as sincerely concerned as their wives for the happiness of their children'. The kids are all right: Sandbach (1978) 145 n. 49 'The responsibility lies with the nature of young human beings, which is such that the wisest of parents will be lucky to attain a relation with his child that will be perfect at all points'?

'. . . *istuc recte* . . .': I have no brothers. I have no sons. I am neither a youngest nor an eldest child. I am no theatre-goer. Still. My credentials?

. . . istuc recte . . .

References

Abbott, F. F. (1907) 'The theatre as a factor in Roman politics under The Republic', *Transactions of the American Philological Association* 38 149–56.

Altman, R. (ed.) (1981) *Genre: The Musical, A Reader*, London Routledge & Kegan Paul/British Film Institute.

Anderson, W. S. (1984) 'Love plots in Menander and his Roman adapters', *Ramus* 13, 124–34.

André, J–M. (1977) *La philosophie à Rome*, Paris, PUF.

Arnott, W. G. (1975) *Menander, Plautus and Terence*, G & R New Surveys 9, Oxford, Clarendon Press.

Astin, A. E. (1967) *Scipio Aemilianus*, Oxford, Oxford University Press.

Astin, A. E. (1978) *Cato the Censor*, Oxford, Oxford University Press.

Atkins, G. D. and Johnson, M. L. (eds) (1985) *Writing and Reading Differently: Deconstruction and the teaching of Composition and Literature*, University of Arkansas Press.

Bassnett-Maguire, S. (1980) *Translation Studies*, New Accents. London, Methuen.

Beard, M. and Crawford, M. (1985) *Rome in the late Republic*, London, Duckworth.

Beare, W. (1964) *The Roman Stage*, London, Methuen.

Bloch, M. and Parry, J. (eds) (1982) *Death and the Regeneration of Life*, Cambridge University Press.

Bonner, S. F. (1977) *Education in Ancient Rome*, London, Methuen.

Bristol, M. D. (1985) *Carnival and Theater*, London, Methuen.

Callier, F. (1982) 'A propos des *Adelphes* de Térence; le personnage d'Mégion et la morale aristocratique', *Latomus* 41, 517–27.

Carrubba, R. W. (1968) 'The rationale of Demea in Terence's *Adelphoe*', *Dioniso* 42, 16–24.

CHCL II (1982) Kenney, E. J. and Clausen, W. V. (eds) *The Cambridge History of Classical Literature Volume II: Latin Literature*, Cambridge, Cambridge University Press.

Clavel-Lévêque, M. (1984) *L'Empire en Jeux* CNRS.

Coarelli, F. (1977) 'Public building in Rome between the Second Punic War and Sulla', *Papers of the British School at Rome*, 32, 1–23.

Dixon, S. (1985) 'Polybius on Roman Women and Property', *American Journal of Philology*, 147–70.

Docherty, T. (1983) *Reading (Absent) Character*, Oxford, Oxford University Press.

Drakakis, J. (ed.) (1985) *Alternative Shakespeares*, New Accents, London, Methuen.

Duckworth, G. E. (1952) *The Nature of Roman Comedy* Princeton, NJ.

Duret, L. (1982) 'La comédie des "Adelphes" et l'indulgence d'Horace', *Review des Etudes Latin*, 248–65.

Earl D. C. (1961) *The Political Thought of Sallust*, London.

Earl, D. C. (1962) 'Terence and Roman politics', *Historia* 11, 469–85.

Earl D. C. (1967) *The Moral and Political Tradition of Rome*, London, Thames & Hudson.

Ehrman, R. K. (1985) 'Terentian prologues and the parabases of Old Comedy', *Latomus* 44, 370–6.

Fantham, E. F. (1968) 'Terence, Diphilus and Menander' *Philologus* 112 196–216.

Fantham, E. F. (1971) '*Hautontimorumenos* and *Adelphoe*: a study of Fatherland in Terence and Menander', *Latomus* 30, 970–98.

Foulkes, A. P. (1983) *Literature and Propaganda*, New Accents, London, Methuen.

Geffcken, K. (1973) 'Comedy in the *Ero Caelio*' *Mnemosyne Suppl.* 30.

Giglioli. P. P. (ed.) (1972) *Language and Social Context*, Harmondsworth, Penguin.

Gloversmith, F. (ed.) (1984) *The Theory of Reading*, Brighton, Harvester.

Gold, B. K. (ed.) (1982) *Literary and Artistic Patronage in Ancient Rome*, University of Texas Press.

Graham, J. F. (ed.) (1985) *Difference in Translation*, Ithaca, NY, Cornell University Press.

Grant, J. N. (1971) 'Notes on Donatus' Commentary on *Adelphoe*', *Greek, Roman and Byzantine Studies*, 12 197–209.

Grant, J. N. (1973) 'The role of Canthara in Terence's *Adelphoe*', *Philologus* 117 70–5.

Grant, J. N. (1975) 'The ending of Terence's *Adelphoe* and the Menandrian original', *American Journal of Philology*.

Greenberg, N. A. (1979–80) 'Success and failure in the *Adelphoe*', *Classical World* 73, 221–36.

Grimal, P. (1982) 'Considérations sur les *Adelphes* de Térence', *Comptes Rendus de l'Academie des Inscriptions et Belles Lettres* 38–47.

Hunter, R. L. (1985) *The New Comedy of Greece and Rome*, Cambridge, Cambridge University Press.

Irwin, J. T. (1975) *Doubling and Incest, Repetition and Revenge: A Speculative Reading of Faulkner*, Baltimore, Md, Johns Hopkins University Press.

Johnson, B. (ed.) (1982) 'The pedagogical imperative: teaching as a literary genre', *Yale French Studies*, 63.

Johnson, W. R. (1968) 'Micio and the perils of perfection', *University of California Studies in Classical Antiquity*, 171–86.

Knapp, C. (1919) 'References in Plautus and Terence to plays, players and playwrights', *Classical Philology* 14, 35–55.

Konstan, D. (1983) *Roman Comedy*, Ithaca, NY, Cornell University Press.

Leach, E. W. (1971) 'Horace's *pater optimus* and Terence's Demea: autobiographical fiction and comedy in *Sermo* 1.4', *American Journal of Philology*, 92, 616–32.

Lloyd-Jones, M. (1973) 'Terentian technique in the *Adelphi* and the *Eunuchus*', *Classical Quarterly*, 23.

Lord, C. (1977) 'Aristotle, Menander and the *Adelphoe* of Terence', *Transactions of the American Philological Association* 107, 183–202.

Ludwig, W. (1968) 'The originality of Terence and his Greek models', *Greek, Roman and Byzantine Studies* 9, 169–82.

McBride, R. (1977) *The Sceptical Vision of Molière*, London, Methuen.

MacKendrick, P. (1954) 'Demetrius of Phalerum, Cato and the *Adelphoe*', *Revista di Filologia é instruzioe classica*, 32, 18–35.

Maltby, R. (1979) 'Linguistic characterization of Old Men in Terence', *Classical Philology*, 72, 136–47.

Marshall, A. J. (1984) 'Symbols and showmanship in Roman public life', *Phoenix* 38, 120–41.

Martin, R. M. (1976) *Terence Adelphoe*, Cambridge, Cambridge University Press.

Millar, F. (1984) 'The political character of the Classical Roman Republic, 200–151 BC', *Journal of Roman Studies*, 74, 1–19.

Orlandini, A. (1982) 'Lo scacio di Micione (Ter. *Ad.* 924–997)', *Gionde Italiano de Filologia*, 99–112.

Pêcheux, M. (1982) *Language, Semantics and Ideology*, London, MacMillan.

Postman, N. and Weingartner, C. (1971) *Teaching as a Subversive Activity*, Harmondsworth, Penguin.

Rank, O. (1971) *The Double*, University of North Carolina Press.

Rawson, E. (1973) 'Scipio, Laelius, Furius and the ancestral tradition', *Journal of Roman Studies* 63, 161–74.

Rawson, E. (1985) *Intellectual Life in the Late Roman Republic*, London, Duckworth.

Revesz, M. B. (1968) 'Si duo dicunt idem, non est idem' *AAntHung* 16, 205–21.

Rogers, J. (ed.) (1969) *Teaching on Equal Terms*, London, BBC.

Roszak, T. (ed.) *The Dissenting Academy*, Harmondsworth, Pelican.

Salmon, E. T. (1982) *The Making of Roman Italy*, London, Thames & Hudson.

Sandbach, F. H. (1977) *The comic tradition of Greece and Rome*, London, Chatto & Windus.

Sandbach, F. H. (1978) 'Donatus' use of the name Terentius and the end of Terence's *Adelphoe*', *Bulletin of the Institute of Classical Studies* 25, 123–45.

Scullard, H. H. (1981) *Festivals and Ceremonies of the Roman Republic*, London, Thames & Hudson.

Shershow, S. C. (1986) *Laughing Matters: The Paradox of Comedy*, University of Massachusetts Press.

Slater, N. (1985) *Plautus in Performance. The Theatre of the Mind*, Princeton, NJ.

Suleiman, S. R. (1983) *Authoritarian Fictions. The Ideological Novel as a Literary Genre*, New York, Columbia University Press.

Tränkle, H. (1972) 'Micio und Demea in den terenzischen *Adelphen*', *Museum Helveticum* 29, 241–45.

Trencsényi-Waldapfel, I. (1957) 'Une comédie de Térence, jouée aux funérailles de L. Aemilius Paullus', *AAntHung* 5, 129–65.

Ulmer, G. L. (1985) *Applied Grammatology*, Baltimore, Md. Johns Hopkins University Press.

Walbank, F. W. (1975) '*Symploke*: its role in Polybius' *Histories*', *Yale Classical Studies* 24, 197–212.

Wood, D. and Bernasconi, R. (eds.) (1985) *Derrida and Difference*, University of Warwick, Parousia.

Zetzel, J. E. G. (1972) 'Cicero and the Scipionic Circle', *Harvard Studies in Classical Philology* 76, 173–9.

· *10* ·

Sunt aliquid manes: personalities, personae and ghosts in Augustan poetry

ROWLAND COTTERILL

In this chapter I attempt a deliberately, I fear provocatively, summary survey of some features of certain texts which will be recognized when I refer to them under the familiar – and yet somewhat oxymoronic – rubric 'Augustan poetry': these two adjectives, indeed, and their doubleness as well, are no doubt part of what is there, somewhere, to be surveyed. I shall invoke styles of discourse for which I am, certainly and (given the antiquity of the texts involved) appropriately, indebted to other scholars and critics,[1] distinguished in this field and in others too: but, apart from what this footnote acknowledges, I have avoided the nomenclature of either parricide or parasitism, and chosen rather to use the space this format allows[2] to expatiate a little upon two bodies of text which have particularly seized me and which permit at once a concentration and a diffusion of many of those features of the larger 'Augustan' corpus to which I shall be attending. These are the *Epistles* of Horace and the fourth book of Propertius' *Elegies*. In the last and longest section of this chapter I discuss these in relation to the place of history, society, truth and desire in Augustan poetry – and vice versa – and, again, in relation to the function of what (if a portmanteau word can claim the excuse of brevity) one might hopefully name 'authoriality' as it stands towards these places, placings, displacements and replacements. The three preceding, shorter sections consider respectively some general issues of critical theory, the notion of 'Augustan poetry' and a few of its refractions in the last generation of classical critical scholarship.

The grammatical mood of 'to deconstruct' may perhaps be irretrievably — as here — infinitive. Or perhaps my 'here' may paradoxically legitimize for it at least one place, time and subject (should one rather call it an 'accusative of respect'?) — that of textuality. Textuality deconstructs. Deconstruction is textual. Deconstruction is — within reference to — text.

And: people — to put it at its most absolute, most crude — deconstruct texts. Shall we say — to mitigate the matter — that people manifest textuality, manifest deconstruction? That a time, a place, of textuality does this?

Already this may be to say no more than that constructions — of society, of history, of those modes of productivity which are known as truth (manifestation) and, even, as desire (deconstruction) — take their place in text: that the fading of text is alternate, double, movement into as much as out of focus.

'I do not hate a proud man as I do hate the engendering of . . .' texts (as Shakespeare's Ajax just fails to say).[3] Texts engender. The engendered, the generic, is the self-sufficient — and it is, of course, always, already, the text 'itself'. 'As if a' text 'were author to himself/And knew no other kin'[4] — the pathos of Coriolanus (at once distinctively Roman and exemplarily un-self-deceived) is critical for the nature of the text; textual, for the nature of the critic; natural, for those who have taken their places as (critical) deconstructors of texts. 'This thing of darkness I acknowledge mine':[5] so says the deconstructor of that infinitive, that textuality, that whose language, well taught it by its successor and inheritor on that space which can never be owned except 'in common', profits by cursing;[6] curses its profiteering inheritors, whose property (in their own innovation, their own deconstruction, their own) is thus appalled.[7]

Can the text (as economic object, object and yet still always paternal engendering authority of its critical profiteers) be — really — the text (place of multiplicity, genre, meaningful ghost of itself)? 'Single nature's double name/Neither two nor one was called'.[8] It is not, of course, that the multiplicity of signification is simply a product of (the complex changes of) economic politics, of (our distanced place in) history, of (our energetically pluralized) readings. (Better, no doubt of it, to say that society, history, and whatever forces unleash reading, are themselves textualized, in text, intertext.) Still: within (let us call it) politics the multiple text occupies constituted places, contests its places, constitutes what it contests: here, too, belong those shadowy and devolved beings, the author, the reader, the world: that is, here – in politics – are the origins, the supplements, and indeed the definable disseminations of textuality: constructed. That is, the thematics of criticism – say of Augustan poetry – is political. (Also, it is, just so, in textuality that these origins and so forth are deconstructed. Which is by no means to say that they fail to take place in textuality.)

And more it is in politics – where else? – that textuality, multiple signification, is posed as (a) value. Even this is insufficient: nothing less in this sense, than politics, could *name* 'multiplicity' (textuality has not learnt to count). Every deconstruction of a text, as every claim to construct a text, belongs to political economics: just as, in textual 'space', there is not this (particular) construction or deconstruction. Little can be said of Textuality, of deconstruction: and (rightly, necessarily, politically) much is said of these things.

'Augustan poetry' names, in a manner we all receive as exemplary, the imbrication of textuality with politics to which my last paragraph, my first section, draws attention. That literature, at least this once, took (its) place in history, that history was, and therefore (we may say) has been, still, transmitted and imprinted by literature – that time elicited value and in so doing conferred immunity from time on that which it valued – that (to put this another way) discontinuity and validity play box-and-cox in that theatre of the classical which the reading of these texts figures for us: no less than this is at stake in the constitution of such a moment, such a haunting possibility. In this moment textuality and politics wink at one another, practise a conscious blindness, supplement each other while (to a malign eye) seeming to contest each other's prerogative of origin (had Augustus nothing better to do . . .? 'sed omnes illacrimabiles/urgentur ignotique longa/ notce, carent quia vate sacro').[9]

'Augustus' names a politics of restoration. Restoration, in turn, is that turn of ideology which seeks to denote an origin as, by unique good fortune, succeeding that which it originated, a present with sovereign competence to re-present a past, itself at once the tolerant condition and the only possible goal and resolution of remembered historical turbulence – itself thus outside history and in need of history for definition and legitimizing. And, if present is also remote past, the future can only be the recent past, the (as now one might well realize) (un)necessary (sic) intermission between plenitude and plenitude. The Augustan future is not generation but genre – only the 'princeps' can define the 'capax imperi', only 'imperium' can function as norm of its bearers (' . . . nisi imperasset').[10] The dissimulations of the Tacitean emperor are those of the Augustan poem, true to nature only in their closures. 'Laudantur simili prole puerperae,/culpam poena premit coems'.[11]

The triumph of Augustan politics was double – like the triumph of its most representative panegyric, the fifth ode of Horace's fourth book: to generate, both at once and both seemingly innocent of each other's potential sovereignty, the god and the common man, each the ghost to the other's machine:

> condit quisque diem collibus in suis,
> et vitem viduas ducit ad arbores;
> hinc ad vina redit laetus et alteris
>   te mensis adhibet deum . . .
>
> 'longas o utinam, dux bone, ferias
> praestes Hesperiae!' dicimus integro
> sicci mane die, dicimus uvidi,
>   cum sol Oceano subest.[12]

The drunk (pseudo-) peasant praises the 'god' who guarantees his private property both in land and in song. And thus a religion is born.

Augustan politics and Augustan religion both stand in constitutive need of, what they all but define out of existence, the potentially different past (future) and the potentially dissenting (and therefore significantly consenting) individual. For both politician and writer, to be an author is to be authorized by another: it is to take place under authority.

Here, then, are some of the resonant themes of that poetry which is Augustan: a transversion of history, wherein origin becomes present: a compression of future into simultaneity, diversity, 'artistic value' – or what we may call, what we and they (its authors) both value as, textuality; let Virgil's *Aeneid* and the aetiologies of Propertius and Ovid (among others) stand in for the

former, and, for the latter, Roman Callimacheanism. Horace's
epistle to Augustus captures both strands –

> *quod si tam Graecis novitas invisa fuisset*
> *quan nobis, quid nunc esset vetus? . . .*
>
> *scribimus indocti doctique poemata passim.*[13]

Whose is this appeal? Who are 'we'? – we are between wisdom
and its absence: we are bound to the past and from our bondage
renew the present – perpetual novelty is what we commemorate;
our poetry is born of mourning –

> *singula de nobis anni praedantur euntes;*
> *eripuere iocos, Venerem, convivia, ludum;*
> *tendunt extorquere poemata . . .*[14]

And thus we may name two more 'Augustan' concerns – with a
wisdom, a 'truth' that is at once the goal and the origin of pursuit:
with a desire, an absence, a loss that excites in its subject self-
sufficiency – or that excites, exacerbates to itself a 'subject', subject
of loss, subject immune to any possible loss, subject for whom loss
is the name of the game. For these concerns, let the texts of
Horace's epistles – enervations and perfections of earlier Roman
satire – and of elegiac love poetry stand in place.

This is a haunted poetry, whose textualized presence to itself is
at one and the same time its diffusion from itself of those ghosts
that haunt it – history, imitable secular society, practical wisdom,
and the symbolisms of desire: in the specificity of these hauntings
the poetry becomes Augustan, becomes the trace of Augustus'
pretentious re-founding of Rome and of Roman imperial polity:
the trace, as well and indeed above all, of the self-sufficiency and
the illusions of the impotent senatorial class, bought off with the
(fulfilled) promises of consumption, clients, continuity and the
impotence of conspiracy. These are the readers, the authorizers,
the material world that, as I say, haunt Augustan texts and turn
them into political and economic value. And this necromantic
politics has its medium: prolific, engendering, self-impregnated as
a medium must be – and, equally, distinguished by the mask of
intervention. *Larvata prodit persona.*[15]

The notion of the 'persona' was put into play within the field of critical scholarship on Augustan poetry as a key tool in a relatively early enterprise of deconstruction. Such criticism constructed for itself a model of past scholarship as having founded its perceptions of poetry upon 'Romantic', 'genetic' and 'biographical' assumptions. Involved in these assumptions were (it was argued) the unargued, metaphorical and misleading conceptions of a poet standing over against a poem – a relationship, this, between demonstrably and politically distinguishable entities – of the poet as the origin (not without, probably, interesting labour) of the poem, and, in turn, of the poem as a document capable of yielding, if carefully handled, reliable and independent information concerning its author. The circular arguments involved in this (alleged) movement of thought indicated, then, not so much an order of importance, or chronology, between two objects separably definable, but rather a mutual parasitism, revealed, for that matter, by the language of 'labour' (the poet's labour-pains on the production of the poem, and no less the labour of critical parturition by which such a poet is constructed from the – now disjunct, rather than organically interrelated – elements of the poetic text). And in place of these two objects (so it was proposed) there was to be set one – the poetic text: of its origin little or nothing could be said (the 'intentional fallacy'), little too of its effects (the 'affective fallacy'), much however of its internal structure. And the 'persona' began (in this field) critical life as a stop-gap, a placebo: the appearance and not the (unavailable, irrelevant) reality of textual origin – speaker of, and in, a discourse whose claims to veridical status could be appropriately resumed under the rubric of theatre.

A certain doubleness soon enough emerged within this acceptance of the term. The theatrical mask, after all, conceals by revealing – its ostentatious revelation is, thus, the locus of its powers of concealment: and herein lies, perhaps, much of its power. (Is there a 'real' Ajax, in Sophocles' play, author of deception and definable into truth, over against it, by his suicide? Surely not: 'Trugrede' and suicide speech jostle one another in their claims upon, their claims to re-present, the reality of an Ajax who is to be found, if anywhere, precisely in the distance between the pliable and the immobilized, the wearer of masks and the mask worn.) Nor were the 'internal structures' of many of the Augustan poems subjected to such interpretations so economically or symmetrically built as to relegate questions of their origin, their archaeology, to insignificance and anachronism – such 'flaws' of structure being, indeed, one of the chief props of inquiry directed towards biographical origins (and historical contextuality). Perhaps a persona might change in mid-poem, might be credited with the mobility of the poetic textual imagination itself? Perhaps a persona might *act* – might simulate, dissimulate, disclaim what it claimed? Could a persona, perhaps, adopt a persona?

A major initial self-recommendation, in turn, of what I shall refer to as 'generic theory' was its short way with such haunting questions (questionable hauntings).

Often the logic of a classical poem or speech appears to be intentionally incomplete or inconsistent. . . . The solution is that the poems and speeches of classical antiquity are not internally complete individual works but are members of classes of literature.

'Such an approach makes unnecessary the psychoanalytic examinations, the inopportune hypotheses of irony, the anachronistic applications of the out-of-date critical techniques of scholars in other fields'.[16] The class makes good, then, the apparent (or are they, on this view, still more than merely apparent!) deficits of the individual member.

And, yet, these classes (the 'genres') have their own origins – 'real life' – and their credentials – rhetorical manuals several centuries later (as the state of our knowledge stands at present) than these Augustan (and earlier) poetic texts to which their application is in question: not, perhaps, an anachronistic application in the normal sense, but a dyschronistic argument and also a nice instance of my earlier claim that Augustan poetry produces the future as the present, the unknown as the multiple, change as the engendering of the self-sufficient. The genres may also include, and be included in, one another. Their constituent 'topoi' – commonplaces – may defy their parent genres and assert their own mutual commonality by emigration from one genre to another. Primary elements of a genre may fail to appear, or appear in inverted form, within a poem without any infringement of apparentation or any breach of rational classification being involved. Most tellingly of all, genres (we come to learn) acquire, or associate to themselves speakers (ghosts in even this most well-oiled or critical machine?) – for, an apparent deviation of poem from generic predictability may be accounted for by 'speaker-variation': thus, the public creator 'of' Horace's Ode 3.14, enacting as he does an

apparent retreat from public matters to private considerations . . . is not diminishing his public role; he is attempting to demonstrate the sincerity of his speeches in the public field, by showing that he is also involved in what he is saying as a private individual.[17]

And so roles, personae, and their mobilities, re-infiltrate the purity of the discourse of textual bricolage. '[Personam] expelles furca, tamen usque recurret. Et mala perrumpet furtim fastidia victrix.'[18]

Any appositeness there may be in this Horatian deformed quotation is perhaps not accidental. In the tenth epistle of his first book Horace sets the 'city' over against 'country' – in order to suggest that the qualities of the country do and in any circumstances will, infiltrate, inhabit, take over the specificities of the city: hypothesizing that the 'natural life' is the object – 'vivere naturae si convenienter oportet'[19] – he, as in the passage cited above, displays its emergence as the subject of human efforts. Just so the critical constructions of persona and of genre are set over against the (equally critical) constructions of a Romantic and biographic geneticism – they are its successors and yet it is the historical victor: just so the 'topoi', the commonplaces which are posited as the common ground of Graeco-Roman poetic imitation, cultivate for themselves one place, in which they may grow and from which as its products they may emerge – and this place, this site, is voice. Dead matter begins to speak – if only to announce its own death. 'Sunt aliquid Manes' – 'Graecia capta ferum victorem cepit':[20] in both cases it is the survivor, the victor, the legatee, who in commemorating finds voice accruing to the speechless, the conquered; the taken over takes over.

This, of course, is an assessment of the success, not the failure, of generic theory. For it is a genetic theory too. Indeed it supersumes that geneticism which it constructed itself by expelling: in much the same way one can argue that a theory of imitation – such as generic theory is – will become, will appear as having always already been, a theory of multiplicity, diversity, productivity, even a theory of the grotesque. Born from moments of (modern) critical rivalry, contestation, from perceptions of historical movement and gestures of nervous confidence (consider the functioning of the words 'solution', 'inopportune' and 'anachronistic' in my quotation from Cairns above), the theory of generic imitation reveals its genuine contiguity with the phenomena of the Augustan poetry, to which its applications so regularly direct themselves, nowhere more than in its appropriations by which it appropriates, its engendering of that which it seeks to expel.

What is the programme of Propertius' fourth book of elegies? What does the text posit for itself as its origin and its goal?

> *sacra diesque canam et cognomina prisca locorum*
> *has meus ad metus sudet oportet equus.*[21]

The goal, the future of the poetic text is to be the resuscitation of the past. And resuscitation is the enterprise of the whole book, indeed – even of those poems frequently seen as standing apart from the rest in their concern with love, whether in others (the third and perhaps fifth elegies) or in the poet himself (the seventh and eight elegies). Arethus posits her perhaps barely legible text as the relic of her death –

> *aut si qua incerto fallet te littera tractu,*
> *signa meae dextrae iam morientis erunt*

(the perfect legitimation for speculative textual criticism) and correspondingly ruminates on the presence to her of one who is absent –

> *cum totiens absis, si potes esse meus.*[22]

The 'lena' of the fifth elegy is at once dead matter, buried and dubiously monumentalized –

> *Terra tuum spinis obducat, lena, sepulcrum –*

and unwillingly animate still –

> *et tua, quod non vis, sentiat umbra sitim.*[23]

And in the last poem of the book the speech of the dead takes over completely from the living: Cornelia, unlike Cynthia in the seventh elegy, can speak to readers without a medium, can defy even the law of inaccessibility to which she offers such eloquent testimony –

> *Te licet orantem fuscae deus audiat aulae:*
> *nempe tuas lacrimas litora surda bibent*[24]

(but to the extent that she answers, by reprobating, them his tears have not found her deaf.)

And yet the project is, of course, mal-apropos from its very start.

> *Quo ruis improudens, vage, dicere fata,*
> *Properti?*
> *non sunt a dextro condita fila colo.*[25]

And it is the speaker's own past and future that must be resuscitated and predicted. The subject of the text becomes, in this giddying transversion midway through the first elegy of the book, its object – just as speech, the voice of the resuscitated past, takes over, in the second, fourth and ninth elegies, and represents past as present, de-authorizing the authority of the necromantic poet.

'External' and 'internal' material, objective and subjective programmes, assumptions and contestations of authority to speak – these are the matter and the manner of the book at large: the objects of the programme of archaeology and aetiology are as elusive and deceiving as his position in speaking of them –

> *mendax fama noces: alius mihi nominis index.*[26]
> *nil patrium nisi nomen habet Romanus alumnus.*[27]

The past is what the present makes: it is also what the present makes of the past's self-making – a doubleness which is communicated in the mixture of nostalgia and modern irony in the tone of Propertius' aetiological speaker –

> *quot gradibus domus ista Remi se sustulit! olim*
> *unus erat fratrum maxima regna focus . . .*
> *nulli cura fuit externos quaerere divos,*
> *cum tremeret patrio pendula turba sacro.*[28]

The Augustan claim to be the past's true presence to itself, its modern origin, is celebrated and subverted here – or rather, celebration engenders subversion and subversion celebrates. One might, of course, compare the function of Dido and Turnus – if not of Aeneas himself – in Virgil's *Aeneid*: the past praises the labour precisely by virtue of its labours towards, whether to build or to undermine it –

> *tantae molis erat Romanam condere gentem.*[29]

And no less labour, or doubleness, is requisite in one who would found a new Latin textuality:

> *ludentis speciem dabit et torquebitur, ut qui nunc Satyrum, nunc agrestem Cyclopa movetur. praetulerim scriptor delirus inersque videri, dum mea delectent mala me vel denique fallant, quam sapere et ringi.*[30]

Such a writer will in turn convert past into present and present into past within language too.

> *audebit, quaecumque parum splendoris habebunt et sine pondere erunt et honore indigna feruntur,*
> *verba movere loco . . . obscurata diu populo bonus eruet atque proferet in lucem speciosa vocabula rerum . . . vehemens et liquidus puroque simillimus amni fundet opes Latiumque beabit divite lingua.*[31]

In so doing he will fertilize his object while himself metonymically acquiring the properties of the fertile text.[32] The labour, like the play, of the Augustan textual project ineluctably engenders the labourer and the player, at once parasites and masters of the texts they inhabit. The labour, the play, are converted into 'artistic value'.

Of course labour could generate value in other ways. The poet could intervene, legislate, dictate. The text could energize, disturb, displace, at least modify its readers. It could project its author's, or its readers', futures. Some of these enterprises seem, in Horace's first book of Epistles, to be in question.

> *nunc itaque et versus et cetera ludicra pono;*
> *quid verum atque decens curo et rogo et omnis in hoc sum;*

condo et compono quae mox depromere possim . . .[33]
nemo adeo ferus est ut non mitescere possit,
si modo culturae patientem commedet aurem . . .[34]
Nil admirari prope res est una, Numici,
solque quae possit facere et servare beatum.[35]

Here is, it would seem, a changeable society and a changeable personality, and a writing that may at least play its part, take a share of the labour involved, in these changes. It is worth seeing how the book puts into practice this programme. The 'verses', the literary textual play, abjured in the first poem of the collection becomes in the second (and with good traditional backing) the fount of that wisdom for which they were, earlier, to be laid aside –

Troiani belli scriptorem, Maxime Lolli,
dum tu declamas Romae, praenest relegi;
qui quid sit pulcrum, quid turpe, quid utile, quid non,
planius ac melius Chrysippo et Crantore dicit.[36]

The substance of moral-philosophical wisdom cannot be possessed and should not even be too strenuously pursued –

insani sapiens nomen ferat, aequus iniqui,
ultra quam satis est virtutem si petat ipsam.[37]

Perhaps it can be subjected only to negative, rather than positive, definition –

virtus est vitium fuguere, et sapienta prima
stiltitia caruisse.[38]

– or perhaps this is only some (first) part of a virtue which none the less, in any fuller body, remains elusive; still to be gathered and acquired as late as the end of the eighteenth epistle of the book – 'aequum mi animum ipse parabo'[39] – still uncertain in its origins and operations –

virtutem doctrina paret, naturane donet;
quid minuat curas, quid te tibi reddat amicum[40]

– such are indeed the questions to be studied: but that in the mode and moment of their being posed there lies also the answer. Friendship, ease, with oneself is both the programme and its goal. Virtue leaves all as it found it, and there an end[41] – only, it removes those barriers to the coincidence of the real with the true which are set up by the inveterate human refusal of limit, (that is) the cultivation of desire ('admirari'). Even against desire (this is the provocative structure of the sixth epistle) virtue can bring no weapons of its own making: to every potentially limitless desire, including the desire of itself, it can only give its dismissive permission. Its end is its beginning –

dimidium facti qui coepit habet; sapere aude; incipe.[42]

And its beginning, by being reiterated throughout the several epistles of the book, comes equally to be its end.

Perhaps a little more than this can be said: perhaps poetry, textuality, wisdom, does leave its deposits –

ludus enim genuit trepidum certamen et iram, ira truces inimicitieas et funebre bellum.[43]

This reprehensible engendering of new from old, unlike from like, contestation from presence – the most dynamic process of the whole book – is what may be expected to come about when an author is inferred from a text, a licence of imitation from an author – and, in turn, invidiousness from imitation, as every imitator sets up as new author. The nineteenth poem of the book thus inscribes a specifically literary productivity: while the twentieth and last envisages the separating out of text from author and the uneasy separation, too, which is the condition of the erotic courtship between text and readers – 'carus eris Romae donec te deserat aetas',[44] only to discover them newly imbricated with one another –

cum tibi sol tepidus admoverit auris, me libertino natum patre et in tenui re maiores pennas nido extendisse loqueris, ut quantum generi demas virtutibus addas . . .[45]

'Nil patrium nisi nomen habet Romanus alumnus'. Something, some body, certainly seems to have grown.

Desire, one might have predicted, finds Augustan poets at their

most playfully strenuous. There are imprecations, dismissals, pleas
for admittance: contests, enjoyments, invitations: there is, between
the figures of lovers, the figures of love, space, across which energy
may carry. If the poetry is metaphor for love, love in turn is
metaphor for the metaphor, for just this transmission between
figure and figure. Love is oscillation: desire is the play between
absence and presence: no author can be held by the objects of
desire, no more than by any objectivized text. Text cannot commit
author, and, familiarly if painfully, text cannot hold 'Woman'.
This is the art of Roman generic love – elegiac and lyric alike:
love's art is a teaching of techniques, of the repeated and predictable, rather than any assessment of the politics or the economics
of love's possessions.

Into such enchanting textualized disenchantment, shadowily,
emerges something that should not be there.

> *Sunt aliquid Manes: letum non omnia finit,*
>   *luridaque evictos effugit umbra rogos.*
> *Cynthia namque meo visa est incumbere fulcro,*
>   *murmur ad extremae nuper humata viae,*
> *cum mihi somnus ab exsequiis penderet amoris,*
>   *et querer lecti frigida regna mei.*[46]

The apparition is intimate and threatening; intimacy is what it
threatens. The speaker is asleep and not asleep. The bed is a
kingdom, however desolate – and also the dominion belongs to
the one who has left the bed. Just so, at the end –

> '*. . . nunc te possideant aliae: mox sola tenebo:*
> *mecum eris, et mixtis ossibus ossa teram.*'
> *haec postquam querula mecum sub lite peregit*
> *inter complexus excidit umbra meos.*[47]

The ghost completes its case, announces its claim to possession –
and escapes the one who would seek to possess it. Through this
amazing poem, love, the bodiless, the weightless, has acquired a
body, a past haunts a present, makes itself present, makes the
present its own, makes good the omissions and gaps of the past
with the present –

sic mortis lacrimis vitae sanamus amores:
celo ego perfidiae crimina multa tuae.[48]

Love's wounds, its gaping holes, its sources of energy, are healed and made good (or, if one should read 'sancimus', are ratified) by lovers: and to heal is at once to name and to conceal wounds. The ghost is the most concrete body of Augustan love: the most ineluctably realized personality. 'Quisque suos patimur Manes'.[49]

Notes

1 Among the books I have profited from reading are: S. Greenblatt, *Renaissance Self Fashioning*, London, University of Chicago Press, 1982; C. Norris, *Deconstruction*, London, Methuen, 1982, J. Drakakis, (ed.), *Alternative Shakespeares*, London, Methuen, 1985, particularly the essay by Malcolm Evans, 'Deconstructing Shakespeare's comedies'; L. Tennenhouse, *Power on Display*, London, Methuen, 1986; G. Williams, *Tradition and Originality in Roman Poetry*, Oxford, Oxford University Press, 1968; G. Williams, *Figures of Thought in Roman Poetry*, New Haven, Conn, Yale University Press, 1980; F. Cairns, *Generic Composition in Greek and Roman Poetry*, Edinburgh, Edinburgh University Press, 1972; J. Warden, *Fallax opus.*
   C. O. Brink, *Horace on Poetry. Epistles Book II: The Letters to Augustus and Florus*, Cambridge, Cambridge University Press, 1982.
2 An earlier version of this paper was given to a seminar organized by the Centre for Research in Philosophy and Literature at the University of Warwick in October, 1985. I learnt much from the comments of Andrew Benjamin, John Fletcher, David Imrie and David Wood — none of whom bears any responsibility for the remaining failings of the present version.
3 Shakespeare, *Troilus and Cressida*, 2.3.154 (all Shakespeare references are to the 1981 paperback version of the edition of the *Complete Works* by Peter Alexander).
4 Shakespeare, *Coriolanus*, 5.3.35–6.
5 Shakespeare, *The Tempest*, 5.1.275–6.
6 Shakespeare, *The Tempest*, 1.2.363–4.
7 Shakespeare, *The Phoenix and Turtle*, 37.
8 Shakespeare, *The Phoenix and Turtle*, 39–40.
9 Horace, *Odes*, 4.9.26–8 (all my Horatian references use the Oxford edition of E. C. Wickham, reused by H. W. Garrod): 'But all [these brave men], unwept and unknown, are borne down upon by perpetual night, because they lacked a bard to praise them.'

10 Tacitus, *Histories*, 1, 49: 'fit to rule . . . had he not ruled'.

11 Horace, *Odes*, 4.5.23–4: 'mothers are praised for the likeness of offspring to parents: sin is at once suppressed by punishment.'

12 Horace, *Odes* 4.5. 29–32, 37–40: 'each man passes the day on his own property in the hills, marrying the vine to the widowed trees: home he returns, gladly, to his wine and at his second cup hails you as a god . . . "Long let them be, the holidays, that you, our good ruler, provide for Italy!" – so we say, sober, in the morning with the whole day ahead of us, so we say, drunk, when the sun sinks into the sea.'

13 Horace, *Epistles*, 2.1.90–1, 117: 'But if the Greeks had hated novelty as much as we [Romans] do, what would there be for us now to call archaic? . . . Unlearned and learned alike, we're writing poems all over the place.'

14 Horace, *Epistles*, 2.2.55–7: 'the passing years despoil us of the things that are ours, one by one; they have snatched away laughter, love, feasting, gaming; they are trying to twist my poems away.'

15 'Masked, there advances – the "persona".'

16 Cairns, op. cit., pp. 5–6, 31.

17 Cairns, op. cit., p. 182.

18 A distortion of Horace, *Epistles*, 1.10.24–5: 'you may drive our [the "persona" – originally 'Nature'] with a pitchfork, still it will always return, and secretly, victoriously, she will break through misguided contempt.'

19 Horace, *Epistles*, 1.10.12: 'if the task is to live in accordance with nature.'

20 Propertius, *Elegies*, 4.7.1. (all my quotations from Propertius' fourth book use the edition of W. A. Camps, Cambridge, 1965): '[perhaps] They have real substance, then – ghosts': Horace, *Epistles*, 2.1.156: 'Conquered Greece conquered for barbarous conquerors.'

21 Propertius, *Elegies*, 4.1.69–70: 'I shall sing of holy things, festal days, and archaic place-names: this should be a goal to make my poetic steed sweat.'

22 Propertius, *Elegies*, 4.3.5–6,2: 'or if you miss the sense of any falteringly written letter, it will be the sign of my dying hand . . . if you can indeed be mine, as often as you are.'

23 Propertius, *Elegies*, 4.5.1,2: 'May the earth hide your grave, your band, with thorns – and, as you'd most hate, may your shade suffer thirst.'

24 Propertius, *Elegies*, 4.5.1,2: 'Though the god of the dark hall might hear your prayer, still your tears will be drunk by deaf shores.'

25 Propertius, *Elegies*, 4.1.71–2: 'Wayward Propertius, where are you rushing in your foolish zeal to be a prophet? No well-omened distaff spins the threads for you.'

26 Propertius, *Elegies*, 4.2.19: 'Lying Rumour, you harm me: I have another to explain my name' – that is, myself; I follow the first of

Camp's two interpretations, indeed a strange (as he says) but not an inappropriate sense.

27 Propertius, *Elegies*, 4.1.37: 'the Roman progeny owes nothing to paternity but its name.'

28 Propertius, *Elegies*, 4.1.9–10, 17–18: 'see how many steps lead up there to the high-raised temple of Quirinus! once a single hearth was the brother's whole domain . . . no-one toiled to search out foreign gods, then, when the people hung on their inherited rites, trembling in awe.'

29 Virgil, *Aeneid*, 1.33: 'so great was the labour of founding the Roman people'.

30 Horace, *Epistles*, 2.2.126–8: 'The poet will give the appearance of one who is merely playing: he will twist and turn himself, like one who dances at one moment the satyr's part, at the next the boorish Cyclops. I would rather be seen as an insane, inept writer – so long as my faulty poems pleased or deceived me – than snarl at others and be wise.'

31 Horace, *Epistles*, 2.2.111–13, 115–16, 120–1: 'he will have the courage to do away with any words that may be found to have lost their brightness, their weight, and their true value . . . the good poet will pluck forth and bring into the light those fine words which have long been unknown to the mass of people . . . strong and clear, like a river of pure water, he will pour forth his wealth and fertilise Latium with the riches of his tongue.'

32 See Brink and loc. op. cit., pp. 339–43.

33 Horace, *Epistles*, 1.1.10–12: 'Now, accordingly, I lay aside both my verses and all other toys: I seek out truth and right, I enquire after that, in this I am totally absorbed: I store up and put together what I may in due course be able to put forth to others.'

34 Horace, *Epistles*, 1.1.39–40: 'No-one is so wild that he cannot be tamed if only he will lend a willing ear to good teaching.'

35 Horace, *Epistles*, 1.6, 1–2: 'The one and only rule, Numicius, to make and keep someone happy is this: absorb yourself in nothing.'

36 Horace, *Epistles*, 1.21–4: 'While you, Lollius Maximus, practise rhetoric in Rome at Praenesfe I have reread the author of the Trojan war – clearer and wiser, as a teacher of what is noble or base, what serves us well or ill, than Chrysippus or Cantor.'

37 Horace, *Epistles*, 1.6.15–16: 'Let the sage be called fool, the just unjust, if he desires even goodness to a degree beyond what suffices.'

38 Horace, *Epistles*, 1.6.15–16: 'Avoiding vice, dispelling one's foolishness – this is virtue and wisdom (at least for a start).'

39 Horace, *Epistles*, 1.18.112: 'A poised spirit is something I shall acquire for myself.'

40 Horace, *Epistles*, 1.18.100–1: 'whether study produces goodness or

whether it is a gift of nature: what reduces anxieties, what puts you on good terms with yourself.'

41 Shakespeare, *Troilus and Cressida*, 1.1.86–7.

42 Horace, *Epistles*, 1.2.40–1: 'To begin is to be halfway: dare to be wise: begin.'

43 Horace, *Epistles*, 1.19.48–9: 'For play tends to generate fearsome strife and ire: thence, bitter enmities and deadly war.'

44 Horace, *Epistles*, 1.20.10: 'At Rome you'll be priced highly, until you lose your freshness.'

45 Horace, *Epistles*, 1.20.19–22: 'When the evening sun brings you a fair court to listen, tell them about me – son of a freed slave, I was born to poverty, and my wings grew too great for my nest: as you belittle my origin you magnify my qualities.'

46 Propertius, *elegies*, 4.7.1–6: 'They have real substance – ghosts: death is the end – but not of everything – and the pale shade escapes the grasp of the funeral pyre. For Cynthia appeared to me, leaning down over my bed, she so lately buried at the edge of the unquiet road – while sleep hung back from me after my love's funeral, and I grieved over the desolate domain – her domain – my bed.'

47 Propertius, *Elegies*, 4.7.93–6: ' "let other women claim you for now: soon I alone will grasp you: you will be with me, bones ground on my bones". As she thus ended her bitter complaint to me, she slipped, a shadow, through my embraces.'

48 Propertius, *Elegies*, 4.7.69–70: 'Thus with the tears of death we heal the loves of life' (or perhaps 'we ratify . . .').

49 Virgil, *Aeneid*, 6.763: 'To each of us his own spirits to endure.'

All translations are my own.

· *11* ·

Concealing revealing: a perspective on Greek tragedy

DAVID HALLIBURTON

The main idea of this essay can be put in various ways. One way is to suggest that whatever ancient Greek tragedy reveals it also conceals. Another is the converse, that whatever ancient Greek tragedy conceals it also reveals. A third way of stating the idea, and the one the present discussion will pursue, is that either way might as well be the same way: that the issue is neither concealing or revealing, nor, as C. K. Ogden would say, its enantiamorph, which would be revealing or concealing. The issue is precisely concealing revealing.

Some thirty years before E. R. Dodds specified three heresies of Sophoclean interpretation – the moralistic, the fatalistic, and the formalistic – Heidegger, inspired at least in part by Karl Reinhardt's 1933 study of the playwright, had already found a way around them.[1] In more positive terms, he located the fulcrum of Sophocles' tragedy in the strife between being and appearance.

At the beginning Oedipus is the savior and lord of the state, living in an aura of glory and divine favor. He is hurled out of this appearance, which is not merely his subjective view of himself but the medium in which his being-there appears; his being as murderer of his father and desecrator of his mother is raised to unconcealment.[2]

The appearance of the hero has nothing to do with the dualism of a later epistemology. Neither subjective nor objective, it is the very mode in which he lives his being – a mode of concealment, which resists revelation. In his appearance the two 'poles' of concealment and revelation may be said to be reciprocal and intertwined, and thus to conceal even as they reveal. Such a view of appearance differs from the view of Plato, who tends to reduce appearance to mere appearance, semblance, thus degrading it, while at the same time raising idea to a transcendental level beyond the senses. But without appearance, one may reply, there would be no concealment to disclose, hence no revelation of being, which is precisely and paradoxically the concealing through which being appears. This view sees in appearance as such a condition of concealing revealing.

Such a cool account does not do justice to the urgency of the thinking, informed as it is by the *pathos* that Heidegger sees in the highest achievements of early Greek culture. A similar passion can be felt in some of the deconstructions of Derrida, and even more in Girard. For these Heidegger could be speaking when he states:

Our relation to everything that makes up being, truth, and appearance has long been so confused, so devoid of foundation and passion, that even in our manner of interpreting Greek poetry and making it our own we barely suspect the power wielded by this poetic discourse in Greek being-there.[3]

Oedipus can be revealed in another aspect. More than a fallen hero, 'we must see him as the embodiment of Greek being-there, who most radically and wildly asserts its fundamental passion, the passion for disclosure of being.'[4] Revelations of being, radical and wild assertion, and fundamental passion doubtless reflect Heidegger's own intellectual, one might as well say spiritual passion. They also echo the views of Reinhardt, whose study of Sophoclean thought Heidegger praises so highly. Calling Oedipus 'the mighty revealer',[5] Reinhardt describes the interweaving of appearance and reality (Heidegger's being) as 'no longer external, no longer pragmatic, but daimonic, embracing the whole being, the soul itself and language itself', producing 'the tragedy of the man hurled down from his realm of appearance' (p. 103). By way of partial proof of this thesis, Reinhardt observes that no chorus in the play sings of fate, while a very prominent one sings of human illusion (1,189 ff).

How Derrida relates to such views is a complex issue. 'Plato's Pharmacy', itself hermetic, stresses concealment: 'A text is not a text unless it hides from the first comer, from the first glance, the law of its composition and the rules of its game.'[6] Translators err when they match a single term, such as remedy, with *pharmakon*, for this destroys Plato's anagrammatic writing, which is a network of actual and virtual citations. That is, every instance of *pharmakon* anywhere in Plato invokes every other instance, while 'certain forces of association' (p. 129) connect such a use with all other terms in the Greek language. The *pharmakon* reveals a 'structure of ambiguity and reversibility' (p. 112) whose meanings are layered, such that the interpreter finds ever new depths offering new but concealing revelations. What Derrida says of one Platonic scene applies to any of the metaphors at issue: it at once 'shelters and exposes' (p. 143), a Heideggerean way of suggesting that revelation works concealingly and vice versa. The secret is not to discern all the words that appear in the text but to discover the chain that connects them. Derrida assumes that this can be done whether or not the chain is concealed to the author; whether an author even exists is something Derrida does not concede. Girard, too, seeks such a chain, though the connections he finds turn up more often in events than in particular words, and the connections are finally unitary.

Derrida comes closest to Girard when he studies the *pharmakon* as at the time of the Thargelia, recalling that the rite of purification, resulting in the death of the scapegoats, aimed at relieving the city from some calamity. But, whereas in Derrida sacrifice is only one of the issues associated with the *pharmakon*, in Girard it is the central one.

Girard likes to quote the degree speech from *Troilus and Cressida*:

> *Take but degree away, untune that string,*
> *And, hark, what discord follows! Each thing meets*
> *In mere oppugnancy . . .*

Whether in Shakespeare or primitive religion or Greek tragedy, it is not difference but the loss of difference that produces violent confusion. Loss of difference may occur during a plague when everyone becomes just as susceptible to contagion as everyone else. Violence is another equalizer, the greatest in fact, though the fact remains generally concealed. Girard emphasizes what he calls essential violence: 'A primitive society, a society that does not possess a judicial system is exposed, it has been said, to the escalation of vengeance, to the annihilation pure and simple that we shall henceforth call essential violence.'[7] Such violence reduces differences in that each agent plays the same role; each is the other's double, indifferently the same. The solution is sacrifice: since everyone is anyone, the death of anyone will channel the contagion out of the community, the single victim having taken on his person the violence that threatened everyone else.

Girard's primitive society resembles Hobbes' state of nature, in which general warring occurs because everyone wants what everyone else wants: 'I put for a generall inclination of all mankind, a perpetuall and restless desire of Power after power, that ceaseth onely in Death.'[8] Hobbes proposes a covenant made by all in behalf of all, establishing one person as sovereign under obligation to each and every one who is party to the covenant. Such should be, and is, the commonwealth. This does not much resemble the Girardian scapegoat at first glance. But the selection in both cases is arbitrary and universal, and the person elevated in Hobbes' scheme can be pulled down. In this connection we recall the frequency with which ritual scapegoats are not the lowest members of society but the very highest, Oedipus having been put forward as a leading example.

Tragedy derives its dynamics from the same indifferentiation, reciprocal violence and exculpatory sacrifice as pre-judicial society. Myth works differently. In the myth as such, it is not a question of identity and of reciprocity between Oedipus and the others. One can affirm at least one thing about Oedipus that is true of no other person. He is the only one guilty of parricide and of incest. He appears to us as a monstrous exception; he resembles no one and no one resembles him (p. 108). In tragedy, by contrast, everyone resembles everyone else in an order of balanced reciprocities: in tragedy there is nothing of difference (p. 50), but rather a 'conflictual symmetry' (p. 105) that is altogether 'perfect' (p. 75). According to Sophocles' tragic reinterpretation of the Oedipal myth,

Laius, inspired by the oracle, removed [*écart*] Oedipus by violence, fearing that this son will take his place on the throne of Thebes and in the bed of Jocaste.

Oedipus, inspired by the oracle, removed Laius . . . with violence and he takes his place, etc.

Oedipus, inspired by the oracle, contemplates the destruction of one who perhaps imagines taking his place . . .

Oedipus, Creon, Teresia, inspired by the oracle, see, to move apart [*s'écarter*] reciprocally . . . (p. 75)

By the way he discloses these reciprocities, Sophocles gives us a glimpse, not of the myth behind the tragedy, but of the catharsis of the scapegoat behind the myth. That event being unrecorded, or rather recorded through the concealing revealing of myth, which replaces indifference with difference, one resorts to hypothesis. In so doing, Girard proceeds much as Kenneth Burke does when he prophesies after the event: one tries to discover everything that must have been the case, whether or not any direct evidence exists, such that the elucidation of it all leads inevitably to the phenomenon being investigated. Sartre proceeds in a similar way in what I call his virtual history, as when he recounts the paradigmatic moment when Genet's foster parents called him a thief, making him one. That is the way it happened, says Sartre: that or some other way.

The premise is that the community, desiring to lift the plague, needs to locate some random victim whose sacrifice will be purgative. Since the community must proceed in line with the oracle, the victim must be revealed to be the right victim, someone who fits the prescription, which requires that the victim's identity as someone chosen arbitrarily will remain concealed.

Oedipus is a scapegoat in the fullest sense *because he is never designated as such*. For the genuine recollection of the crisis, which allows for no differentiation whatever between all the *doubles*, the two differentiated themes of the myth are substituted. The original elements are all there, but rearranged and transfigured in such a way as to destroy the reciprocity of the crisis and polarize all its violence on the wretched scapegoat, leaving everyone else a passive victim of that vague and undefined scourge called 'the plague'.[9]

Noting that many other investigators have been intrigued by the same fundamental problems, Girard concludes that their results have been disappointing because they have tried to find historical documentation for a direct link between some particular ritual and the Oedipus myth. Hence Girard's indirect but global attempt to reveal explicitly what Sophocles reveals concealingly. This he does by playing on the reciprocities of which I have spoken, a powerful structuring device that pulls in the direction of sacrificial events preceding the myth. If there is torsion in the play, it is at least in part because, even while half-revealing concealed things, it draws upon the myth to establish that his hero is, after all, entirely unique, the truth of the myth thus vying with the truth 'behind' the myth.

As regards historical linkage, a correlate of sacrifice, ostracism, has been linked to specific civic procedures. Following Carcopino, Vernant explains how the assembly, working outside the tribunals, decides who shall be the right victim. In a preliminary session participants raise their hands not to join a debate or to propose a name but merely to decide whether ostracism will occur during the year. If the answer is yes, the participants reconvene to vote. Again, no debate transpires, no names are revealed as candidates. Rather, each voter conceals his choice, which he etches on to a potsherd. As though to support Girard's stress on a sudden contagion that can be ended only by an anonymous and spontaneous act of scapegoating.

The vote takes place without there being any appeal to reason, political or judicial. Everything is organized to give to the popular feeling which the Greeks call *phthonos* (both envy and religious mistrust in regard to one who rises too high, succeeds too well) the occasion to manifest itself in the most spontaneous and unanimous form (it requires at least six thousand voters) outside all rule of law, all rational justification.[10]

Without a doubt this is concrete social history, and further aspects of such history will be touched upon below. In two respects, on the other hand, this piece of history points in other directions: towards the mythical in that the procedure in question singles out one person as being uniquely suited for punishment, toward the tragic in that, while preserving this uniqueness, it exemplifies anonymous, violent reciprocity. Within Girard's three-phase continuum of techniques for controlling what he calls 'interminable vengeance', by which he means always violent acts, we find a spectrum of increasing efficacity. The first and least effective technique entails preventive measures that channel sacrificial deviations. The second technique involves pre-judicial controls and constraints, such as arbitration or trial by combat, 'whose curative action is still precarious'. The third technique is 'the judiciary system the efficacity of which is without equal' (p. 38). The ostracism procedure represents the second type of technique. It points, again, in two directions, toward a sacrificial solution, on the one hand, and toward a more judicial system on the other (consider, for example, the secret ballot). It remains, however, a rather makeshift arrangement, an in-between procedure superior to the 'magic' of the first way but not yet 'medical' enough to cure or 'legal' enough to operate rationally in the third way. That the intermediate way is precarious is confirmed by Louis Gernet, who explains how ostracism came to an end. Two men of high rank, expecting to be ostracized in a proceeding of 417, conspired together to transfer their burden to a third party, a man of lower rank who was already unpopular. With the ostracism of this man the institution ended; for, 'horror-stricken by this "shunting error", which underlines at the same time the polarity and the symmetry of the *pharmakos* and the ostracized, the Athenians were forever disgusted with the institution.'[11]

A longer-lasting institution of a specifically juridical nature provides an important background to the complexities and ambiguities of tragic discourse. It has recently been argued that the true significance of Draconian law-making was the creation of a substitute for the venerable practice of family retaliation against the victim of a homicide. This substitute was the *ephetai*, a court whose purpose was to determine the intention of the killer; should the act prove to have been unintentional, the killer would be provided with a safe-conduct to leave the country. By the time of Aristotle, no fewer than five types of homicide courts are in operation. The Council of the Areopagus inquires into homicide or wounding with intention, as well as fatal poisoning and arson. A Palladium court focuses on involuntary homicide, homicide carried out by an intermediary, and murder of a slave, a foreigner, or a resident alien. At the Delphinium a third court hears murder cases when the plea is what we would now call justifiable homicide. Meeting at a coastal location, another court decides cases in which someone already in exile is accused of another instance of homicide or wounding. Finally, the king-*archon* and leaders of the four hereditary tribes of Athens examine deaths caused by animals or inanimate objects. The factor of intentionality, made central by the *ephetai*, has clearly become highly differentiated and contextualized. Guilt or innocence comes increasingly to turn on the particulars of a situation as they constrain, incite or delimit intentionality and its consequences. The question of responsibility is no longer resolved, as under the old law, by arbitrary vengeance, but by a network of arbitrations.[12]

The significance of juridical thought and procedure has been a well-established fact since the work of Gernet early in this century; legal language, often of a quite technical nature, runs through tragedy after tragedy, including those of Sophocles. Under the authority of the *eponymous archon*, tragic contests are held, at the climax of which, as in other types of contests, judges elected by lot from a pool of Council-approved candidates, one from each of the ten traditional tribes, cast secret ballots.

Tragedy is contemporaneous with the City and with its legal system. In this sense one can say that what tragedy is talking about is itself and the problems of law it is encountering ... Not only does the tragedy enact itself on stage, but most important, it enacts its own problematics. It puts in question its own internal contradictions, revealing (through the medium of the technical legal vocabulary) that the true subject matter of tragedy is social thought and most especially juridical thought in the very process of elaboration.[13]

When one allows for the different modes in which the two interpreters function, Vernant here parallels Heidegger when the latter says that the hero's appearance in *Oedipus* is the medium of his being-there. What Vernant calls the medium of the legal vocabulary is precisely an aspect of appearance, as are the kingship of Oedipus, his relations to his wife and the seer, the city, and everything else.

In a second observation by Vernant a hermeneutics of suspicion edges to the fore, enabling a return to the suspicions of Girard.

The tragic poets utilize this vocabulary of Law in playing deliberately with its uncertainties, its vacillations, its incompleteness: imprecision of terms, shiftings of meaning, incoherences and oppositions, which reveal discordances in the heart of juridical thinking itself.[14]

In other words, through the language of law tragedy reveals social thought; then through the language of law tragedy reveals what is discordant in one kind of social thought, the juridical. In a Girardian spirit one may go on to suggest, first, that tragedy reveals mythic thought in its discordances; and, second, that the discordance in mythic thought derives conjointly from the explicit difference of the hero, which revealingly conceals; and, on the other hand, his implicit identity with the other characters, which concealingly reveals.

A Structuralist might wish to reduce such a statement to a binary opposition, concealment being one term, revelation its opposite. The same attempt at reduction could be made on unconcealment, the Heideggerean rendering of *alētheia*, the privative prefix serving as one member of the opposition, concealment the other. Such attempts miss the point entirely, while creating more problems than they solve. In the first place the Structuralist model of opposition is one of unproblematic neatness and extremity: the members of the opposition must be balanced antitheses, such as life and death, peace and war, male and female, raw and cooked. But this is only one type of opposition, and by no means a paradigmatic one. C. K. Ogden diagrams fourteen types of opposition that lend themselves to visualization, including inside/outside, A/Not A, opposite banks of a river or a street, and the enantiamorph, or mirror image (also illustrated by the left and right of a pair of gloves). This leaves oppositions that are in general richer and more interesting, such as good and bad, before and after, or kind and unkind, which yields 'two cuts and three pairs of opposites': 'Kind–not-kind, Kind–unkind, Kind–cruel'. All of the terms in this latter series are conspicuously contextual. To make sense of any of the relations one needs to know, as do the judges in the courts described above, or as do partners in a conversation, the particulars of the context, the role played by intention, and numerous other differentiae. Now some practitioners who go by the name of Structuralist, or have simply been stuck with the label, know this. The Edmund Leach of 'The Legitimacy of Solomon' is one such exception. But not Lévi-Strauss. To comprehend how the Tewa people can employ the same word for coyote, mist and scalp he marshals no evidence about their culture, their habitat, their history or even their language. The answer is to be found by abstract analysis, such that, between the opposition of herbivorous and carnivorous animals, the coyote, as a grazer who eats meat, becomes the mediating term between the opposition of herbivorous and carnivorous animals; and so on.

For his part, Ogden gets in trouble because of the same visualism and 'diagram-ism' that is such a defect of Structuralist virtue. The trouble, which verges on the comic, lies in time, a theme that is implicit in the arguments I am making in this essay when it is not explicit. The model Ogden adopts to explain before and after hypostatizes time as a mode of space:

Since the time-series is diagrammatized by a single directional line, exactly like *in front of* and *behind*, the most obvious account of the opposition is as a metaphor from this spatial direction. Before = in front of a given moment to which we progress along the line; and on the other side we come to what is (behind it or beyond it or) after it.[15]

As if to acknowledge in advance the befuddlement in which the model will entrap him, Ogden confesses that 'in no other case does language present such curious anomalies'. For instance,

What is behind, as opposed to what is in front of, the cut in this progression might well be the future. But what we call 'behind' is the past. Again, what has passed a given line towards which we are progressing, and is therefore past, is something in front of us. What is 'in front of' us is in the future, so that what is past is clearly in the future. But since what is in the past is 'what has gone before us,' and 'what has gone before us' is what is now before us, viz., the future, the future is clearly in the past.[16]

Here time comes to serve as the abstract 'other' of an equally abstract space. Understood more fundamentally, time is what Heidegger calls 'original time', in which expecting, retaining and presenting are grasped in their essential connectedness. What accounts for this connectedness is not time but temporality, which is the unity of times as they are commonly comprehended: 'The original unity of the future, past, and present which we have portrayed is the phenomenon of original time, which we call *temporality*. Temporality *temporalizes itself* in the ever current unity of future, past [having-been-ness], and present.'[17] A closer look at the fundamental modes of temporality will clear the way for a transition from temporal experience as known to the modern west to the temporal experience of Greek tragedy.

The world into which human beings are thrown already is, is

present, and is going on. What it goes on to we call the future, the realm of expectation, which is a way of conceiving that we are presently already ahead of ourselves, presently gathering from an earlier time toward a later that is already coming to be. Temporality is characterized by this continuity of spanning or stretching. An example may help. First, any question one poses has a 'past' for it is already the assumptions that went into it, the thinking that formulated it and that the posing retains; and so on. Meanwhile it presences, as on a threshold, in the stretch of the posing wherein the expectedness it foretells is already coming to be. A question is an early phase of its answer, an answer a late phase of its question; in which case the 'present' may be seen as the stretch in which the phases are 'on time'.

Temporal modes are differently the same, each being in its own way an *ecstasis*, originally meaning a standing-outside, and later referring to removal or displacement: '*Temporality is the primordial "outside-of-itself in and for itself"*. We therefore call the phenomena of the future, the character of having been, and the Present, the "*ecstases*" of temporality'.[18] The ecstases are the same in that they are equally primordial,

but the modes of temporalizing are different. The difference lies in the fact that the nature of the temporalizing can be determined primarily in terms of the different ecstases. Primordial and authentic temporality temporalizes itself in terms of the authentic future and in such a way that in having been futurally, it first of all awakens the Present. *The primary phenomenon of primordial and authentic temporality is the future.*[19]

This discussion pertains to *Dasein*, human being-there, which is the focus of *Being and Time* as a whole. In Heidegger's subsequent 'turn' early Greek thinking, not least because it differs so much from the Judaeo-Christian tradition that Heidegger problematizes, comes increasingly into play, and the question of Being as such, more than the question of human beings or entities, moves to the forefront. In the later writings the epochal character of human being meanwhile becomes more explicit: a Japanese *Dasein* is identified, for example, and an early Greek way of being-there is posited. How well does the original interpretation of the temporal ecstases sort with early Greek experience, or rather with Greek tragedy? It seems to me that the three modes are valid, and that they are differently the same for the reasons already advanced. The problem lies in the stretch between the already and the futural. Another look at tragedy, of which Sophocles' *Oedipus* may be taken as representative, may help to address it.

At the start of the drama the protagonist's future appears to lie 'before' him as the later time toward which he presently moves from the time when he rose to pre-eminence in Thebes. From such a standpoint it would appear that the future is primary. But this appearance is limited, as the audience knows, to human temporality, which is dissynchronous with the transhuman temporality in which the gods design futurity, making future events an after-phase of the already, and letting the oracles give hints in the mode of concealing revealing. Oedipus imagines the murderer he seeks as someone he will overtake when he is himself in fact already overtaken. The crises of *anagnorisis* and *peripeteia* are precisely the moments when he realizes that that other temporality is overtaking him: the most dynamic junctures in tragedy frequently involve just this synchrony, this coming together of human and transhuman time. Synchrony shifts that which is later to be toward that which has already been. Anything further from a Judaeo-Christian framework is hard to imagine, though the latter exhibits a synchrony of its own in chiliasm and epiphany; and there is another instance of coming-together in the eternity of after-life. In such a framework what we call the future is of the essence; and it may be that Heidegger's early emphasis on *Dasein* works best within the tradition that variously derives from and complements the Judaeo-Christian framework as it becomes more secularized and technologized.

But all of this is a later story. The early story, the story of tragedy, is one of temporal overtaking and synchrony; it is also one of revelation inasmuch as the synchronous moments are moments when some crucial truth emerges from concealment. In the Judaeo-Christian tradition, again, revelation as apocalypse is a supreme climax or as Torah is ongoing.[20] In *Oedipus*, by contrast, a climax comes with each recognition of being overtaken; the climax is in fact that moment. With the revelation that he murdered his father, committed incest with his mother and fathered his own siblings, Oedipus knows the worst, but he does not yet know everything. He does not know where he will end his life, for instance, or the fact that Antigone and Creon, each guided by a different view of *nomos*, will enter into an inevitable conflict leading to Antigone's death. All this remains concealed. Though the plot of that later time has been composed, the dramatis personae selected, and the scene set, nothing can be revealed until the overtaking comes, as come it must. Illumination then may linger, like the after-image of a light flashed into the eye, but sooner or later the two times part, designed as they are to experience the same differently, the one waiting while knowing little if anything of what will come, the other waiting while knowing everything.

John J. Winkler's strong new theory about the origin of tragedy brings several previously established lines of evidence together. Winkler argues – in a degree of detail that cannot be reproduced here – that tragedy emerged as a complex, liminal, drill-like procedure aiming at the *ephêboi*, or 'ephebes', 18- to 20-year-old military cadets, with the aim of disciplining them for their mature roles in the *polis*. In the ritual of the tragic performance, Winkler argues, the members of the chorus were ephebes.

If true, this would allow us to sense a complex and finely controlled tension between role and role player, for the ephebes are cast in the most 'disciplined' part of the tragedy – disciplined in the exacting demands of unison movement, subordinated to the more prominent actors, and characterized as social dependants (women, slaves, old men) – while the actors, who are no longer ephebes, perform a tale showing the risks, the misfortunes and sometimes the glory of ephebic experience. What most makes the tension come alive is the scrutiny of the watchful audience. ...These social tensions in the audience are focused on the crucial and central transitiion figures of the ephebes, who are (as it were) the growth point, the bud and flower of the city. Tragedy is the city's nurturance of that precious youth by a public ritual of discipline, enacting tales (more often than not) of its blight.[21]

The liminality of such a public ritual is futural by helping the initiates on the way to what they are to become, an outcome of high social relevance. But, again, standing out or displacement occurs at two other junctures as well. Here the guidelines come from the anthropology of Van Gennep, who points out the importance of each of three phases. In the first the initiate is separated from the collectivity in question, this being a necessary condition of the second or threshold state through which the initiate passes. At the other 'end' of the temporal spectrum comes another ecstasis, a passing into the community whose members presently wait for those who belong already to the collective future. This enabling, it should be added, entails the giving up of one type of behaviour, the exercise of deceit or cunning, and the acceptance of another, honourable behaviour toward the enemy. The deceit is exemplified by a story in which one opponent called the other's attention to an apparition looming behind the latter, causing him to turn and expose his back to the former's spear. Honour is exemplified, on the other hand, by the practice of submitting a formal challenge to an enemy force before hostilities can begin.

A connection can be envisaged as well with the legal language in tragedy. Here is a pluri-signifying language, as Philip Wheelwright would say, with words meaning one thing in one context and another thing in another; hence the readiness, almost the eagerness, with which modern interpreters insist on its complexity and ambiguity. Multiplicity is an apt word, too, especially if one of the offices of the tragic experience is, on behalf of the audience and hence of the *polis* at large, to open it to new possibilities of interpretation and, on the basis of that, of social decision-making. If Vernant goes too far right in saying that through its language tragedy questions divine justice, certainly its authors face the problematic aspects of human justice as these play upon the nerves. Which is to say that, with respect to its civic office *vis-à-vis* the public, it involves itself in what later political theorists call legitimation. Which is in turn to say that for the spectator-citizen the questioning in tragedy may be assimilated and integrated into the social fabric in such a way as to prompt not only more questioning by the spectator-citizen himself, but also, in a manner appropriate to the *polis*, if not to tragic art, more 'answering'. An historically documented scenario demonstrating all this would be invaluable. *Faute de mieux*, an imaginable social scenario, in three phases, goes something like this. First, in the courts a discursive nexus evolves, ramifying in a variety of ways (the meaning of which, from a strictly legal point of view, falls outside the present focus). The assimilation of this discourse by tragedy, in the transition to a second stage, involves change. In being uprooted from its concrete texts, key words from the courts undergo, as the Russian Formalists say, *ostranenye*, estrangement. While the terms could, it is true, retain exactly the sense they had originally, it is more likely that they take on new colorations, and even different identities. In

decontextualizing this language the dramatist perforce *recontextu-*
alizes: to make the assimilated discourse his own, he must, in this
second phase, de-estrange it for his audience. If we now take a
look at the qualities in this phase we find complexity, ambiguity,
liminality – the qualities already connected with issues surrounding
ephebic initiation, mythic residues, concealed essential violence,
and the like; for in this second, threshold state, we linger in the
concealing-revealing liminality of tragedy itself.

Far from being self-contained, tragedy spills over, as it were,
into the *polis* at large. (Artaud likens theatre to plague because
both spread contagiously: negative implications notwithstanding,
he has a point.) The third and final phase has begun. Resuming
the role of citizen, the spectator, reinforced by the mnemonic function of familiar narratives vividly relived, carries his *mathesis* into
the *polis* at large, the theatre itself already being, of course, an
important component of that life. In the *polis* one is forever
learning and relearning, training and retraining. The ephebic
passage to reintegration into the community on a more advanced
level illustrates such learning and training, while extensive learning
and training must have gone on to produce the multiplicity of
discourse in the courts. Is it too much to say that tragedy, at least
in certain respects, is itself concerned to train? The latter term
may be too closely associated with 'low-level' practices such as
preparation in sports or in the military. Wittgenstein, however,
not only uses the term, but also emphasizes its centrality in the
constitution of meaning. At any rate, and at a minimum, learning
and relearning eventuate from tragedy, as from the other institutions indicated above. The particulars of situations, the shifting
role of intentionality and responsibility, the question of justice and
authority, all with their own peculiar ambiguities and multiplicities:
these are phenomena of the *agora* as well as the theatre, and the
theatre performs a kind of enabling with respect to them. Here, in
this third stage, new, renewed, and renewing opportunities present
themselves, opportunities to look at things from a fresh angle and
to make decisions that will be different in that they depend on the
historical power and purport of reconfigured contexts.

The threefold patterns surrounding tragedy are striking. While
the topic, which has broad implications, cannot be addressed in
detail here, and while there did exist a two-tragedy contest with
no satyr-play, one notes the convergence in Thespis (on Else's

reading) of impersonation, the epic hero, and iambic verse; the three phases of ephebic initiation; the three phases described above, in which, as in the ephebic design, discourse is separated from its original legal contexts, recontextualized in tragedy, and integrated into the life of the *polis*, and around and through all this, the three ecstases of temporality. Although it embraces a longer temporal framework than the latter, the Girardian interpetation, also socially oriented, elucidates tragedy as it derives from myth as myth itself derives from originary violence. Finally, concealing revealing is itself threefold as a threshold between the policies of concealment and revelation respectively.

Several additional points remain to be made, both about temporality and about concealing revealing.

The first point, an obvious one, is that the debates in Sophocles, whether on the subject of the gods or their justice or human discourse, are not in the same dimension as divine design. The temporality of the latter, as it instigates overtaking, remains as transcendent as it remains, in its purpose, concealed. Its flashes of too-bright light disclose that one's future of intended acts is already superseded by unintended acts already performed; when the light fades uncertainty returns: all one knows of future suffering is that it will occur. Whatever one thinks about Else's views on Thespis, the former's remarks about 'the hero's *situation*, his fate' say something valid about tragedy in general. The focus of this situation is

not what the hero does but what he suffers, not his display of prowess, his moment of glory on the battlefield or in council, but his moment of disaster or failure: death, loss, humiliation. I propose to call this moment the hero's *pathos*: borrowing a term from the *Poetics* but giving it a somewhat wider extension than Aristotle does.[22]

The same consideration bears upon the chorus as well. Dwelling mainly upon the hero's superhuman achievements could make him seem too remote from ordinary human beings. The dramatist accordingly dwells on

that which allies him with us: death, mortality, suffering. For the same reason Thespis did not present the hero quite alone. He added another element, the chorus, to be a sounding board for the heroic passion. The chorus is made up of ordinary mortals like us, and through their emotional participation in the hero's fall we too are drawn into the ambit of his *pathos*. The chorus is our link with him.[23]

The revelations touching on the temporality of the gods and their design for destiny are themselves problematic, being at best partial; and when their light fades the darkness seems darker than ever: as Hölderlin put it, King Oedipus had an eye too many. By contrast, revelations touching on human laws and interpretations are relatively straightforward; what is problematic *here* is those laws and interpretations themselves. In their own discrete realms this or that pattern of discourse presumably leads a life of its own, undisturbed by its divergence from other patterns. But the playwright makes them quarrel, as it were, as they linger, proleptically, in their peculiar liminality. Putting the matter this way suggests a qualitative similarity between this approach and the ephebic theory, which also stresses ambiguity and complex tensions and is notably, so to speak, full of threshold.

An overtaking destiny accords with the office tragedy performs for the *polis* through the participation of the ephebes. Without ever sinking to the level of a 'message', the *pathos* at once entails *mathesis* with *mneme*. Audience and performer alike learn or relearn lessons in authority, hierarchy, tradition. Through the disorder in tragic experience order emerges; tragedy *is* an essential ordering from disorder. The learning, however, is actually relearning; tragic ordering is precisely mnemonic, yet another manifestation of overtaking: everyone learns what everyone already knows.

So general a lesson speaks to a general apprehension. A modern counterpart of the latter would appear to be Rousseau's *volonté générale*. This is merely analogy, however, and one that can be misleading. Will is a post-classical construction. Ancient *boulesis* pertains to wishing and *proairesis* to choosing; in neither case do we find the individualistic inwardness that characterizes true willing, which is a creation of the Judaeo-Christian tradition. In Hannah Arendt's *Willing* Epictetus, born, we recall, in the first century of the Christian era, is the first Greek to treat of will in a manner that the latter tradition can assimilate.

More than one sense of the term apprehension is relevant here. Apprehension signifies, *inter alia*, a view, notion or opinion, but also the anticipation of something adverse (*OED* II.5 and II.6 respectively). While it can signify a more accurate cognition as well, this is less to the point than a conflation that suggests a kind of credulous anxiety or nervous knowing. I am aware of no Greek word that quite fills this bill, but the quality at issue pervades many choral utterances. Then there is the institution of ostracism, at which a brief second glance is in order. Though the participants vote openly on the issue of whether the procedure should be held, and although lobbying sometimes occurred beforehand, when the ceremony is actually held concealment reigns. No discussion takes place. No names are mentioned or even hinted at. In unbroken silence each participant inscribes a name, ostracism occurring when at least six thousand names prove to be the same. But six thousand voters could not hit upon the same *pharmakos* if there did not exist a general apprehension. General apprehension is precisely the state of being that makes it possible for such concealment to pass so smoothly into such revelation.

In this tribunal, in other words, the participants are overtaken by their own concealed consensus. Entering the voting site, each man knows already the name he will inscribe; what is concealed to each is just this already-existing agreement. In a fashion the judges play god to this name's Oedipus. Until the vote is finally revealed the latter is blind to what the future holds, and when the moment of revelation comes he sees that the one he has overtaken is himself.

In epistemological terms overtaking suggests the emergence of revelation from concealment. The experience of revelation conveys knowledge of what is already designed as futurally present, or to say the same thing another way, knowledge of what is already present as futurally designed: designed rather than determined because destiny, ever at the heart of tragedy, requires human participation. Omnipotent as they are in their own dimension, the gods need that human dimension to realize fateful fullness. Only when mortals act as they must, according to immortal design, does destiny come into its own. This is no attempt to smuggle in modern 'liberal' notions of freedom, such that tragic personae can choose without constraint what they wish to do. In the society in which tragedy briefly flourished, constraint is everywhere, though in two ways its severity lessened. First, in a characterological way: Oedipus is headstrong; when Iocasta, aware of what has already happened to the future/past of her husband/son, tries to deter his investigations, he presses on heedlessly. Second, divine design writes the script but does not necessarily stipulate the tempo or pace of the characters' acts. The gods are authors more than directors. To use another analogy: though the gods may leave open certain aspects of the hero's character and of timing, these are *obbligati*, and if you are free to play them in your own style or tempo, nothing in your playing will alter the score or even the orchestration.

The relation of concealment and revelation is a thoroughgoing reciprocity. When Heidegger speaks of 'the reciprocal intimacy of revealing and concealing', taking Heraclitus as a point of departure, he speaks of intervolvement, to borrow a word that Milton spun out of *intervolve*, to wind together. Intervolving, revealing and concealing wind in and through together, like the various aspects of Heraclitean fire, *pur*. While tragedy is a work of *poiēsis* bodying forth *alētheia*, the same revealing-concealing may be discerned in *phusis*, which Heidegger links with *to mē dunón pote*, 'the never going into concealment' that 'never falls prey to concealment only to be dissolved in it, but remains committed to self-concealing, because as the never-going-*into* ... it is always a rising-*out-of* concealment.'[24] Having neither the vocabulary nor the syntax to render this adequately, we may once more take recourse to analogy. Rising out of concealment – what I have been calling concealing-revealing – may be likened to a light appearing out of the dark in such a way that its shining is shadowed into a darkling illumining, lingering in its threshold. Recourse to the analogy of light is a trademark of western metaphysics, of course; one can only ask the reader to tolerate this as one way of figuring the quasi-emergent quality at issue here. Or we may imagine a sound emerging from silence, just audible, a little like the voices in some of Samuel Beckett's late monologues, or like the sound that we would listen to if Keats' heard and unheard melodies were the same.

Temporality, the horizon 'against' which concealing-revealing occurs, apparently shifts from epoch to epoch, suggesting that a study of major works would disclose what is epochally distinctive in this sphere, just as a study of temporality would disclose that it too varies epochally: that is the ecstases recur, but dynamics and relative emphasis vary. In the latter connection I have suggested that Greek tragedy privileges overtaking and the power of the already. Although I have arrived at this conclusion by my own route, Heidegger, taking another, arrives at a supportive conclusion. In ancient Greek ontology, he observes, the *eidos* or look of something precedes its *morphē* or form:

This founding relationship can be explained only by the fact that the two determinations for thingness, the look and the form of a thing, are not understood in antiquity primarily in the order of the perception of something. . . . We must rather interpret them with a view to production.[25]

'With a view to production' elicits both the earlier and the later aspects of this temporality: the thing to be created takes shape according to its anticipated look or *eidos*. Such anticipation is the expectation of the thing as it was beforehand and hence of the thing as it must be. 'Beforehand' and 'it will be' indicate the future's obligation to what already is.

Therefore the anticipated look, the *eidos*, is also called *to ti en einai*, that which a being already was. What a being already was before actualization . . . is at the same time that whence what is formed properly derives. The *eidos*, that which a thing already was beforehand, gives the kind of the thing, its kin and descent, its *genos*.[26]

To the modern way of thinking, at least in the west, the reverse obtains. To put it one way, emphasis shifts from production to perception: the thing in question is not formed beforehand as it will be, but is primarily an occasion for cognition. We do not look back through the *morphē* to its *eidos*, as it were, but at the *eidos* for which its *morphē* is responsible. From its look we perceive what it is and, since perception is an ongoing process essential to human activity, we perceive what it will be for us. Without such a reversal a Kantian world view cannot be imagined. To put the matter another way, the shift in temporality is exhibited in the difference between the anticipated and the anticipatory. In Greek ontology, as we have seen, the anticipated is that which a being already was, before production realizes the former's beforehand state. By contrast, the anticipatory, which is characteristic of the modern west, privileges the futural: if production is an end, perception is a start. Moreover, the willing that is absent from Greek antiquity prior to Epictetus is here presupposed. 'The Will's blind force functions not only in purely mental activity; it is manifest also in sense perception. This element of the mind is what makes sensation meaningful.'[2] Willed futurity holds sway pervasively, in the theory and practice of human 'development', in the contagion of planning, in the recurrent and related themes of Utopia and apocalypse, and in other ways too numerous to mention.

Against the horizon of the already and of overtaking, temporality finds itself disclosed in the concealing-revealing of tragedy. The disclosure does not merely show the nature of this temporality, but shows its transition into a now already passing into the future, hence our feeling that concealing revealing, instead of being polarized at one or another 'end' of the temporal spectrum, hovers on a threshold. There overtaking suddenly reveals the presently futural as the already and just as suddenly vanishes into concealment. The general effect is one of ambiguity and liminality, the same qualities that pertain, as we have seen, both to ephebic aims and to the language of civic law. The Girardian theory of violence, for its part, aims to reveal what is concealed before anything else, before the ephebic nexus or the nexus of language and law. But here too concealing-revealing and overtaking are at stake. In the first place, the tragedy may be seen to unfold in the ways indicated above. The truth of what has already been is originally concealed, then partly unconcealed, then revealed, whereupon the future becomes once again unknown. In accordance with divine design, Oedipus has overtaken himself. All of this, however, is itself a network of concealment. What turns Oedipus ultimately into a *pharmakos* is not divinely ordained justice but the process by which an earlier state of violence was brought under control. The plague exemplifies the indifferent victimization characteristic of that state. At any time the plague may claim anyone; anyone is everyone. Then suddenly a difference is revealed. One alone is after all responsible for the pollution and this same one, by being removed, effects purgation. Now all of this transpires before our very eyes, and can hardly be said to be concealed. But if the all-important overtaking originates not from divine but from human design, then the tragic version of its origin, which the drama climactically reveals, is itself a tour de force of concealment. If such is the case, the overtaking actually comes not from the temporality the tragedy indicates, that of the gods, and not from the temporality of the myth that tragedy reworks; the overtaking comes, if not all the way from the pre-mythic stage in which *pharmakos* purgation was instituted, at least from the later civic institutions that were contemporaneous with tragedy. On such a reading tragedy becomes a kind of palimpsest, each level of which reveals another level that it may well have been designed to conceal.

Notes

1 See Hugh Lloyd-Jones, *The Justice of Zeus*, 2nd edn, Berkeley, Calif., University of California Press, 1983, pp. 104 ff.

2 *Introduction to Metaphysics*, trans. Ralph Manheim, New Haven, Conn., Yale University Press, 1959, p. 106.

3 *Introduction to Metaphysics*, p. 107.

4 *Introduction to Metaphysics*, p. 107.

5 *Sophocles*, trans. Hazel and David Harvey, Oxford, Blackwell, 1979, p. 6.

6 Jacques Derrida, *Dissemination*, trans. Barbara Johnson, Chicago, Ill, University of Chicago Press, 1981, p. 63.

7 *Violence and the Sacred*, trans. Patrick Gregory, Baltimore, Md, Johns Hopkins University Press, 1977, p. 50. Further citations to this volume are noted parenthetically.

8 *Leviathan*, ed. C. B. Macpherson, Harmondsworth, Penguin, 1968, p. 161.

9 'The Plague in literature and myth', *Texas Studies in Literature and Language* 15, 1974, p. 843.

10 'Ambiguity and reversal: on the enigmatic structure of *Oedipus Rex*', *New Literary History* 9, 1978, p. 491. John J. Winkler points out that the outcome of the balloting may have been affected by lobbying for votes and by the fact that some participants appear to have voted several times.

11 Jean-Pierre Vernant and Pierre Vidal-Naquet, *Tragedy and Myth in Ancient Greece*, trans. Janet Lloyd, Atlantic Highlands, NJ, Humanities Press, 1981, p. 118.

12 This account mainly follows Raphael Sealey, *A History of the Greek City States, ca. 600–338 BC*, Berkeley, Calif., University of California Press, 1976, p. 103. For a more specialized discussion of legal considerations, see D. M. MacDowell, *Athenian Homicide Law in the Age of the Orators*, Manchester, Manchester University Press, 1963.

13 'Greek tragedy; problems of interpretation', in Richard Macksey and Eugenio Donato (eds), *The Languages of Criticism and the Sciences of Man: The Structuralist Controversy*, Baltimore, Md., Johns Hopkins University Press, 1970, p. 279. Kathy Eden's informative *Poetic and Legal Fiction in the Aristotelian Tradition*, Princeton, NJ, Princeton

University Press, 1987, which the author let me examine in page proofs after the present essay had been written, identifies the apposite modern discussion of the legal-tragic nexus (p. 7), examines the role of intentionality (pp. 20 ff.), and considers the crucial relation of 'Poetry and Equity' (ch. 2, pp. 62–111). On the wide range of implications for tragedy of law and legality see Charles Segal, *Interpreting Greek Tragedy*, Ithaca, NY, Cornell University Press, 1986, p. 141.

14 'Greek tragedy: problems of interpretation', p. 347.

15 *Opposition: A Linguistic and Psychological Analysis*, 1932; rpt Bloomington, Indiana University Press, 1967, p. 85.

16 *Opposition*, p. 86.

17 *The Basic Problems of Phenomenology*, trans. Albert Hofstadter, Bloomington, Ind., Indiana University Press, 1982, p. 266.

18 *Being and Time*, trans. John Macquarrie and Edward Robinson, New York, Harper & Row, 1962, p. 217.

19 *Being and Time*, p. 329.

20 Bruce Rosenstock, of the Department of Classics at Stanford, called this distinction to my attention and contributed additional insights to a draft of this essay, as did Herbert S. Lindenberger, Professor of Comparative Literature and Humanities at Stanford.

21 'The Ephebes' Song: *Tragôida and Polis*', *Representations* 11, 1985, 44–5. The following discussion is indebted to Winkler not only for this article but also for several suggestions for improving the present study.

22 Gerald F. Else, *The Origin and Early Form of Greek Tragedy*, 1965, rpt New York, Norton, 1972, p. 65.

23 Else, pp. 65–6.

24 Heidegger, 'Aletheia', in *Early Greek Thinking*, trans. David Farrell Krell and Frank A. Capuzzi, San Francisco, Calif., Harper & Row, 1975, p. 114.

25 *Basic Problems of Phenomenology*, p. 106.

26 *Basic Problems of Phenomenology*, p. 101.

27 Hannah Arendt, *The Life of the Mind*, New York, Harcourt, Brace, Jovanovich, 1977, II, 100.

Index